D0722371

JAMES FITZJAMES

JAMES FITZJAMES

The Mystery Man of the Franklin Expedition

WILLIAM BATTERSBY

DUNDURN PRESS

TORONTO

This book is dedicated to the memory of the late Major G.L. Dean, BA, Intelligence Corps, retired. In his old age, Admiral E.P. Charlewood described Captain James Fitzjames as 'my dearest friend'. Guy was mine.

Copyright © William Battersby, 2010
Published in the UK by The History Press 2010

First published in North America in 2010 by Dundurn Press, Ltd.

Library and Archives Canada Cataloguing in Publication

Battersby, William, 1958-
    James Fitzjames: the mystery man of the Franklin Expedition / by William Battersby.

ISBN 978-1-55488-781-1

1. Fitzjames, James, 1813-ca. 1849. 2. Sailors--Great Britain--Biography. 3. Explorers--Great Britain--Biography. 4. Franklin, John, Sir, 1786-1847. 5. Arctic regions--Discovery and exploration--British. 6. Northwest Passage--Discovery and exploration--British. I. Title.

FC3961.1.F58B38 2010   917.19'52041092   C2010-901498-7

Care has been taken to trace the ownership of copyright material used in this book. The author and the publisher welcome any information enabling them to rectify any references or credits in subsequent editions.

J. Kirk Howard, President

www.dundurn.com

Dundurn Press
3 Church Street, Suite 500
Toronto, Ontario, Canada
M5E 1M2

Gazelle Book Services Limited
White Cross Mills
High Town, Lancaster, England
LA1 4XS

Dundurn Press
2250 Military Road
Tonawanda, NY
U.S.A. 14150

Typesetting and origination by The History Press
Printed in Great Britain

CONTENTS

FOREWORD

On 24 March 1845, Commander James Fitzjames, RN, sat down in his cabin on board the newly commissioned HMS *Erebus* in Woolwich Docks and began to write:

> Captain Fitzjames presents his compliments to Mr O'Brien and sends him as long since requested a rough summary of his services.

> For further details of the services of himself, Commander E.P. Charlewood (now superintendent of Dover Railway) and Lieut. Henry Eden (now commanding HMS Lizard) he would refer him to the Supplementary Report on Steam Navigation to India, in 1838, which gives Col. Chesney's dispatches on the subject.

> HMS Erebus
> Woolwich
> 24 March 1845

The Mr O'Brien (actually O'Byrne) to whom Fitzjames was writing was compiling a complete 'Naval Biography' of every serving Royal Navy officer and he had sent Fitzjames a detailed questionnaire. This questionnaire was the 'rough summary of his services' which Fitzjames was struggling to complete before his ship sailed. He detailed with care every ship he had served on, even down to short, detached duties of a few months. He completed the questionnaire meticulously, squeezing his writing small where necessary to fit all the information into the correct boxes on the form. His responses overflowed onto an extra page and a half, which he carefully attached to the original form. But he left blank the second box on the front of the form, which asked: 'Dates of Birth and Marriage, name of Wife, and number of children? If possessing any Relatives in the Service? Their names?'

Why?

Six weeks after posting the partially completed questionnaire, James Fitzjames completely and quite unexpectedly disappeared. For ever. This book was written to answer a simple question: who was this man who hid all reference to his family and background?

I started the research which led to this book simply because I was interested in the Franklin Expedition and wanted to know where and when each member of it was born. I found that it was easy to get that information for most members of the expedition, but material on James Fitzjames was incredibly difficult to pin down. I had to go back to contemporary sources to establish anything and by the time my research was complete I had, in effect, written an entire book on this remarkable man.

Although most of what appears here is based on my own research, I have been helped by many other people. So many that it is difficult to list them all here, so to anyone who helped me and who does not appear now, I can only apologise. My thanks must first go to Glenn M. Stein FRGS, one of today's finest polar historians, and to Martin Crozier who is, of course, related to Captain Francis Crozier, captain of HMS *Terror*. Both have been enormous sources of strength and encouragement. I would also like to thank Simon Hamlet, my publisher at The History Press, for all his support.

Many librarians and curators have helped me and must have been puzzled by the strange twists and turns of my research as I hounded the shades of Captain James Fitzjames through dusty byways of the world's archives. Thanks to everyone at The National Archives in Kew, the British Library, the Royal Geographical Society archive, the National Maritime Museum, the Scott Polar Research Institute at Cambridge, the National Library of Australia, the Hoare and Company archive, the Bank of England archive, the National Gallery archive, the Derbyshire Record Office in Matlock, the Hertfordshire archives at Hertford and the Wirral Archives Service at Birkenhead. Since, in many cases, I never knew your names, please do not be offended if I do not thank you in person, but I would especially like to record my thanks to Heather Lane, Naomi Boneham and Lucy Martin of the SPRI and Pamela Hunter of Hoare & Co. Many people at the National Maritime Museum have been generous with their time including Barbara Tomlinson, Virginia Llado-Buisan, Bernie Bryant, Doug McCarthy and Melissa Viscardi. I also much appreciate the kind help of Bruno Pappalardo at The National Archives. Others to whom I owe a debt of thanks include David Woodman and Ann Savours, William Wills, the great-grand-nephew of Lt Le Vesconte of HMS *Clio* and HMS *Erebus*, Dr Michael Bailey of the Newcomen Society and the indefatigable Russell Potter, Professor of English at Rhode Island University. Professors Russell Taichman and Richard Simons have also been helpful in sharing their opinions and insights. Several descendants or relatives of people mentioned in the book have been most generous including Professor Robin Coningham, Georgina Naylor-Coningham and Marilyn Hamilton. I'm most grateful to Jack Layfield, Jennifer Snell and Carol Holker for showing me at first hand so much of Sir John Barrow's life at Ulverston. I would like to thank Captain (then Commander) James Morley, RN, then captain of HMS *Lancaster*, and the officers and company of that beautiful ship for their hospitality when I spent several days on board some years ago and experienced a little of life in the Royal Navy.

Lastly, but by no means least, several friends and relatives have been a great source of help and encouragement, including my old friend and drinking partner from the Institute of Archaeology, Julian Bowsher, and Dr Michael Michael. I should particularly like to thank my friends and family for much help, especially my parents Celia and Brian Battersby and my friend Rainer, Baron von Echlin, for rigorous proof reading and comments on the later drafts of the book, and my wife Julia for extremely insightful analysis of the opening sections of the book. My children Maddie, Hannah and Jamie should especially be mentioned for their initiative in baking me a fiftieth birthday cake decorated with the face of Captain Sir John Franklin and a representation of the headless skeletons in the ship's boat at Erebus Bay – undoubtedly a first in Franklin studies.

Acknowledging that I could not have written the book without many people's assistance, there are undoubtedly errors and omissions in this book and for them I alone am responsible.

Most of all, I hope that somewhere in the frozen shades the spirit of Captain James Fitzjames, RN, will have been amused by my attempts to wrest him back to reality. If there is an afterlife, and if he recognises something of himself in this, then it will all have been worth it.

FAMILY TREE 1 – JAMES FITZJAMES

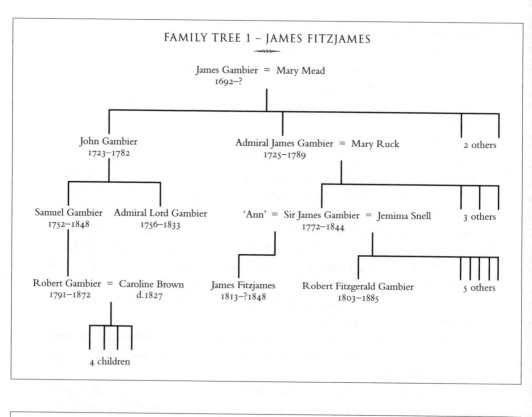

James Gambier = Mary Mead
1692–?

John Gambier
1723–1782

Admiral James Gambier = Mary Ruck
1725–1789

2 others

Samuel Gambier
1752–1848

Admiral Lord Gambier
1756–1833

'Ann' = Sir James Gambier = Jemima Snell
1772–1844

3 others

Robert Gambier = Caroline Brown
1791–1872   d.1827

James Fitzjames
1813–?1848

Robert Fitzgerald Gambier
1803–1885

5 others

4 children

FAMILY TREE 2 – WILLIAM CONINGHAM

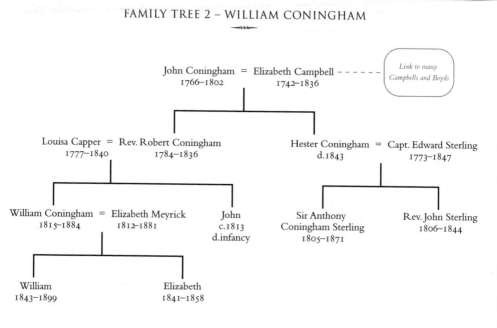

John Coningham = Elizabeth Campbell – – – – – *Link to many Campbells and Boyds*
1766–1802   1742–1836

Louisa Capper = Rev. Robert Coningham
1777–1840   1784–1836

Hester Coningham = Capt. Edward Sterling
d.1843   1773–1847

William Coningham = Elizabeth Meyrick
1815–1884   1812–1881

John
c.1813
d.infancy

Sir Anthony
Coningham Sterling
1805–1871

Rev. John Sterling
1806–1844

William
1843–1899

Elizabeth
1841–1858

Introduction

JAMES FITZJAMES AND ME

Like many people, there are times when I have had to travel for my work. And like all regular travellers I tend to have my own little habits. One of these is that I usually call in at the bookshop at Heathrow airport and treat myself to a history book or a historical biography before I leave. Several years ago on a regular run to San Francisco, I picked up a book by Fergus Fleming which I had seen reviewed called *Barrow's Boys: A Stirring Tale of Daring, Fortitude and Outright Lunacy*. I started to read the book as the aircraft took the great circle route over northern Greenland, Nunavut and the Canadian Arctic. Visibility was good. Even travelling at nearly 600mph it takes many hours to cross the icy, rocky wastes of these northern parts. Looking out of the window I could see a vast and inhospitable landscape of rock and ice which didn't look like planet Earth at all, but more like pictures of one of the moons of Jupiter.

Fleming's book described the incredible adventures of groups of Royal Navy explorers sent to these uninviting wastes in the early nineteenth century. While some men died and some ships were lost, all returned to tell their tales of adventure. Except the Franklin Expedition. Fleming's book closes this remarkable chapter in history by highlighting the horror of Sir John Franklin's Third Expedition, which simply disappeared somewhere in the far north of the American continent. I was transfixed by Fleming's remarkable account, and especially by this passage:

> Within two years the expedition was destroyed – vaporized would be a better word – by an unknown calamity that sprayed human debris across the dark, unknown heart of the Arctic. In decades to come, explorers would pick wonderingly through the bundles of cloth, whitened bones, personal articles, stacks of supplies and scraps of wood that comprised the remains of the best-equipped Arctic fleet to have left England's shores. Two of Franklin's men were eventually found. They lay in a boat drawn up on the shore, with loaded muskets and a small supply of food by their sides. One, obviously an officer, wore a fur coat. Their skeletal grins gave no answer to a question that would burn for more than 150 years.

I didn't realise then that this purple prose actually underplays the true, macabre horror of that scene. Neither skeleton 'grinned' because something, or rather someone, had removed both men's skulls although their jawbones lay nearby. Dead men do not remove, dismember and carry away their own skulls after they have died. The clear implication, that someone else had taken the heads away as food, is almost too horrible to contemplate.

I decided to find out more about the Franklin Expedition. I wondered whether there was something unique about it, which had made it fail and everyone on it die when so many people on other expeditions had survived? I soon found I was not alone. Many other people had asked themselves the same question. I started to read other books on the Franklin Expedition and the huge literature surrounding it. Ever since the expedition became overdue in 1848, men have been searching for it; first for survivors, then for written records and, since the 1860s, simply for answers. Literally hundreds of books, papers and articles have been written about it and more ships and lives lost in these searches than on the expedition itself.

I found that even today basic facts, like the cause of the disaster, are disputed. Some said it was caused by dietary problems, some by climate and some by the cultural arrogance of Expedition members. There was surprisingly little consensus about anything. I read in Owen Beattie and John Geiger's *Frozen in Time* that the expedition had been poisoned by the lead in their tinned food. Then I read Scott Cookman's book *Ice Blink*, which said they were poisoned by botulism. The best all-round history of the expedition, I found, had been written by a doctor from Cheltenham called Richard Cyriax and published in 1939. I was lucky enough to obtain a signed copy of this book. But while Cyriax summed up the facts about the expedition very clearly and gave a wealth of sources, he was a cautious man. He did not give any 'cause' for the failure of the Franklin Expedition other than suggesting that the men were crippled by a bad outbreak of scurvy.

I started to appreciate that the Franklin Expedition was more than just a mystery for archaeologists and sailors. I found that, since the 1850s, its combination of real-life mystery and horror has inspired a remarkable range of fiction writers too. A diverse range of authors have been drawn to write about it, producing literature which ranges from philosophical and social discussion to downright horror. In the nineteenth century, books, plays and articles were written about it by Wilkie Collins, Charles Dickens, Swinburne and Jules Verne. And the inspiration lives on today. In the last twenty years the Franklin Expedition has formed the central event in a huge genre of fiction, including Sten Nadolny's *The Discovery of Slowness*, Mordecai Richler's *Solomon Gursky Was Here*, William Vollmann's *The Rifles*, John Wilson's *North with Franklin: The Lost Journals of James Fitzjames*, Dan Simmons' *The Terror* and Clive Cussler's *Arctic Drift*. And, from the nineteenth century on, it has also inspired a wide range of songs, poems and paintings. The respected Canadian novelist Margaret Atwood has gone as far as to say that the Franklin Expedition has become more than mere history and now lives on as a universal myth.

I realised that what had attracted my attention had inspired many others. This was not just an archaeological puzzle. The elemental horror of a community of men, for such is the company of a ship, cut off from all humanity in a frozen desert and condemned slowly to die touches people everywhere.

I originally trained as an archaeologist so I was accustomed to the concept of collecting disparate data and then trying to makes sense of it through objective analysis. Having exhausted the published books, I started to collect facts and figures about the expedition for myself. I wanted to see if I could make sense of the disaster. It was clear there were so many layers of writing about the expedition that perhaps a fresh and objective approach could yield more answers. Could I spot something that others had missed?

I found that in most cases the facts and figures were relatively easy to come by and to confirm. The plans of the ships, beautifully photographed by the National Maritime Museum, enabled me to understand how and where the men had lived and, in some cases, died. Disease seemed key, so I wanted to understand their health. I started to collect evidence of their lives. And here I came up against James Fitzjames. For most of the officers and even the men it was quite straightforward to collect material on their lives, families and careers. There are several biographies of Sir John Franklin and Francis Crozier. The lives and careers of the sailors and the Royal Marines have been clearly documented by Ralph Lloyd-Jones in his two papers published in the *Polar Record* in 2004 and 2005.

But although all the authorities agreed that James Fitzjames was a highly influential young man on the expedition, there were very few hard facts about him. No one agreed even, for example, on how old he was. The more I searched for information about him, the less I understood.

Because James Fitzjames is a well-known figure. He wrote the Victory Point note, which is the key historical document from the expedition and one of the few records to survive from it. He features prominently, not only in the histories of the expedition but also in the fiction. He appears in Dan Simmons' bestselling horror novel *The Terror*, which is set on HMS *Erebus* and HMS *Terror* during the Franklin Expedition. Simmons says Fitzjames had been acclaimed a hero 'before his first ship' for rescuing a man from the sea at Liverpool and was rewarded with a silver plate. He was 'the handsomest man in the Navy' and 'a well-bred young gentleman'. He had led raiding parties against Bedouin tribesmen, suffering a broken leg and imprisonment in the process. He had behaved heroically in the Opium War and was wounded. After commanding HMS *Clio*, he was left ashore with no job until the opportunity to be Franklin's deputy on the *Erebus* gave him his second chance. Simmons says that in public Fitzjames' demeanour was 'an easy mix of self-effacing humor and firm command' and that he spoke in a confident voice with a slight upper-class lisp. Simmons has Fitzjames die of botulism about two-thirds of the way through the novel, thus missing its supernatural climax.

Fitzjames is also the principal subject of a best-selling work of fiction: *North with Franklin: the Lost Journals of James Fitzjames*, by the Canadian novelist John Wilson. Wilson describes how he was inspired by letters Fitzjames had written in the early weeks of the expedition to an Englishwoman called Elizabeth Coningham. These captivated Wilson and he wrote the book as 'a labour of love'. It is an imaginative reconstruction of the journal Fitzjames would have kept from the point where he disappeared. It has an apparent ring of authenticity, because in the early parts of the book Wilson freely raids Fitzjames' letters, so it is sprinkled with comments and observations which Fitzjames actually made. It is fine writing, although still fiction, and through it James Fitzjames has won a spark of immortality.

Fitzjames also makes a cameo appearance on the very first page of Clive Cussler's novel *Arctic Drift*. He is only a peripheral character in this thriller, which opens with a description of this 'bright and affable man' who had 'quickly risen through the ranks of the Royal Navy'.

So though James Fitzjames died over 160 years ago, his position as third-in-command of the cursed Franklin Expedition has kept him in the public eye. But why could I not find out more about him?

Before answering that question, we need to review the story of the Franklin Expedition. Its loss was a shock to contemporary British society, comparable to that of the *Titanic* disaster or the loss of the space shuttles to modern American society. Exactly as with the *Titanic*, its disappearance and the macabre revelations of its grisly fate had the effect of signposting a turning point on the road to a more sober and less optimistic society.

The Franklin Expedition was the largest single disaster in British exploration history. The impact of its failure reverberated around the world. For Britain and the proud Royal Navy, it was a shameful defeat as every last man on it died. For the Inuit peoples of the far north it was even more dramatic. Before Franklin, they were masters of their own land and had few fleeting encounters with westerners. Searching after Franklin, wave after wave of British, American and other searchers had scoured the Arctic and mapped it. By the time the search was over, the Inuit found that, without being asked, they had become Canadians. Canada's sovereignty over its far north owes much to this Expedition. Even before it was sent the Franklin Expedition had political significance, being a statement of British possession of the far north at a time of tension between Britain, Russia and the United States. And ironically, the shared effort to rescue it helped to heal this potential conflict and foster the eventual political settlement in North America.

For all humanity the story stands as a truly horrific chapter in history. The expedition was a living nightmare in which men fought for their lives in miserable conditions, possibly for years, before succumbing to cold, exhaustion, starvation and perhaps even murder. There is clear evidence of horrific disease and cannibalism visible in the pathetic scraps left by its last survivors.

While all the details, perhaps thankfully, will never be known, the bare facts are clear. The expedition was commissioned by the Admiralty to complete the discovery of, and then pass through, a 'seaway' through the ice to the north of the American continent from the Atlantic to the Pacific. This was called the North West Passage and had been a British obsession for centuries. There were several drivers for the expedition. The political settlement in Canada was fragile and in 1845 Britain needed to maintain a quasi-military presence in the north as proof of sovereignty to both the United States and Russia. There was also important magnetic and scientific research which could only be carried out in that part of the world.

But it would not have happened in the form that it did without Sir John Barrow.

Barrow is an extraordinary figure. He was born in 1764, the son of a Lancashire farmer, and although of modest origins, had a very good education. He was essentially an accountant, a surveyor and an administrator. After working as a clerk at an iron foundry and on a whaling ship, he wangled a position on the first British embassy to China in 1792. He became a valuable member of the embassy, adding a mastery of the Chinese language to his organisational skills. He wrote authoritatively on the embassy and on aspects of Chinese culture. This made his reputation with the British ruling class as a hard-working 'fixer' and won him the trust of the influential Lord McCartney. When Lord McCartney was sent to South Africa to establish the new British colony of the Cape of Good Hope, he naturally took the useful and capable Mr Barrow with him. Barrow was appointed Auditor-General in Cape Town, married a local girl, Anne Maria Trüter, and settled there. The couple's first child, George, was born and died there. But power-politics intervened. Under the Peace of Amiens of 1802 the British agreed to hand the new colony back to the Dutch, so the Barrows sold up and moved back to England in 1804. Barrow had earned the trust and respect of some very powerful people in British society and on his return he was appointed Second Secretary to the Lords of the Admiralty. He was a workaholic, a tireless networker and writer and held this post almost continually for forty years. Under him it became a position of huge influence as he directed and ran the Royal Navy. As the years of his career extended, so did the extent of his influence.

Barrow was a keen proponent of exploration and surveying and, with the close of the Napoleonic Wars in 1815, he sent out innumerable Royal Navy ships. It was a personal ambition of this powerful and obsessive man to see a British ship sail through the North West Passage in his lifetime. And although in 1845 he boasted that he could still read without spectacles, by then he was 80 years old.

The conventional account of the expedition notes that Sir John Barrow had wanted Fitzjames to lead it because of his high birth and friends in high places. But the Admiralty rejected Fitzjames because of his youth. Then Sir James Clark Ross turned the opportunity down flat, so Sir John Franklin was chosen to lead the expedition by default at the age of 59. Most accounts suggest Fitzjames was around 33 years old. Francis Crozier was never considered to lead the expedition, despite being the Royal Navy's most experienced polar exploration captain after Ross, so was offered the second-in-command position instead. Crozier's recent biographer suggests that 'his Irish pedigree was regarded as an impediment by the stuffy civil servants and admirals whose positions owed so much to the British class system'. This seems unlikely as many senior British officers had similar Irish roots. It was the Duke of Wellington, himself Irish, who famously retorted that 'being born in a stable does not make one a horse' when challenged over his origins. Many of Britain's most acclaimed nineteenth-century polar explorers came from Ireland, including Sir Leopold McClintock, who was born in Dundalk, Sir Robert McClure from Wexford and Sir Henry Kellett from Tipperary.

The expedition took two ships, HMS *Erebus* and HMS *Terror*. They had been used for Ross and Crozier's outstandingly successful exploration of the Antarctic from 1839 to 1843. For the Franklin Expedition they were fitted with steam engines and crammed with technology advanced for the day. They were packed with three years' supply of food. Their tinned food has attracted huge attention. In the 1850s it was said that it was rotten, supplied by a cut-rate provisioner called Stephen Goldner. Goldner became a scapegoat for a wave of anti-Semitic opprobrium. We have seen that the American author Scott Cookman suggested the food was riddled with botulism, and John Geiger and Dr Owen Beattie claim it was poisoned with lead from the solder of its tins. This allegation has been repeated so often that it has become an urban myth. For many people, indeed, almost the only thing they 'know' about the Franklin Expedition was that the men died of lead poisoning from their tinned food.

The expedition set off from Greenhithe in May 1845 with 24 officers and 110 men in an atmosphere of great confidence. After stopping for three days in the Orkneys, it anchored off Greenland to transfer extra supplies from a transport ship to the *Erebus* and *Terror*. Five men were sent home. The remaining 129 men and the ships were last seen in early August 1845 waiting to cross to Lancaster Sound, after which they disappeared.

The story of the expedition credits Franklin's wife Jane with being a key figure. She harangued the Admiralty to get her husband his appointment, then from 1848 shamed the Admiralty into instigating a belated search for the lost ships and men. At its peak in the early 1850s, this involved hundreds of men and no less than eleven British and two American ships. In 1850 searchers found relics of the expedition on Beechey Island where inscriptions on the graves of three men proved that the expedition had wintered there from 1845 to 1846. In 1859 a note was found, written by Fitzjames and Crozier, which was dated 25 April 1848 and explained that the ships had first tried to sail north, then doubled back south to become permanently locked in ice off King William Island in September 1846. It said that Franklin had died on 11 June 1847 and that the 105 men alive at that point apparently intended to walk to safety via the Back River to Canada. In 1854 the explorer Dr John Rae had been told by an Inuk that thirty-five to forty men from the expedition had died near the mouth of the river and that there had been clear signs of cannibalism amongst them. This caused an outcry in England. Lady Franklin orchestrated a campaign to denigrate Rae and the Inuit. Disgracefully, she induced the novelist Charles Dickens to write a polemic which traduced this with much offensive and racial abuse. Dickens called the Inuit accounts a 'vague babble of savages' demonstrating that one can be a writer of genius but a very poor archaeologist and forensic scientist. Archaeological evidence since uncovered has completely validated the Inuit account. Other searchers in the 1850s and 1860s brought back more Inuit accounts which backed up Rae and added much macabre detail to the stories of suffering and death.

Research has continued to this day. In the 1980s Dr Owen Beattie analysed scraps of bones from Franklin Expedition members on King William Island and found they had suffered from scurvy, cannibalism and lead poisoning. He autopsied the three men buried on Beechey Island and suggested they had died of pneumonia and tuberculosis aggravated by lead poisoning.

Inuit recollections of their ancestors' memories of the expedition continue to bring out more information. David Woodman and Dorothy Harley Eber have both contributed a great deal by analysing these memories. Recently the Canadian government has established a major research programme, led by Robert Grenier, the senior marine archaeologist with Parks Canada, to uncover fresh evidence and to reconcile this with the known Inuit testimony. And to this day descendants of the Inuit bridle at the way they were ignored and then slandered by many of the searchers.

Like everything to do with the Franklin Expedition, Fitzjames' posthumous reputation has swung dramatically since he vanished in 1845. First, Franklin's men were eulogised as martyrs to British imperialism. At the turn of the twentieth century, the slightly sinister Sir Clements Markham held Fitzjames up as 'among the most promising officers in the navy at that time ... strong, self-reliant, a perfect sailor, imaginative, enthusiastic, full of sympathy for others, a born leader of men, he was the beau ideal of an Arctic commander'. Markham was 15 years old when Fitzjames disappeared so, although the two men never met, he knew people who had known Fitzjames. His description carried weight. Markham presented Fitzjames as the idealised picture of the Royal Naval officer he wanted the British to send to conquer the South Pole. It was Markham's fantasy of Fitzjames that Captain Scott died trying to emulate.

Since then, Fitzjames has conformed to a different stereotype which holds the Franklin Expedition up as a classic example of nineteenth-century British imperial hubris. Here it is a blinkered attempt to export a hidebound and class-ridden society to the Arctic. Fitzjames and his brother officers never attempted to adapt to their environment; instead they simply sat in their ships being served preserved food by their servants, which they ate with silver cutlery off fine crockery. To add a final, delicious irony to this case, it is often stated that the food they ate was poisonous – 'tainted' or poisoned with lead or botulism. We have seen that Simmons has Fitzjames killed off by botulism in *The Terror* and Cussler takes a belt and braces approach in *Arctic Drift*, plumping for botulism and lead poisoning as the cause of his death.

It was clear to me that there were many unanswered questions about the expedition and especially Fitzjames' place in it. But I found that stereotypes and posthumous grandstanding were not the only reasons for confusion in the memory of James Fitzjames. There are some very mysterious gaps and inconsistencies in all the records which relate to his life and Royal Naval service. Even information like the ships he served on, dates and ranks is contradictory and does not tie up with the questionnaire he submitted to O'Byrne. This has prevented researchers from piecing his life together from the usual contemporary sources.

Like many others who have wondered about the Franklin Expedition, I puzzled over some strange questions about him. Why was Sir John Barrow so determined the expedition should be led by this 'engaging and able officer with friends in the right places but with no Arctic experience', as Crozier's biographer Michael Smith describes him? Why, when thwarted, did Barrow still send Fitzjames as Franklin's deputy on HMS *Erebus*? And who actually was James Fitzjames? There are no reliable details of his age or family background in any of the standard works on the Franklin Expedition.

I found that all the modern writers based their understanding of Fitzjames on what Sir Clements and Sir Albert Markham had written about him. It was the Markhams who said that Fitzjames had been orphaned at an early age. John Wilson, in *North with Franklin*, says he was orphaned at the age of 7 and imagines Fitzjames having a dim recollection of his parents. Clive Cussler has Fitzjames writing letters to his family on the expedition and in *The Terror* Fitzjames shares a bottle of Scotch with Crozier, which he says was given to him by his father.

Another strange question was this. Everyone seems to agree that Fitzjames had great influence – 'friends in high places' – but no one could say why or where this influence came from. And who was this family of his?

Richard Cyriax, the great historian of the Franklin Expedition, says nothing at all about Fitzjames' family or life before he joined the Royal Navy in 1825 except that he was 'about thirty two years old' in 1845. There is nothing about him in Owen Beattie and John Geiger's best-selling history of the Franklin Expedition *Frozen in Time*. Other historians give contradictory information. Scott Cookman in *Ice Blink* gives Fitzjames' age as 33 and describes him as 'well-educated, aristocratic, wealthy, of good family, Church of England, fast rising in the service – and thumpingly, lispingly English to the core'. Cookman says Fitzjames was 'aristocratic and of good family'. But how can this be so if nobody knew who his family was? Simmons in *The Terror* follows this, even down to the 'upper-class lisp'.

Once I started to collect information about him I found that there were few facts about James Fitzjames, and much that was written about him was conflicting so that he himself became another of the mysteries of the Franklin Expedition.

The Royal Navy's records relating to him are very confused and incomplete. I looked for his 'passing certificate' in the index at The National Archives in Kew. Every officer in the Royal Navy at the time had to pass an examination before being appointed lieutenant and on this certificate would be given a record of his prior service. Fitzjames said he passed this exam in 1833, yet his name was missing from the index altogether. Why?

I had a second-hand account of his service from the O'Byrne directory of naval officers. This was written from the questionnaire Fitzjames had been completing on the *Erebus* just before she sailed. I tracked down the original questionnaire which Fitzjames had sent to O'Byrne. After publishing the directory, O'Byrne had kept all the completed questionnaires, and after his death they had been deposited in the manuscripts section of the British Library. From this I could see that O'Byrne hadn't just missed out information about Fitzjames' family. Fitzjames himself had actually refused to give any information about them or himself at all. Not even his own date of birth.

I wanted first-hand information so I spent days at The National Archives in Kew tracking Fitzjames' career back through the ships' muster books. I found that there were gaps and inconsistencies in these too. For example, in his O'Byrne questionnaire Fitzjames said he had entered HMS *St Vincent* on 15 December 1830 and served on her until 1833 as a volunteer and a midshipman. Yet in the muster books I found that this was not true. He had entered *St Vincent* when he said he did, but not as a midshipman. The contemporary muster book showed that actually he entered as master's assistant, which was an entirely different and civilian position. It then told me that he had been dismissed from *St Vincent* after only a month, in January 1831, and entered HMS *Asia* as a midshipman. Then he rejoined *St Vincent* in February, but this time as a midshipman. What was going on? Why should his career be so confused? Why had he apparently concealed information about some things, like the ships on which he had served, in the same way that he seemed to be hiding the identity of his parents and family?

There were more puzzles like this.

More fundamentally, I could not fathom why Fitzjames was supposed to have had such influence on the Franklin Expedition. And if it was true that he had so many 'friends in the right places', why was he not selected to lead it? If he was so capable and well-connected, why did he accept the lowly position of third-in-command of the expedition? After all, he had already served as captain of a previous ship, HMS *Clio*. This seemed strange.

The biggest puzzle was this: who was he? The very first question O'Byrne's 1845 questionnaire asked Fitzjames was to give details of his family background.

O'Byrne said this question was optional but most officers answered it at considerable length because, in their society, their families, their social origins and their naval pedigrees mattered. Fitzjames' refusal to name his parents or even say when he was born is very strange behaviour for someone 'of good family'. It suggested to me immediately that what we read about James Fitzjames may not be true. If he was a well-connected young officer in the class- and family-based Royal Navy of the time, then surely his connections would be plain and he would want people to know them? But if he had no family or connections, then how could he possibly be 'well connected'? If no one can identify his family, how can anyone say that he was 'lispingly English'? That is especially ironic given that Francis Crozier was supposedly held back because his parents were Irish. Why was Fitzjames promoted so fast if he apparently had no parents at all?

I went back to Sir Clements and Sir Albert Markham, who seem to have been used by all succeeding historians for information on Fitzjames. I consulted the Markhams' published books and a handwritten manuscript by Sir Albert for a book he never published on the Franklin Exhibition which is deposited in the archive at the Royal Geographical Society. In this he wrote nothing about Fitzjames' education, wealth or breeding, which is a puzzle since succeeding writers seem to be convinced that he had plenty of all three. But the Markhams did give what appeared to be two facts about Fitzjames' family.

The first was that Fitzjames was said to be the brother of Elizabeth Coningham, the lady to whom he wrote the last letters which inspired John Wilson. The second was, rather strangely, that Fitzjames was the nephew of her husband William Coningham, as they tell us Coningham's father Robert was Fitzjames' uncle.

By now Fitzjames seemed to me to be a bit like Woody Allen's Zelig. Everyone seems to know him, yet he appears to have sprung fully formed from nowhere. He was a young man who 'rose without trace', as Peter Cook memorably said of the television personality David Frost. I thought that with what Sir Clements and Sir Albert Markham had said I could trace his family and fill in the gaps in his career. Little did I know then that the accepted story about James Fitzjames simply didn't add up.

This book reveals who James Fitzjames really was and it will cause quite a few surprises. The truth, revealed for the first time here, will enable historians of the Franklin Expedition to understand Fitzjames' position and his influence on the expedition. But what is much more exciting, and what I had not expected, was that it brings back to life the exciting story of the real James Fitzjames. The true picture of the man that has emerged does not conform in the slightest to any stereotype. No one has ever understood him because no one has ever put together all the information he left behind.

One

TRACKING DOWN JAMES FITZJAMES

James Fitzjames joined the Franklin Expedition at the start of the photographic age. Pictures were taken of the officers of the expedition, including Franklin, Crozier and Fitzjames. These pictures are not photographs but daguerreotypes. A daguerreotype is something between a photograph and a painting. Like a photograph, it is a mechanical image, but like a painting it is unique in that it can never be reproduced. This makes them precious and to handle the original daguerreotypes, as I have been privileged to do, gives you a unique connection with the subject (see plates 1 and 2).

The often mistranslated Chinese proverb that 'a picture's meaning can express ten thousand words' is certainly true of these portraits. Franklin and Crozier are identically posed. Both have problems with their hats. Franklin is wearing an archaic fore-and-aft hat and looks ill, while Crozier looks tired and wan and is wearing an improbably huge cap. Fitzjames has a rather large cap too, but as he is holding it the absurdity seems less. Two daguerreotypes were taken of Fitzjames. In one he holds a telescope, the symbol of an officer, and in the second he has put it down. He looks more relaxed and confident than Franklin or Crozier – a more modern figure. One of the daguerreotypes of him has been lost, but a photograph of it survives so both images are reproduced in this book.

These daguerreotypes are well known yet even they have concealed significant information which generations of Franklin researchers have missed. The researcher Peter Carney noticed that reflections can be seen in the peak of Fitzjames' cap in both pictures and that, since Fitzjames held his cap at a slightly different angle, by enlarging the two images it is possible to 'see' what Fitzjames was looking at when he sat for his pictures. On Fitzjames' left stood Sir John Franklin, who can be discerned wearing his fore-and-aft hat. In the centre was a mast with a lower spar and a furled sail visible from one of the ships, possibly HMS *Erebus*. And on the right can be seen the tripod of the daguerreotype machine. It is eerie that Fitzjames' own image has retained, unseen for 165 years, an image of his own view of his commander Sir John Franklin and (probably) of his ship HMS *Erebus*.

The Markhams were the starting point for my quest for the truth about James Fitzjames, especially the handwritten draft of Sir Albert's unpublished book on the Franklin Expedition. The other recognised source for information on Fitzjames is the published set of letters he wrote to Elizabeth Coningham, who Markham had said was Fitzjames' sister.

Less well known is the archive of Fitzjames' papers held at the National Maritime Museum. This includes the certificate of his baptism at the church of St Mary-le-Bone in London. It records that his father was James Fitzjames, gentleman, and his mother Ann Fitzjames, and that he was born on 27 July 1813 and christened on 24 February 1815.

Now I had confirmation of the identity of his family; but who were Ann and James Fitzjames? I tried to find out more about them. Even though detailed census records did not exist in 1815, there are many other sources of information, especially for someone who was a 'gentleman'. Many parish records are now accessible through the internet. I tried everything. But in every single case I drew a blank. I even searched trade newspapers and Court Circulars for some sign of the 'gentleman' having had some sort of independent existence somewhere. There was no one of that name in the Royal Navy. I looked through the marriages and deaths registers for their parish church, St Mary-le-Bone, from 1790 to 1820, but there was nothing. There were no candidates for either Ann or her husband on any registers or databases of births, marriages and deaths. If Fitzjames was their first child and if they were supposed to have died a few years after his birth, then there ought to be a trace somewhere. The baptismal certificate proved that at some stage on Friday 24 February 1815 a couple had brought their 1-year-old baby to be christened at that church. Yet it was frustrating because I could go there and stand at the very spot where they had stood with James Fitzjames in their arms, but could not find any more information about them. They seemed to walk into the church from nowhere and then walk out again into a void.

I wondered if I could trace them through Fitzjames' 'sister', Elizabeth Coningham. Here the parish records were easily accessible and proved beyond doubt that she had been born Elizabeth Meyrick in the little town of Burford in Oxfordshire. Unlike the records relating to the Fitzjames family, her family records are complete. They show that she did not have a brother called James, nor did she have any relations called Fitzjames. I checked her father's will and again drew a blank. It seemed impossible that the sibling relationship alleged by Markham between Elizabeth Meyrick and James Fitzjames could have existed.

Markham also described Elizabeth's father-in-law, whose name was the Reverend Robert Coningham, as Fitzjames' uncle. This had seemed strange, but if Fitzjames was not Elizabeth's sister, perhaps he was really related to her husband

William. Again, parish and genealogical records enabled me quite easily to prove that Fitzjames was not associated with Coningham's family tree in any way.

I noticed that in his letters to Robert Coningham, Fitzjames had addressed the older man as 'uncle'. Markham must have seen this. Then I found official letters to the Admiralty from both Robert Coningham and James Fitzjames in which both men made it quite clear that Robert Coningham was Fitzjames' guardian and they had no blood relationship. In most of his letters, Robert Coningham said that Fitzjames 'was placed at a very early period of his life under my charge, and was carefully brought up under my own roof till the time of his going to sea, when he was just twelve years of age'. Sometimes Coningham says that Fitzjames came into his household at age 7. John Wilson seems to have picked up on that.

This proved that Fitzjames was not related to any of the Coninghams, but got me no closer to the elusive 'Ann and James Fitzjames'. I started to think that perhaps Fitzjames was illegitimate and these names were false. Illegitimacy was not unusual and the accepted practice was for the resulting child to be born discretely and then quietly and informally fostered elsewhere.

It was usual for illegitimate children to be given a surname constructed from their father's name. The illegitimate son of King James II was called James Fitzjames and the Duke of Clarence gave his illegitimate children the surname FitzClarence. It is a coincidence which threw me for a while that I found evidence of an unrelated, but clearly illegitimate, James Fitzjames who was born in 1802, entered the Royal Navy as a volunteer at age 12 and died on active service in 1822. His strange story is given in Appendix I.

So was 'my' James Fitzjames illegitimate too? If so then his name, which has the meaning of 'James, the son of James', might suggest that his father also had the first name 'James'. And the fact that his father, if he concealed his real name, adopted the name 'James Fitzjames' for himself suggested to me that Fitzjames' grandfather might also have been christened 'James'.

Over the years there have been many different suggestions for Fitzjames' true family. The name is unusual and at the time had strong connotations of Jacobinism (support for the exiled Stuart line of claimants to the throne). The exiled Stuart royal line used the surname Fitzjames and some have suggested that James Fitzjames' father might have been one of them. Others have noticed that James Stephen, the famous anti-slavery lawyer, named his son James Fitzjames Stephen and have suggested that Fitzjames may have been an illegitimate son of James Stephen. A further suggestion, on the basis that Fitzjames is a common surname in Ireland, is that perhaps he was Irish. Many Irish parish records were destroyed in the early years of the last century, so this would explain why I could find no trace of Fitzjames' ancestry in any search there.

I had spent about a year puzzling over this, exploring blind alleys and loose ends until one day, reading some Admiralty files at The National Archives at Kew, I found a personal letter which proved categorically that Fitzjames was illegitimate and conclusively identified his father. James Fitzjames' natural father was not called 'James Fitzjames', was not Sir James Stephen, was no Jacobin pretender and was certainly not Irish. He was no relative of Elizabeth Coningham either. Proof of Fitzjames' paternity lies in Admiralty file ADM1/2559, letter S10, dated 27 January 1831. This was a private letter between two senior officers, Captain Fleming Senhouse of HMS *Asia* and his friend Captain George Elliot, who was First Secretary to the Admiralty. In the letter, Senhouse refers to Fitzjames as 'Mr Jas Fitzjames, a son of Sir Jas Gambier and who having served in the *Pyramus* under Captains Gambier and Sartorius is now on board the *St Vincent* as assistant master'. This was my man and my proof. It enabled me to reconstruct the story of James Fitzjames. And the story it reveals is far more remarkable than anyone could possibly have guessed.

Fitzjames' true father, Sir James Gambier, was born in 1772 and died in 1844, shortly before James Fitzjames sailed on the Franklin Expedition. Fitzjames was not orphaned at an early age, nor at the age of 7. Sir James Gambier was a member of a prominent British family in the eighteenth and early nineteenth century. He was descended from a French Huguenot called Nicholas Gambier, who had moved to England from Normandy in about 1690 to escape sectarian persecution. The family had prospered in the eighteenth century and most of its male members had chosen careers either in the Church of England or the Royal Navy.

Sir James' father had been Admiral James Gambier, who was born in 1723 and died in the year of the French Revolution, 1789. My hunch about the forenames of Fitzjames' father and grandfather had been correct. Admiral Gambier had fought in the American War of Independence as second-in-command to Vice-Admiral Lord Howe and had briefly been commander-in-chief at New York after Howe resigned his command.

There was a second Admiral Gambier, both more famous and more controversial, who was 57 years old at the time of Fitzjames' birth. This was Admiral Lord Gambier (see plate 3), whose first name was also James. He was Fitzjames' father's first cousin. He had fought with great distinction in one of the early sea battles of the French Revolutionary Wars, the Glorious First of June in 1794, but his career ended in controversy after the Battle of Basque Roads in 1809. After this battle he was accused publicly of cowardice by Admirals Lord Cochrane and Sir Eliab Harvey after he refused to close with and destroy the trapped French fleet. Harvey told Gambier to his face, 'I never saw a man so unfit for the command of a fleet as Your Lordship'. Lord Gambier was cleared in the subsequent court martial but never went to sea again.

Why had Admiral Lord Gambier not moved in for the kill at the Battle of the Basque Roads? The reasons lie in his personality. Lord Gambier was a career naval officer who was known for his profound Christian belief. He seems to have been unable to accept responsibility for the bloodshed which would follow an assault on a large body of French sailors unable to defend themselves.

Lord Gambier was active in missionary work and a leading light in such organisations as the Marine Society, the various Bible societies and the Church Missionary Society. Like Sir John Franklin, he was a man who was regarded as particularly pious even by the standards of the time. He was a member of the Clapham Sect, the group of committed evangelical Christians centred on William Wilberforce who worshipped at the Church of All Saints in Clapham. He was actually related to the Reverend Venn, the vicar of All Saints and spiritual leader of the Sect. Gambier's pious nature was well known throughout the Royal Navy and made him deeply unpopular. Officers found the assertive teetotaller an uncomfortable messmate and the sailors, who evidently did not appreciate his fervent sermons, nicknamed him 'Dismal Jimmie'.

Sir John Barrow told a story about Gambier's behaviour at the Battle of the Glorious First of June. Gambier had been captain of the HMS *Defence*, a relatively small ship of 74 guns, which seemed about to be overwhelmed by a huge 120-gun French ship bearing down upon her. One of his lieutenants momentarily, and understandably, panicked at this terrifying sight and shouted to Gambier: 'Damn my eyes, sir, here is a whole mountain coming down upon us; what shall we do?' Gambier was more offended by this oath than by the sight of the French ship and replied solemnly: 'How dare you, sir, at this awful moment, come to me with an oath in your mouth? Go down, sir, and encourage your men to stand to their guns like brave British seamen.' When an incredulous Sir John Barrow later asked Gambier whether this was true, Gambier apparently murmured that 'he believed something of the kind had occurred'.

It was probably this that prevented Gambier's court martial from finding him guilty. It would have been extremely embarrassing for this venerable seadog and pillar of the Church to be convicted of cowardice in the face of the enemy.

This mixture of Church of England and Royal Navy was the heritage of Sir James Gambier. But Sir James broke away. He was neither clergyman nor sailor. After brief service in the Royal Navy he joined the army by purchasing a commission in the Life Guards. Then he became a diplomat, being appointed British consul-general at Lisbon in 1803. This became a vital post with the outbreak of the Peninsular War. When the Portuguese royal family went into exile in Brazil in 1808, to escape the invading French armies, Gambier was appointed British consul-general in Rio de Janeiro. Portugal and Brazil then shared the same royal family. Gambier served in this role until 1814, when the allies reached Paris and forced Napoleon into exile on Elba. Gambier returned to England in August that year at the age of 42. In 1815 he went abroad again, being appointed British consul-general to the Netherlands in The Hague, where he remained until at least 1825.

Britain's relations with Brazil and Portugal were vital during the Napoleonic Wars and the War of 1812, and Gambier's role had been critical. From 1808 British land forces were continually engaged with the French in Spain and Portugal in

the bitter Peninsular War. Brazil was a key British trading partner and ally, especially once the cool relations between Britain and the United States descended
into open warfare in 1812. Compounding British difficulties was the start of the
protracted Latin American revolt against Spanish and Portuguese colonial rule
in which Lord Gambier's nemesis, Admiral Lord Cochrane, played an important
role. This series of revolutions might have been expected to act against British
interests and favour France as the revolution in North America had forty years
earlier. But skilful diplomacy, aggressive trading and selective use of the force of
the Royal Navy enabled Britain to maintain a positive position in the turbulent
world of Latin American politics and to exploit these relationships to counter-
balance France and the United States. Sir James Gambier played a vital part in
this balancing act, working with the Portuguese royal family in exile in Rio de
Janeiro from 1808 until 1814.

The life of the Portuguese expatriates in Brazil was exotic and licentious. Sir
James fully entered into this and his life in Brazil was one long social whirl of lux-
urious living. We have an eyewitness account of this from the diary of Elizabeth
Macquarie, who visited Rio and met Sir James and his wife and six children in
August 1809 while on her way to Australia. She tells us that Sir James and Lady
Gambier lived in a beautifully situated house called 'Bolto Togo' which Gambier
had bought outright. The house was situated 'in a most romantic spot' on the sea
shore surrounded by an orange grove. Elizabeth Macquarie found the smell of
the orange blossom overwhelming. The house was approached by a grand drive
which skirted the beach. It overlooked the harbour and the Sugar Loaf Mountain.
The interior was decorated in the regency style and furnished in the latest English
taste. As Gambier's bankers would later attest, the family lived a life of 'unbounded
expense' in which Lady Gambier fully shared. Elizabeth Macquarie described
Lady Gambier as 'one of the most elegant and pleasing women we had ever seen,
and very handsome'. The Gambiers continually entertained the English community and passing English visitors and when the Macquaries visited they insisted
on organising a ball for the officers of Colonel Macquarie's regiment. At this ball,
Elizabeth Macquarie met not only 'all the English persons of distinction at Rio
consisting for the most part of naval officers', but also senior members of the
Portuguese nobility and the Papal Nuncio.

But at some point in this exotic, elegant, extravagant and no doubt alcohol-
fuelled life, Sir James strayed. Since James Fitzjames was born in July 1813, it is
clear that in or around November 1812 Sir James was conducting an affair, as it
was then that James Fitzjames was conceived.

Who was James Fitzjames' mother? There are no clear pointers in the English
records. But it seems most likely she was an unmarried woman of some social
importance. Had the mother been a lower-class woman the Gambier family
would not have been obliged to take responsibility for the baby. And had she
been married it is likely that her family would have brought the baby up as if it

had been conceived by the mother's husband. Right from the top, the Portuguese royal family and nobility in exile were notoriously licentious. Dom João, the regent, was heir to the thrones of Portugal and Brazil. He was well known for his personal ugliness, indolent nature and corpulent physique. His wife Carlota Joaquina, daughter of the King of Spain and a member of the illustrious Bourbon family, was an even more eccentric figure. Although lively and flighty, she was renowned for her quite astonishing unattractiveness and it is a little ungallant to record that contemporary paintings of her fully bear this out. She had a persistent reputation for promiscuity. She had little in common with her husband and the couple led very separate lives under different roofs. Between 1793, when she was 18, and 1820, when she was 45 years of age, she bore twelve children, although the last three were stillborn or died in infancy. Rumours about the paternity of at least some of these children seem to have been more than just gossip.

The Gambiers would have known this family and it appears that 'Bolto Togo', the name Elizabeth Macquarie gave for Sir James Gambier's house, was actually Botafogo, where the estranged Carlota Joaquina set up her home in exile. It is tempting to suggest that this apparently highly sexed woman was herself James Fitzjames' mother and it is biologically possible. But it seems to have been her practice to bring up all her offspring within her family, irrespective of paternity, so there doesn't seem to be any reason why this baby should have been brought up differently had she had an affair with Sir James Gambier. It is more likely that Fitzjames' mother was an unmarried woman in her social circle. She was presumably a daughter in one of the Portuguese noble families in exile or possibly even a member of the royal family. But without some documentary evidence it is difficult to see how we will even be able to identify this lady.

This exotic and promiscuous sub-tropical life may not have been the only attraction of Rio de Janeiro to Sir James Gambier. His bank records in the archives of Hoare and Company in Fleet Street, London, do not make pleasant reading. He was plainly an extravagant and irresponsible man who borrowed vast sums. In November 1814 he owed Hoare's and others over £9,000, which in today's earnings is equivalent to over £5 million. When he returned to England he tried to avoid Hoare's, but they tracked him down and he was forced to place his financial affairs in the hands of trustees before he could take up his next posting. This new information linking Sir James Gambier means that now, for the first time, we can describe Fitzjames' origins and reconstruct his early life.

It turns out that James Fitzjames, the 'thumpingly English' officer of Franklin legend, was actually born in Rio de Janeiro, in sight of the Sugar Loaf Mountain. The hot, humid air of Brazil, laden with the scent of orange blossom, was the first he breathed. Perhaps his mother's first name was Ann or Anna as this was the name given to her when Fitzjames was baptised in London in 1815. She was almost certainly Portuguese and there is evidence that Portuguese was Fitzjames' first language. It is possible that the name his mother gave him when he was born was not even James and it is also feasible that, as she would have been a Roman Catholic, he may have been christened at birth as a Roman Catholic.

Life changed dramatically for Sir James Gambier and his extended family in August 1814 with the apparent end of the Napoleonic Wars – nobody predicted Napoleon's dramatic re-emergence during the 'Hundred Days' – and his recall to London. Sir James had to face up to some serious problems. His first problem was his creditors as his recall to London put him squarely in their hands. By November 1814 the family had taken lodgings at 130 Lower Grosvenor Street in Mayfair and it was here that Hoare's tracked him down and forced him to place his affairs in the hands of trustees.

Sir James' distinguished cousin, Lord Gambier, took it upon himself to try to sort out the mess of his dissolute relative's life. At this time Lord Gambier was a busy man. He was part of the British delegation negotiating a way out of the war of 1812 with an American delegation in neutral Ghent. The treaty was finally signed at Ghent on 24 December 1814.

Sir James' second problem was to find another job. His fifteen years in Lisbon and Rio de Janeiro had made him an expert in Portuguese and Brazilian affairs but with the apparent peace there was little call for this expertise. It is perhaps not a coincidence that Sir James' next posting was as British consul-general to the Netherlands. It looks very likely that Lord Gambier was able to obtain this position for Sir James, one which was away from the metropolis of London but not so far away that he would be beyond control. Lord Gambier took the lead in sorting out Sir James' tangled financial affairs, established a creditors' trust and managed it. Sir James was allowed to keep part of his salary and under Lord Gambier's watchful eye his debts were slowly paid off over the next fifteen years.

Sir James does not seem entirely to have lost his taste for high living. He next appears in the historical record as a guest at the Duchess of Richmond's famous ball given in Brussels on 17 June 1815, the evening before the Battle of Waterloo. Sir James had already taken up his appointment as British consul-general. He had spent less than six months in England since returning from Brazil. This ball must stand as perhaps the most glamorous social event ever. It was here that the Duke of Wellington announced that the battle would be fought the next day. Some guests left early, but other officers were said to have gone straight to the field of battle from the ball and fought in evening dress. This sounds a tall story, but Fitzjames' friend Sophia Percy remembered, as a child of 7, being shown the coat her uncle Henry had worn for the ball and then fought in at the battle. She recalled that it had a 'large stain of blood on one shoulder of it'.

The third problem in Sir James' life could almost certainly be found in the form of a one-year-old infant in his household at Lower Grosvenor Street – the young James Fitzjames. While it might be acceptable in Brazil to have illegitimate children in your extended household, it certainly was not in England. Sir James had brought the young James back across the Atlantic. A one-year-old baby would have needed careful care to survive such a voyage. This suggests that someone, perhaps a Portuguese nurse, came with him. It's doubtful whether the grown-up Fitzjames will have had any memory of his early life in Brazil or his first sea journey.

On 24 February 1815, a couple took this child to be baptised at the nearby church of St Mary-le-Bone. Presumably the man who gave his name as 'James Fitzjames, gentleman' was actually Sir James Gambier, and 'Ann Fitzjames' was either Lady Gambier or the Portuguese nurse who had brought him across the Atlantic.

There is no suggestion Fitzjames ever lived in the Gambier household in Ghent so it seems that shortly after the baptism Fitzjames was handed over to his new foster parents, Louisa and Robert Coningham. We have seen that Coningham usually said this happened when Fitzjames was 'at an early age'. In an almost unbearably moving letter she wrote to Fitzjames on Robert's death, his widow Louisa makes it overwhelmingly clear that Fitzjames, who she called 'my dear afflicted child', entered her household and affections as an infant. Coningham's 'at the age of seven' was evidently a way of obscuring how close his links with Fitzjames really were. We know from Captain Sartorius that at the age of 14 Fitzjames was fluent in Portuguese. Portuguese was not commonly spoken in Hertfordshire. This strongly suggests that Fitzjames' first language was Portuguese and that when he lived in the Coningham household he was cared for by a Portuguese speaker, presumably the nurse who accompanied him over the Atlantic. This may be the person he referred to in a letter he wrote at the age of 12 as 'Rumb'.

But what is the link between the unwanted baby James Fitzjames and the household of Robert Coningham?

Lady Gambier, at that time an attractive 39-year-old, had been born Jemima Snell. It seems very likely that it was her family who stepped in to find an appropriate and discrete foster family for Sir James' unwanted son. Her father William Snell was a prosperous but elderly retired gentleman whose family had lived on the attractive Salisbury Hall estate in Hertfordshire for over a century. He seems to have been the link to the Coningham family as they were well connected into the squirearchy of Hertfordshire, and Salisbury Hall lies just 10 miles from the Abbots Langley area where the Coninghams settled.

Lord Gambier may also have known Robert Coningham through the Clapham Sect. He was a prominent member of it and was related to its spiritual head, the Rev. Venn. Like many members of the Sect, Robert Coningham was educated at Cambridge University and may have had close connections with it.

What was the family of Robert Coningham like and what can we learn about Fitzjames' childhood?

The Coninghams' only natural son to live to maturity, William Coningham, was one of Fitzjames' closest friends. Fitzjames put up a portrait of William in his cabin on HMS *Erebus* and it can be seen in the *Illustrated London News* picture published in 1845. William was born on 26 June 1815 and christened three weeks later at Madron, Penzance, in Cornwall. The place of birth was given as Rose Hill, which is a small hamlet outside Penzance. At the time of William's birth, Robert Coningham was 29 years old, having been born in 1784 in County Londonderry, Ireland, where his father had been a merchant. Their family name had been Cunningham and they had originated in Scotland. 'Cunningham', pronounced with a Northern Irish accent, sounds rather like 'Coningham' and it was in Ireland that the spelling changed.

Robert Coningham's wife Louisa was seven years older than him and had been born in India. She was the daughter of James Capper, a colonel in the Madras army of the Honourable East India Company. She must have been a hardy little girl to survive, as the death rate among European infants born in eighteenth-century India was high. Louisa Coningham was an intellectual with strong interests in literature, philosophy and especially in women's education. She wrote and published two books: *A Poetical History of England* and *An abridgment of Locke's Essay concerning human understanding: with some conjectures respecting the interference of nature with education.* The first is a history of Britain in verse, supposed to have been written for the instruction of the 'young ladies' at Rothbury House School in Kennington and published in 1810, the year before her marriage. It was successful enough for a second edition to be published in 1815. Her eldest sister Marianne was married to Robert Clutterbuck, the wealthy heir to a large Hertfordshire brewer. Clutterbuck was an author and a pioneer topographer, who wrote the huge *History and Antiquities of the County of Hertford* in three volumes, published from 1815 to 1827, which is still a valuable resource for local historians today. Louisa's father, Colonel Capper, hailed from Londonderry in Ireland, so we can speculate that it was through an Irish connection that she met Robert.

Their circle had something of the roving, colonial culture about it. Other members of Robert's family had immigrated to the West Indies in the early eighteenth century and become extremely wealthy through the ownership of one of the largest sugar plantations on St Vincent. Their wealth depended upon the ruthless exploitation of a large workforce of slaves.

After attending Peterhouse College, Cambridge, Robert Coningham took Holy Orders in the Church of England and was ordained priest at Ely in June 1810. Although he served as Curate of Abington in Cambridgeshire, he never became a clergyman and took a secular living. Instead, at some point in the 1820s, he bought an attractive country estate called Rose Hill in Hertfordshire and settled down to the life of an educated country gentleman of independent means. Before then the family seems to have lived in Cornwall, Watford and perhaps also Blackheath before settling at Rose Hill.

Their first child, a boy called John, was born either in 1812 or 1813 but died in infancy. Louisa Coningham was 35 when John was born and 37 when William was born. The family was small for those days. John was of almost the same age as the infant James Fitzjames. It is tempting to suggest that he died at about the same time that William Snell was looking for foster parents for an unwanted baby boy and that the grieving Coninghams informally adopted James Fitzjames after the tragic death of their firstborn son.

What was Fitzjames' childhood like? With his fostering and the death of John Coningham, this would have been a time of great emotional turmoil for the Coninghams and for the infant James, but it is clear that through it they were able to build a very stable and loving relationship. Fitzjames remembered Robert Coningham as being a 'dear and kind' man who was 'as fond of me as he was of his own son'. Louisa wrote to Fitzjames that 'I consider you as a son' and William Coningham, writing to Fitzjames to tell him of Robert Coningham's death, made a revealing slip of the pen in referring to Robert Coningham as 'our father'.

Fitzjames retained a great affection for Hertfordshire and seems to have visited the place whenever he could, even after both Louisa and Robert Coningham had died. Twenty years later, in 1836, he wrote to Robert Coningham's mother from the banks of the Euphrates to say how much he loved the countryside of 'sweet Herts. I love it and all connected with it. It is pleasant to look back sometimes when we all were so happy at Watford and the thoughts of seeing once more the dear old haunts gives me new spirits and life'.

Once time had ameliorated the traumas of the death of John Coningham and the adoption of James Fitzjames, the little family settled down in happiness. If it is correct that 'Rumb' was his Brazilian or Portuguese nurse, then she seems to have lived with the family, at least until Fitzjames was 12. Although the environment would have been very different from that which the infant Fitzjames would have experienced in Rio de Janeiro, the consistent presence of the nurse would have reduced the emotional trauma. He would have retained few, if any, memories of his childhood prior to Hertfordshire.

Robert Coningham's widowed mother lived with them. She was clearly fond of James and he referred to her as 'grandmama'. Born Elizabeth Campbell, this formidable lady was linked to a large and close family of Campbells across Britain, and through her Fitzjames was too. Among the closest friends of the Coninghams were a sister and brother called Alicia and Colin Campbell.

Alicia and Colin Campbell had scandalous origins. Their grandmother had also been called Alicia Campbell. The Campbell family's propensity for intermarriage and for using a small set of forenames makes their ancestry very confusing. Alicia, the grandmother, married a Henry Campbell but, after having two children with him, ran away with her cousin Colin Campbell who was also married. Shockingly, they set up home together and had more children. One was a daughter, called Alicia by some authorities but Agnes by others, who married a humble carpenter called John McLiver. The Coninghams' friends Alicia and Colin Campbell were the product of this legitimate marriage which was tainted by their mother's illegitimacy and near-incest and John's humble origins. But blood was thicker than water to the wider Campbell family and Alicia and Colin were looked after. Colin was enlisted in the army under the name of Campbell and the brother and sister thereafter both took the surname Campbell. Colin Campbell had a record of brave service during the Napoleonic Wars and in Fitzjames' childhood he would have been a revered figure, although as he served abroad for most of this time Fitzjames can hardly have known him. But Alicia seems to have been close to Fitzjames and the Coningham family and was a lively and intellectual influence. In later life Bishop William Boyd-Carpenter, another Campbell relative, remembered her as 'dear white-haired, beaming-faced Alicia Campbell. Warm of heart, cheery in manner, breathing kindness a kind of fairy godmother. She brought us books, and they were books which, as a rule, interested us.' This animated, charming and intelligent woman was typical of the circle in which the Coninghams moved.

Rose Hill was a substantial estate. As well as 'Rumb', the family engaged a tutor to educate the two boys and there is no doubt the standard of their education was extremely high. In 1851 the household consisted of two indoor servants, a cook, a labourer, a laundress and a coachman, and there is no reason to assume it was any different in Fitzjames' day. At the back was a courtyard, coach house, stables, barns and other farmyard buildings with pigs, hens, ducks and geese. The estate extended back to about 30 acres of parkland, orchard, kitchen garden, paddock and arable land. In the paddocks lived the family's horses and with their coach the family had a high degree of mobility. They could easily visit London and return home the same day. Fitzjames was fit and healthy and this would have been an idyllic country upbringing for the young boy. The house survived until 1956 and a photograph of it, taken in about 1900, is shown as plate 8.

There were thousands of such households up and down the British Isles. At Rose Hill the Rev. Coningham lived the quiet life of a country gentleman, respected in the neighbourhood and on easy terms with the local intelligentsia and nobility. As a pleasant and healthy area to live with easy access to London, it attracted some large and wealthy households.

Close by was the 'big house', Cassiobury House, the country seat of the Earl of Essex. The earl's wealthy family had connections at the highest level with other members of the aristocracy and the Royal Navy. Another eminent local family were the Percys, relatives of the Duke of Northumberland, who lived at Scotsbridge House in Croxley Green, a hamlet about 6 miles from Rose Hill. Sophia Percy (plate 5) knew James Fitzjames as a teenager. She gave a wonderfully vivid portrait of what life was like in this part of the country at that time in her memoirs, published as late as 1901:

In those days in the country there were always eccentric people of strong individualities to be met with, and they were probably more numerous and more eccentric than in these times of travelling and of wider interchange of ideas. One wishes one could reproduce them and have their photographs. Their angles had not been ground down by going to London and travelling abroad. Some quite well-to-do people of the upper middle class, and even of the landed classes, lived and died in their own homes and on their own properties. Their prejudices were unassailable, and they were narrow-minded and insular to a degree. Such people could scarcely exist nowadays. They were relics of 1800, some even of 1700. They had a profound contempt for 'foreigners', especially for the French, and an entire ignorance of the character and customs of these 'foreigners,' and of their language and literature. They were insufferable bores to live with, but amusing to see and listen to for a short time.

The old-fashioned country poor people of those days were delightful, with their entire absence of education (in the South of England at least), their strong mother wit, and excellent manners.

I wish I had written down the prayers of an old woman I knew who rejoiced in the name of 'Puddifoot.' They were long verses, which she said she recited every morning and night. They were not about God or religion, but about lambs and green fields, and I suspect of great antiquity. They answered the purpose of prayer to her, and doubtless were accepted as such, for she recited them as an act of worship. She used to reckon time as so many months or years before 'the Sally-come-o'er-us' visited or left England. This, I at last discovered, was the cholera which in 1830 visited Rickmansworth. It was the old woman's Hejira, and she counted all events as occurring before or after 'the Sally-come-o'er-us'.

There was much dissent of all sorts, and superstition. Many of the poor people would declare, and firmly believe, that they had 'met the Lord' on such and such a road. Perhaps they did in their hearts. They also would relate how they 'had met the Enemy,' and how he had tempted them, which is also not improbable. The Watford road appeared to be the usual place where this dread personage was to be met with. He seems to have frequented it on market days, when farmers and their men would return from Watford 'market pert' (pronounced peart), as the old Staffordshire expression had it.

[Sophia Percy added a footnote that 'pert' meant drunk]

As well as mixing with their powerful and influential neighbours, Louisa and Robert Coningham were on close terms with other intellectuals in or associated with their extended family. Many of this 'clan' of cousins shared a similar family background being descended from Scottish families which had settled in Ireland.

Louisa was related to some prominent local Hertfordshire families, including that of Robert Clutterbuck, her brother-in-law. At the time of Fitzjames' childhood, Louisa's father, Colonel James Capper, was also still alive. By then he seems to have been in financial difficulties and living in Norfolk. He was a pioneer meteorologist, being a keen observer of the weather. Unfortunately, he attempted to explain weather patterns by reference to the lunar cycle, presumably thinking that the atmosphere, like the tides of the sea, could be influenced by the moon. His theories were, therefore, valueless.

Colonel Capper had two further distinctions, one of which may have been very important in shaping Fitzjames' future life. In the 1780s Colonel Capper had tried to establish whether there was a quicker overland route for transmitting the vital mails between England and India. He sailed from England to Aleppo and then explored the lands of the Middle East and the Arabian Desert before taking a ship to India from Basra on the Shatt el-Arab waterway, in what is now southern Iraq. According to the *Dictionary of National Biography* he was the first person to pen the phrase 'passage to India'. Like many people in the Coningham family circle he was an unconventional thinker and a writer.

Another was the up-and-coming writer John Sterling, who was married to Robert's sister Hester. He was another Cambridge-educated intellectual. Like Robert he had taken holy orders, but his interests lay in writing. He was a perfectionist who published relatively little. To modern tastes John Sterling's writings have little appeal, but in his day his rigour, his ascetic and holy lifestyle and his suffering (he contracted TB) had great appeal. Some of his work remains in print.

Through the Campbells the Coninghams were related to the large family of Archibald Boyd, who lived nearby. The Boyds were yet another Irish family of Scottish extraction who had settled in Hertfordshire. One of the sons, John Boyd, was a childhood friend of Fitzjames who also served in the Royal Navy.

A final significant piece in the cousinly jigsaw was the Gledstanes family. The Gledstanes' were a wealthy family of merchants and bankers who tended to manage the extended family's wealth.

There would have been frequent visitors from London, even before the development of the railways. Stagecoaches ran several times a day and most families of the wealth of the Coninghams also maintained their own coach. Visitors from overseas, from far-off lands and colonies, would have stayed from time to time. Although still very rural, the area was far from a backwater and the young James Fitzjames was exposed to many scholarly people and concepts.

Robert Coningham mixed with other writers and thinkers too, including Thomas Carlyle and his set. The only actual description of Rose Hill which has survived for us is that of the perpetually hypochondriac Jane Carlyle, who stayed with the Rev. Coningham and left a brief description of the household in a letter to Susan Hunter dated 20 September 1835. She described the house as being 'about twenty-five miles from London' and 'a perfect Paradise of a place, peopled as every Paradise ought to be with Angels'. There she 'drank warm milk, and ate new eggs, and bathed in pure air, and rejoiced in cheerful countenances, and was as happy as the day was long' as everyone there 'seemed to have no other object in life but to study my pleasure'.

The family travelled and moved around a lot. Robert Coningham often seems to have stayed at Blackheath with relatives of his wife's family. Louisa Coningham and her son William appear often to have been ill and to have tried various 'cures'. The young Fitzjames' letters to Robert Coningham are peppered with hopes that 'aunt', that is Louisa Coningham, and 'Willy' will be better after their cure at Cheltenham or Switzerland or, less plausibly one imagines, Boulogne. Fitzjames' childhood near-fluency in French suggests that the family may all have stayed in France for some time.

Life at Rose Hill came to an abrupt end for James Fitzjames when at the age of 12 he was enrolled into the Royal Navy and joined HMS *Pyramus* at Portsmouth. Why was this? Everything we know about the Coninghams points to a rather quiet and gentle life and they had no prior connection with the Royal Navy. Their interests seem to have been mainly literary and intellectual. By contrast, everything we know about Fitzjames points to a very different character. As a youth and a man he had a strong sense of humour, a great liking for boisterous behaviour and practical jokes and a keen interest in drink and the opposite sex. It may also be significant that several of the elaborate jokes we know he set up for his friends in adulthood were at the expense of ascetic and 'preachy' clergy or pious types. It would not be surprising if, by the time he entered his teens, his energy and sense of fun was beginning to jar in the gentle rural idyll of Rose Hill.

Fitzjames of course did have naval connections through his natural family, the Gambiers. Robert Gambier, his first captain, was Fitzjames' natural second cousin. He seems to have been selected as captain of HMS *Pyramus* because the ship was on a diplomatic mission to southern and central America where his family name would count for much. The Coninghams may have felt that life at sea would be a good outlet for the energy of this lively, large and energetic youth and the *Pyramus'* commission was a perfect opportunity for a member of Fitzjames' natural family to take charge of him. There does not seem to have been any long-term intention for Fitzjames to have a naval career at this stage.

In those days the first step towards becoming an officer in the Royal Navy was to be taken on as a volunteer by the captain of a ship. The youth would spend several years as a volunteer, under the wing of the captain who recruited him, and would 'learn the ropes'. If he wanted to continue his naval career, greater responsibility would come with the rank of midshipman, before the candidate would finally be commissioned as a lieutenant. With Robert Gambier willing to vouch for the youth, there was no objection to Fitzjames starting on the bottom rung of the naval officers' promotion ladder.

Two

MR FITZJAMES GOES TO SEA

His Maj Ship Pyramus
Portsmouth, 30 June 1825

Sir,
I have to request you will be pleased to solicit the sanction of my Lords
Commissioners of the Admiralty to enter as the second class of Volunteer the
young gentlemen named in the margin. They are of respectable parents, and
their education and requirements even superior to their selection, and they
promise fair to do justice to the vocation they are about to embark in.

I have the honor to be, Sir,
your most obedient servant,

Robert Gambier,
Captain

To Sir George Martin, GCB
Admiral of the Blue

Robert Gambier had just been appointed captain of HMS *Pyramus* and the
margins of this letter tell the whole story of Fitzjames' entry into the Royal
Navy. Down the side of the letter Gambier wrote the names and ages of the
two boys he wished to enrol: James Ashton and James Fitzjames, giving the ages
of both as 13 – incorrect in Fitzjames' case. To enter a 'young gentleman' as a
volunteer, a captain had to vouch for the respectability of the 'young gentleman'
and as James Fitzjames was his true second cousin, Robert Gambier had no
problem in doing so.

The same day that this letter was received at the Admiralty, another hand noted
on it: 'July 1st. Grant leave if there are vacancies. JB.' Thus, with a stroke of his pen,
Sir John Barrow permitted Robert Gambier to enter James Fitzjames into the

Royal Navy. The workaholic Barrow made dozens of such decisions every month and could have no possible idea how inextricably his family would come to be linked with James Fitzjames.

Robert Gambier was only 34 but had already served in the Royal Navy for twenty-one of those years. This was his first sea-going appointment for five years as his last had been ashore as an inspecting commander of the Revenue Coast Guard. Prior to that he had a distinguished Napoleonic War record. His surviving correspondence with Fitzjames shows him to have been a serious and religious man and the association between the two men was rather like a father/son relationship.

Gambier had a young family of three daughters and a son, all rather younger than Fitzjames. Fitzjames moved into the Gambier household at Portsmouth as one of their family and stayed with them until the *Pyramus* sailed. His little cousins, the Gambier children, were excited to have this much older boy staying, but James Fitzjames was not happy. He was homesick for Hertfordshire and the Coninghams. He got bored and then depressed. And as an adolescent about to take on the testing position of volunteer, with many of the privileges of an officer in the violent and macho world of an early nineteenth-century warship, he must have been apprehensive. He hated being treated as a playmate by the little children who were, of course, only a few years younger than him. Here is his first surviving letter to Robert Coningham:

Portsmouth, Sept 21st, 1825

Dearest Uncle,

Although I have not much to say yet it is a great consolation to me to write to you for I am very dull and unhappy without you. The two youngest children are very troublesome and tease me very much. And the eldest is gone to Perbrook. Capt Gambier does not come home till Thursday evening and I hardly know what to do with myself for although I try to be merry I can not help crying whenever I think of you. Yesterday evening I went out with the children but when I came home I felt so heavy hearted I hardly knew what to do. I miss my dear Willy [William Coningham] very much for the children will not leave me alone one minute at the moment they are making such a noise I can hardly write. Pray give my love to Grandmama [Robert's mother Elizabeth Coningham], dear Rumb and Mr Graham. It rains today so I am not able to go out, so went up into my own room to write to you but I was obliged to lock the door to keep the children out for they would not leave me one moment to write my letter. I hope I shall soon see you and my dear Aunt [Louisa Coningham]. Pray answer my letter for nothing would give me more pleasure than to hear from my dear Uncle. I am a great deal more merry since

I have written to you and I hope I shall soon be happy. Do not forget to write to me, in the meantime, I remain, your affectionate nephew,

James Fitzjames

Fitzjames had already been entered onto the books of HMS *Pyramus* on 25 August 1825 as the third in the list of five volunteers, second class. This was the most junior rank of volunteer. He seems not to have been clear how to describe his circumstances. When first entered he gave his age as 14 and his place of birth as Devon. The next month, when asked the same questions, he gave his place of birth as London and age as 12. This age was correct although he could hardly have given his true place of birth, Rio de Janeiro, without revealing his paternity. Ever after he claimed to have been born in London. Already, with his career in the Royal Navy measured in just weeks, he had been forced to lie. It would not be the last time.

HMS *Pyramus* was a 15-year-old frigate of 920 tons mounting 36 guns. She sailed on 19 October 1825 on a diplomatic mission, conveying three important passengers to South and Central America.

One passenger was a Mr Tupper, the British consul to La Guayra. A second passenger was Sir Robert Ker Porter. He was an exotic and intellectual man who had been born in 1777 and had shown early precocious talent as a painter. In 1804 he had been appointed historical painter to the Tsar of Russia and had married a Russian princess. He had travelled extensively and been honoured in Russia, Sweden and Persia, and had been present with the British army in Spain in 1809 at the death of Sir John Moore at Coruña. After his wife died at St Petersburg, he had returned to Britain and been appointed British consul in Venezuela where, amid much involvement in the liberation struggles of South America, he was to find time to paint a portrait of Simon Bolivar. It was to take up this position that the *Pyramus* was conveying him to South America.

The third passenger was the equally striking Mr Morier, the British commissioner designate to Mexico. He had been born in 1782 in Ottoman Izmir and was the son of a Swiss merchant, although he had become a British subject by naturalisation. He had worked for the British diplomatic service in Persia from 1814 to 1818 and was travelling to Mexico to negotiate a commercial treaty. This treaty, which would be ratified in 1827, was a significant diplomatic victory for England. It regularised trade between Britain and the new state of Mexico at a time when Great Britain was in dispute with the United States over Caribbean trade. Hostilities between Britain and the United States had only ended ten years ago. Britain had a strong interest in bolstering the newly independent state as a counter-weight to limit American expansion south and west, especially as the United States had no equivalent trade treaty with Mexico. Fitzjames' fluency in French means that he would have been a natural companion for Morier. In an age when few British officers spoke any language other than English, he was perhaps called upon to translate.

For a lively and intelligent boy, a trans-oceanic voyage to a foreign country must have been a fascinating experience. There would have been much to get used to in the management of the ship. The social divisions between the captain, the officers and the company are complex on a warship and would have been especially so for Fitzjames. He was a member of the company, but on the bottom rung of the promotion ladder to becoming an officer, and with a covert and no doubt much gossiped-about direct relationship with the captain. There is a hint that he was very aware of this. We know from a letter that he wrote to John Barrow, son of Sir John Barrow, much later in his life that he liked the books of Captain Francis Marryat. In the letter he referred jokingly to Medea Culpepper, who was the fat and greedy daughter of a ship's purser in Marryat's novel *Percival Keene*. The subject matter of the novel is interesting. Percival Keene is an extremely naughty boy who is sent away to sea at the age of 12. His mother is young, unmarried and respectable, but becomes pregnant. She does not know whether the father is a handsome but humble Royal Marine or a well-connected but lazy and boring Royal Naval captain. The little boy, Percival, actually believes his father was the Royal Marine but loses no opportunity to advance himself by letting people think that his father might be the captain. It is difficult to believe that Fitzjames and his friend John Barrow did not see something of Fitzjames in this.

There is no doubt that Fitzjames took to the life at sea on this first voyage. His childhood friend Sophia Percy sailed on a similar ship, HMS *Winchester*, in the 1830s and she remembered that 'it was the prettiest thing in the world during the first night watch in the tropics to hear the men singing on the tops, the maintopman starting the song by a verse, and then fore and mizzen tops taking up the chorus; sails set for the trade wind, often a moon and phosphorescent sea, and the soothing sound of the frigate slipping at such a pace through the water'. She was disappointed that the songs they sang 'were very sentimental, singing about lambs and green fields'.

Notwithstanding the romance of the sea and their taste for sentimental airs, the world of the sailors on the ship was very violent and macho and would have been a threatening culture for the young volunteer. There is a direct insight into this world in the recent analysis carried out by the Oxford Archaeology Department on the skeletons of 107 seamen who served in the Royal Navy at this time and whose remains were buried at the Royal Hospital at Greenwich. The excavator says that these remains were 'remarkable for the high prevalence of a wide range of pathological conditions, which clearly illustrated the rigours of life in the Royal Navy at this time', including 'numerous fractures, rickets, tuberculosis, syphilis, scurvy, cancer and a range of non-specific infections. Amputations and craniotomies were also identified.' More than half of these sailors had suffered fractures to the skull at some point and, incredibly, more than 60 per cent of them had suffered fractures to their nasal bones. While it is possible that some suffered these facial and head injuries in battle, the excavator considers that 'falls and interpersonal violence were highly probable causes of fractures ... Falls were a common feature of everyday life aboard ship, whilst the social life below decks was anything but decorous, particularly where alcohol was involved'.

Under his captain's watchful eye, Fitzjames had been flung into a challenging position at what in modern times would be regarded as a very young age, and clearly he had risen to the challenge.

A strange incident took place at Barbados when the ship called in there for water and fresh provisions. Fitzjames would have noticed that at least one of the ship's company, John Williams, was black. He had signed on to the ship as a seaman at Portsmouth, but when he went ashore in Barbados a slave-owner claimed that he was a runaway slave of his called 'Elias' and demanded his return to slavery. Captain Gambier refused to hand John Williams over. It turned out that John Williams had been a slave on a ship belonging to a Mr Tyne, but had been released from the ship at Gibraltar following an order from the governor that, since Britain did not recognise the existence of slavery, no man at Gibraltar could be considered a slave. With this protection, Williams had immediately jumped ship, worked his passage to Britain and enlisted in the Royal Navy. Fitzjames must have been shocked that a ship mate could be considered a chattel but, on the other hand, he must have known that some of the Coningham wealth was derived from slave-owning.

With her passengers safely delivered to the respective countries, HMS *Pyramus* returned to British waters after calling at New York. The ship remained in commission with Fitzjames a volunteer on her and carried out experimental and scientific work in home waters. By April 1826 Fitzjames was writing, chattily informing 'grandmama', Robert Coningham's aged mother, about the testing of the new 'Congreve rocket' life-saving equipment which the *Pyramus* was about to conduct at Liverpool. She may not have understood the technicalities of this rocket but she would have recognised the enthusiasm with which the lad was now enjoying his varied duties.

HMS *Pyramus* was also employed convoying soldiers to Malta, an important British outpost in the Mediterranean. It was here that a tragedy struck which must have caused significant problems for Fitzjames. Gambier's wife was taken ill. Fitzjames wrote to Robert Coningham on 5 July 1826 that 'Captain Gambier has left the *Pyramus* to go to Italy with Mrs Gambier as she is still in very bad health. The new Captain's name is Captain George Rose Sartorius. I do not know much about him but I am sure that I shall not like him as well as Captain Gambier.'

Unfortunately Gambier's wife Caroline died, leaving him a widower with four young children – the ones who had so plagued Fitzjames in Portsmouth a year earlier. Gambier resigned as captain and returned to Britain to bring them up by himself. He never went to sea again and outlived Fitzjames by twenty-five years, dying at the age of 80 in March 1872.

Fitzjames had been taken on personally by Gambier so given his irregular parenting this twist of fate put him in a difficult position. It would have been easy for him to leave the ship with Captain Gambier and return home. He chose the alternative, to stay on board and win the confidence of the new captain purely on ability. Under Sartorius, *Pyramus* became the flagship of Admiral Sir Thomas Hardy, the same man who had been the captain of HMS *Victory* at Trafalgar and had comforted Nelson as he lay dying. Hardy was in charge of the Experimental Squadron, an attempt by the Royal Navy to make a practical assessment of four different ship designs through experimentation. This would provide interesting and challenging work for a well-educated young volunteer like James Fitzjames. We know from his later excellent pass-marks at HMS *Excellent* that Fitzjames had an aptitude for figures and it seems he shone in this work. Another volunteer who served with the Experimental Squadron, three years older than Fitzjames, was someone whose name would have meant a great deal to him. This was William Barrow, son of the famous and powerful Second Secretary of the Admiralty Sir John Barrow.

Fitzjames had an aptitude for languages. In a reference, Captain Sartorius stated that Fitzjames was fluent in Portuguese. With his cosmopolitan background this is not surprising, but Robert Coningham added that he could also speak French, some Spanish and a little Italian. Coningham avoided mentioning Portuguese, presumably to avoid drawing attention to Fitzjames' Brazilian origins. Sartorius found the 14-year-old volunteer invaluable as a translator when *Pyramus* was sent to Portugal to protect British interests at the request of the Portuguese government. After King João VI died in 1826, Portugal started to descend into a civil war triggered by a complex dynastic dispute between two of his sons, Pedro and Miguel. This was complicated by tensions between the two branches of the same royal family in Brazil and in Portugal and by deep fissures in Portuguese society between liberal and absolutist factions. Miguel, who had retired to Brazil, became associated with absolutist factions and returned to Portugal in February 1828. At this point, Miguel was proclaimed king by his absolutist supporters and in May the dispute between absolutism and liberalism broke out into open fighting. Fitzjames felt aligned with Pedro and disliked the absolutists and Miguel.

HMS *Pyramus* arrived at Lisbon on 6 July and, as the Royal Navy's guard ship in the Tagus estuary, was expected to stay there for at least a year to guard British interests. Fitzjames wrote that the weather was so exceedingly hot that 'we can hardly sit up', although he was impressed by the 'sight of the ripening grapes ... and the abundance of peaches, apricots, plums, pears and bilberries'. He was still rather childlike and homesick, adding that 'I can swim a little now and I should like to be able to swim with Willy ...'

Fitzjames was present in Lisbon when Don Miguel landed from Brazil and usurped the Portuguese throne. Many English scholars of the time were attracted to the liberation struggles taking place in Central and South America, Greece and Iberia. Admiral Cochrane, Lord Gambier's nemesis, played a key role in the South American struggles for independence, and Byron and Shelley were both attracted to the cause of Greek liberation. Fitzjames' liberal sympathies in Portugal were shared by many British intellectuals and the Coninghams.

There was an extraordinary link with his tragic future when, on 19 February 1828, the Royal Naval bomb-vessel HMS *Terror* was wrecked at Villanova de Melfontes on Portugal's Atlantic coast. Although only one member of the ship's company lost his life in the wreck, the *Terror* was almost lost. This was the same ship that Fitzjames and Crozier would abandon in the Arctic twenty years later. At the time he wrote that 'she was wrecked about 70 miles to the south of Lisbon. And as soon as the Admiral heard of it, he sent us round to her assistance, with the Lyra brig. We found her lying on a bit of sand surrounded by rocks and the surf beating over her tremendously … After having rendered her all the assistance in our power, we came back to Lisbon.'

Fitzjames had won Captain Sartorius' confidence. Robert Coningham must have been pleased to hear, in a letter from Fitzjames dated 8 June 1828, about the group of twenty French refugees on board who spoke no English, but 'I have spoken to them a great deal. Indeed some of them have taken a great liking to me.' He stayed with them in France and went out riding with them. In the diplomatic and quasi-diplomatic duties into which the ship was drawn, Fitzjames' education and winning personality were useful attributes to his captain.

On 1 July 1828, after almost three years' continuous service, he was promoted 'in the field' by Sartorius to volunteer of the first class. This is significant because it was not an Admiralty sanctioned promotion. Fitzjames had shown himself a competent and confident 'young gentleman' able to thrive without family assistance or patronage.

The Coningham family received their next letter from Fitzjames postmarked Plymouth and dated 22 August 1828. 'We are at last free of that detestable hole Lisbon,' said Fitzjames, adding that 'I am heartily tired of the *Pyramus* and shall be very glad when I am clear of her. I complete three years on the 25th of this month and I have been about 18 months without seeing my aunt or Willy … [and] more than two years since I saw you at Cambridge.' His intention after being paid off was to wait for his second cousin Robert Gambier to be appointed captain of another ship, when 'of course he will take me with him'.

He was paid off on 15 September 1828 at the age of 15, having served just two and a half months as a volunteer of the first class. He reverted to civilian status as, unlike commissioned officers at the rank of lieutenant or above, young men at his level did not serve continually in the Royal Navy. Instead they simply signed on to individual ships for the length of its commission.

Fitzjames was not committed to a career in the Royal Navy and moved back to live with the Coninghams, who seem to have been living at Richmond in Surrey rather than at Rose Hill. While he had been at sea, William Coningham had been sent away to school at Eton College. He seems to have started at Eton at the age of 14 in September 1827 and left sometime between late 1829 and Easter 1830, when he would have been about 16. It's possible the family moved to Richmond to be near William.

With both boys now back home, Robert Coningham withdrew William from Eton and engaged a tutor to continue the education of both boys jointly at home. He later wrote:

> when the *Pyramis* [sic] was paid off he [Fitzjames] returned to my care ... and pursued his studies in company with my own son, their tutor being a graduate of the University of Cambridge, a son of the Master of Emmanuel, Dr Cory, and as Mr Fitzjames' abilities are excellent, he has made very considerable progress in mathematics. He also speaks French fluently, having learned it at a very early age, has a good deal of acquaintance with the Spanish language, and knows something of Italian.

Dr Cory was Robert Cory, a son of the Master of Emmanuel College, Cambridge, and 27 years old at the time.

It seems to have been now that the family settled permanently at Rose Hill and this time fits perfectly with the recollections of the young Sophia Percy, who remembered Fitzjames as 'the strongest, most energetic man I ever saw'.

One of the exciting developments at the time in the Coningham circle was their commitment to the cause of Spanish liberation. John Sterling suddenly developed an enthusiasm for this cause, linking himself to a charismatic Spanish exile, General Torrijos. Thomas Carlyle, who knew Torrijos well, described the general as 'a valiant gallant man; of lively intellect, of noble chivalrous character: fine talents, fine accomplishments, all grounding themselves on a certain rugged veracity'. Like almost everyone who came into contact with him, Fitzjames must have been deeply impressed by the Spanish general.

Torrijos was determined to lead a liberal uprising in his native land. His salon was centred on Sterling's at Regents Street in London. Carlyle says that Torrijos' wife became especially close to Sterling's mother, who was Robert Coningham's sister Hester. Sterling joined Torrijos in plotting a liberal uprising in Spain and soon attracted the idealistic and somewhat young Robert Boyd, elder brother of Fitzjames' childhood friend John. Robert threw himself, body and soul, into the cause. He had some experience as a soldier, having earlier served in the Indian army until, again according to Carlyle, he had 'received some affront, or otherwise taken some disgust in that service [and] had thrown up his commission in consequence'.

By 1829 plans were formed to land in southern Spain and foment an uprising around the figure of the charismatic general, as Napoleon had attempted when he returned from Elba in 1815. But the Hundred Days had failed. Was Torrijos a better plotter than Napoleon, and was Spain riper for revolution than France was fourteen years ago? Sterling and Robert Boyd certainly thought so and Robert sank his entire considerable wealth, £5,000, into it. With this the plot suddenly moved from opera *buffa* to opera *seria*. Arms were purchased, men recruited from among the Spanish exiles of London and a small ship hired.

While this romantic plan was hatched, Fitzjames and William Coningham continued their education at Rose Hill. Fitzjames had liked life at sea and wanted to return to it and pursue the career of a naval officer. But he had no patron in the Royal Navy as Robert Gambier was ashore on half-pay bringing up his children and Captain Sartorius had become so involved in the Portuguese civil war that he had taken a position as an admiral fighting for the liberal forces. It is a useful corrective, to those who have said that Fitzjames' rapid promotion in the Royal Navy was due to his birth and his upper-class connections, to note that at this point he had effectively no worthwhile personal connections at all.

Fitzjames sought an appointment as a midshipman. But the Admiralty recruited midshipmen only from the ranks of those who had already served at least one year as a volunteer of the first class. He had only served two months. As such, Fitzjames was unable to find a position on any ship as a midshipman and it became so difficult to find an opening for him in the Royal Navy that Robert Coningham and Fitzjames' 'friends', presumably his natural family, decided he should abandon his naval career and instead go to Cambridge University.

Fitzjames was adamant that he wanted to continue his career in the Royal Navy. He knew the world of the educated clerical gentleman scholar and it was not for him. Robert Coningham put it that Fitzjames had a 'strong inclination for the profession of his choice' and said that he insisted on being sent to sea again. Coningham finally gave in, 'trusting ... that his own excellent conduct, and qualifications admirably adapted to his profession, would ultimately get the better of any obstacles that might occur in the way of his advancement to the most honourable distinctions of his professional career'.

But Coningham himself had no connections with the navy and little understanding even of its basic career structure. Eventually he managed to enter Fitzjames onto the books of HMS *St Vincent* on 15 December 1830.

Fitzjames travelled to Portsmouth alone to join his ship. The journey overnight in the stagecoach was terrible. He arrived at Portsmouth at 8 a.m. on 15 December 'after a rather tiresome journey of thirteen hours; there were six inside [the coach] every inch of the way and I was in between a fat old lady and an old gentleman who hardly let me have a wink of sleep all night by their fidgeting'. He collected his sea chest from his agent only to find that the contents, including all his uniforms, had gone mouldy.

He located HMS *St Vincent* and reported to her, being introduced to his new captain, Hyde Parker, who he found to be 'a little, odd looking old man with a great cut on his upper lip which makes him speak in a curious way'. Already the omens were not good. 'They say he [Captain Hyde Parker] is not liked and all the Lieutenants are great beasts. Foley the Commander is hardly ever on board ...'

The *St Vincent* was a large warship by the standards of the time. She displaced 4,600 tons, a little more than the Royal Navy's Type 42 destroyers of today. But while the Type 42 carries only one large calibre gun, the *St Vincent* mounted 120 guns. And while the Type 42 has a total complement of 253, the *St Vincent* packed in well over a thousand men. Although launched in March 1815, there had been no need for such a behemoth in the aftermath of the victory over Napoleon, so she was kept 'in Ordinary' until September 1829, when she was commissioned with orders to sail for the Mediterranean.

From his first interview with Parker, Fitzjames realised that Robert Coningham had made a terrible mistake. Instead of being appointed as a midshipman and volunteer of the first class, he found that he was back as a volunteer of the second class and a master's assistant. This was a vital distinction because, while a midshipman and first class volunteer was on the promotion track to become a commissioned officer, a master's assistant was a civilian appointment on a civilian career path, which in time would take him to the civilian position of master. This was not what Fitzjames wanted – he wanted to become a midshipman in the Royal Navy. Added to that, he only now found out that he did not have the necessary qualifications to be appointed as a midshipman, having served less than three months as a first class volunteer.

Quite clearly, neither he nor Robert Coningham had understood any of this. Fitzjames sank into depression, exacerbated by the gloomy quarters he was given on the great ship. As a volunteer of the second class and master's assistant, he messed in a completely dark part of the ship where

> not a soul, except the caterer, an old Mate, has said a word to me ... I had my meals with the rest, but at other times I have done nothing but sit with my hands in my pockets looking at them. If I were a Midshipman I am sure this would not be the case, but because I am in the second class there is no one is speaking to me. If I could I would rather begin over again than stay one day longer in it, but I suppose that it is quite impossible I should ever get into the first class.

A very concerned Robert Coningham struggled to find a way to gain Fitzjames the coveted position of volunteer of the first class and midshipman. Fitzjames was not proud of how the two men engineered this promotion and later concealed the whole story. When he completed his O'Byrne questionnaire in 1845 he claimed that his appointment to *St Vincent* was as a 'Volunteer' – implying, though not actually stating, that this was of the first class – and that his service on *St Vincent* was continuous from 15 December 1830. Neither statement was true.

Throughout his life Fitzjames was ambitious, determined and lived off his wits. He set about engineering a position for himself as a volunteer of the first class and a midshipman. Within five days he understood how it might be done. Somehow he would have to evade the requirement to have already served a year in the first class and then persuade another captain to enter him as a volunteer of the first class and midshipman. HMS *Asia*, commissioning nearby, was the obvious candidate ship.

On Friday 23 December he was invited ashore by a Mrs Campbell, one of the extended Campbell clan related to his beloved 'grandmama', who appears to have been the wife of General Sir Colin Campbell, the Lieutenant-Governor of Portsmouth. At the Campbells' he met their son Major Henry Campbell. He learned that Major Campbell, in turn, had a friend called John Barrow who worked at the Admiralty and was the son of Sir John Barrow, the Second Secretary of the Admiralty. This link looked promising, although Fitzjames had no idea how to take advantage of it.

Fitzjames tried to pull strings with the Gambier family, writing to Captain Gambier, but they could offer no assistance. Patronage was dead for him; he would have to use guile. His time on *St Vincent* dragged. Fitzjames complained that 'the Captain comes on board once a day for an hour or two and says very little to anybody. I have no duty of any sort or kind to do, nor have any in the second class …'

In little over a week a plan emerged. Through General Campbell, Robert Coningham and Fitzjames asked Major Campbell to sound out his friend John Barrow for advice on how Fitzjames might obtain a position as midshipman.

Barrow wrote back to Henry Campbell to explain the procedure and requirements. Fitzjames would have to petition the Board of the Admiralty himself, taking care to address the Board through his captain and then Sir John Barrow, and ask for promotion to the first class. He should explain that his present position as a master's assistant was a mistake and put as strong a case as he could for his promotion. Barrow explained that the Board would be willing to dismiss him from *St Vincent*, but could not appoint him as midshipman on another ship. That could only happen if Fitzjames himself persuaded the captain of another ship 'to receive him as Volunteer of 1st class'. Barrow wrote in the abstract and did not check Fitzjames' service records, so he assumed that Fitzjames knew the service requirement and would not have been asking the question unless he had already served at least one year as volunteer of the first class.

The two men, Robert Coningham and James Fitzjames, planned carefully. Robert Coningham prepared a very impressive reference for Fitzjames. Meanwhile, Fitzjames had an interview with Captain Parker and discussed his unhappiness. Parker was not unsympathetic but explained that he was powerless to help. He pointed to the *Asia* again as the obvious ship to aim for, but said he could do nothing as he did not even know who *Asia's* captain would be. To add to his problems, and not for the first time in his life, Fitzjames was extremely short of money. He had to draw some via the Coningham bankers, the trading business of Gledstanes.

Fitzjames submitted his letter of resignation to the Admiralty on 19 January 1831 without knowing what he would do next. It was very similar to the draft which Major Campbell had passed to him. In it he asked 'that I may be removed from the second class in which I am now serving on board HM Ship *St Vincent*. And I humbly pray that their Lordships may be induced to allow my being removed to the first class it never having been my wish or intention to be brought up in the line of Masters.'

This burned his boats with *St Vincent* and would be the end of his naval career unless he could induce another captain to take him on in the first class. Two days later he read that Captain Fleming Senhouse was to be appointed captain of HMS *Asia*, which was to be the new Mediterranean flagship of Admiral Sir Henry Hotham. HMS *Asia* was his dream. He wrote: 'if I once get rated as Mid in a sea going ship I shall be the happiest fellow living as there is nothing I wish for more than to get out of this horrible class'.

Fitzjames and Coningham desperately sought strings to pull. Fitzjames thought Hotham might be a friend of Robert Gambier. He found out that Senhouse had family in Hertfordshire and he hoped Elizabeth or Robert Coningham might be able to put in a good word for him. But these connections were slight and of no use, especially as he simply did not have the mandatory one year's service as a volunteer of the first class. But he was determined to achieve this promotion by hook or by crook.

On 22 January Sir John Barrow wrote back to say the Board would accept his resignation from *St Vincent* and permit him to be taken on by another captain if he could persuade one to take him. Again, Sir John Barrow wrote in the abstract assuming that Fitzjames had the necessary qualifying service. Knowing that Fitzjames had no powerful patron to intervene on his behalf, Sir John Barrow probably thought this was the last he would hear of the ambitious young man.

John Barrow junior also wrote directly to Fitzjames, and made a slip of the pen. His letter seems to have been ambiguously worded and capable of being read to suggest that Fitzjames had already served a year as a volunteer of the first class. John Barrow would have assumed that Fitzjames had this length of service because otherwise there would have been no point in him applying for the position.

Fitzjames immediately spotted this ambiguity and ruthlessly exploited it. On Wednesday 2 February 1831 he called on Captain Senhouse, the newly appointed captain of the *Asia*, at his lodgings in Portsmouth for the fateful interview. Senhouse was expecting this as he had already written privately to his friend Captain Elliot, First Secretary to the Board of the Admiralty, to check the procedure should he decide he wanted to enter Fitzjames as midshipman. It was in this private letter, accidentally caught up in the Admiralty's files, that Senhouse revealed Fitzjames' paternity.

Fitzjames was an accomplished, well-educated and confident young man. The interview went well. Senhouse decided to offer him a position as midshipman and volunteer of the first class. Senhouse explained that the decision was in his gift but he would have to obtain the consent of his Admiral, Sir Henry Hotham, before doing so. At this point Senhouse does not seem to have been aware that Fitzjames did not have the necessary service and Fitzjames did not tell him. Fitzjames seems to have shown Senhouse John Barrow's letter and allowed Senhouse to conclude from it that Fitzjames had at least a year under his belt as volunteer of the first class.

Hotham did not want to appoint another midshipman but would not override his flag captain, so he permitted Senhouse to enter Fitzjames as a midshipman on HMS *Asia*. On 31 January 1831 Senhouse wrote to the Admiralty asking for 'permission to enter Mr James Fitzjames as Midshipman on board HM ship under my command, who is now serving as Master's Assistant in HMS *St Vincent*', and stating, quite wrongly, that 'Mr James Fitzjames has served more than the required time as Vol. of the 1st class'.

It is not clear when Senhouse realised the mistake about Fitzjames' service but, whenever it was, the deed was done. Rather than risk embarrassment with the Board and with his admiral, Senhouse covered up. Fitzjames' story to Senhouse seems to have been that he thought he had the necessary service and that the Admiralty records were wrong, although of course he must have known this was not true. Equally, Senhouse must have realised that Fitzjames had pulled the wool over everyone's eyes and played fast and loose with the regulations. What the two men said to each other privately cannot be guessed. In a letter to Robert Coningham, Fitzjames said that Senhouse had privately told him not to let him, Senhouse, see Fitzjames' certificates, 'but let him continue in his mistake for if he knows I have not served in the first class he could not be justified in giving me the rating'.

This ambiguous and highly irregular 'fix' was all it took. The Admiralty did not spot its mistake in time so on Tuesday 8 February 1831 Fitzjames received formal notification of his discharge from *St Vincent* and appointment as midshipman to HMS *Asia*. He entered into her service four days later. Fitzjames had won. He would not be going to Cambridge but instead would resume his naval career on the fast track to becoming an officer.

This strange and not altogether creditable story tells us a lot about Fitzjames. He won this position not through patronage but through cunning, personality and ruthless determination. He knew that he was not qualified and in effect lied, at least by omission. He shamelessly broke the rules and engineered a plum promotion over the heads of many young men who were qualified.

A final, unrelated coincidence made it much easier for Fitzjames to cover up the whole disreputable episode. About three weeks after his appointment to the *Asia*, the decision was taken that HMS *St Vincent* should become Sir Henry Hotham's flagship in place of HMS *Asia*. Hotham, Senhouse, Fitzjames and all the officers of HMS *Asia* changed places with their opposite numbers on the *St Vincent*. Fitzjames never referred to this episode again and although his brief service on HMS *Asia* appears in contemporary documents, he suppressed it in his O'Byrne questionnaire. He made out that he had served on *St Vincent*, implicitly as a volunteer of the first class, throughout the whole time. Most authorities since have followed O'Byrne.

Much later Fitzjames flattered Sir John Barrow by crediting him with this appointment, writing in 1845 that 'I never can forget that it is to you, I owe my first footing, when you secured me the rating of Midshipman in the *St Vincent*'. This was completely untrue. Fitzjames had run rings around Barrow and his senior officers. Not for the last time, the precocious Fitzjames had taken big risks with his naval career and won what he wanted.

Three

'A SAILOR'S LIFE'

We hear from those who cannot know
The pleasures of a sailor's life
That when we on the waters go
We pass our days in useless strife
But I contend that one may be
Happier than anywhere else at sea.

First verse of a poem written by James Fitzjames in the back of his journal at
Portsmouth on 20 August 1834

Fitzjames' career was based around *St Vincent* until she paid off on 23 May 1834.
During this period *St Vincent* was based at Malta and was the Royal Navy's
Mediterranean flagship.

The three months before he re-entered *St Vincent* had been extremely stressful
for Fitzjames and it is perhaps not surprising that his health broke down. He was
on the sick list for several weeks with knee trouble, which he reported was being
treated with leeches. *St Vincent* sailed for Malta via Lisbon and Gibraltar and the
great ship arrived at Malta on 18 June 'on a most beautiful Moon light night and
the sea perfectly calm, with just enough wind to send us along'.

His childhood friend John Boyd was another midshipman on *St Vincent* and
the two young men attracted a circle of friends in Malta, mixing with naval officers and also army officers from the local garrison. *St Vincent* spent much of her
time in harbour or moored, acting as flagship and Fitzjames soon became bored.

After reaching Malta, the ship only left harbour once for a twelve-day cruise in
August. This was to visit 'Graham Island', a volcanic island which had appeared
in the Mediterranean and immediately been claimed for England by Captain
Senhouse. He rushed there in a brig to claim this valuable new real estate for
King William IV. Unfortunately for all concerned, the island shortly afterwards
subsided beneath the waves again, so William IV lost this latest little part of his
empire. This was perhaps just as well because the Kingdom of Naples and Sicily

and France also claimed it and, had the island remained, it could have led to a major diplomatic incident. Bizarrely the volcano from which the island is formed periodically erupts so the island has a habit of appearing and disappearing at different times in history. The island last featured in an international incident when American warplanes, patrolling during the confrontation with Libya in 1987, mistook it for a Libyan submarine and dropped a depth charge on it.

Fitzjames was ill when the *St Vincent* arrived at Graham Island but an army friend of his who had come on the cruise was able to land there. An unknown officer painted a delightful watercolour showing this landing party with the *St Vincent* in the background (see plate 9). Fitzjames was rather disappointed at not seeing the island erupting, although 'when we were there a great deal of smoke and steam was coming from the crater which is filled with boiling water'.

Though the sailing was limited his relations with Hotham and Senhouse were good and he became a regular private guest at Lady Senhouse's tea parties. He also regularly attended the opera and took an interest in amateur dramatics, a natural draw for a man who was a born mimic.

Attached to the *St Vincent* was a small cutter called the *Hind*, of only 60 tons, a former revenue cutter (see plate 10). This ship was used to carry mails around the Mediterranean and made regular runs to Constantinople and back, as well as spending time patrolling the lawless Greek archipelago. John Boyd wangled an appointment to this little ship when she sailed to Constantinople in the autumn of 1831.

When the *Hind* next sailed to Constantinople, early in 1832, Fitzjames and Boyd sailed together on her. Fitzjames was entranced by the city and the scenery surrounding it although he found the winter weather very harsh and commented that there had been snow lying on the decks of the little *Hind*.

Boyd and Fitzjames spent six months on the *Hind* cruising the Greek Islands. Fitzjames, with a fine classical education, took a great interest in the culture of ancient Greece, although the whole area was lawless because a political settlement following Greek liberation from the Ottoman Empire had eluded the great powers. He spent some time on this trip at Athens and he had a chance to see the Acropolis and other antiquities there.

But while John Boyd and James Fitzjames continued the social round at Malta, they would have been aware of tension rising further to the west. From 1829 onwards John Boyd's elder brother Robert had been the principal backer and financier of General Torrijos and had become a key figure in his attempt to overthrow the autocratic regime in Spain. Boyd had purchased a small ship and with General Torrijos and a handful of dedicated revolutionaries had sailed to Gibraltar. With only fifty-odd followers this looked foolhardy in the extreme, but they believed that Spain would rise when they raised the flag of revolt. They bided their time and waited for propitious circumstances when they could strike and act as the flame which would set alight a liberal revolution in Spain.

From Gibraltar, Torrijos communicated secretly with friendly contacts in Spain, orchestrating the revolution he would lead. One of these contacts was General Moreno, the regional Governor of Málaga. Moreno assured him that the thousands of soldiers under his command would rally to the flag of liberty as soon as Torrijos could land. If they could reach Málaga, Moreno and his men would fall in under his command and together they could march on Madrid.

The date was set. On 30 November the little expedition sailed from Gibraltar. But things started to go wrong almost at once. The little vessel was harried by Spanish ships. Torrijos and Boyd had to land at the small Spanish fishing village of Fuengirola as Spanish ships cut them off from Málaga.

Moreno himself met them at Fuengirola with several thousand of his soldiers. But it was a trap. Moreno had been acting as a double agent all along and it was estimated that four of Torrijos and Boyd's fifty-odd band were also stool-pigeons. Moreno gave Torrijos a simple choice: the whole band could either be shot down on the spot or they could hand over their weapons and surrender. It was no choice at all. Torrijos, Boyd and the others threw in the towel and were imprisoned at a convent of Carmen in Malaga.

Moreno informed the Spanish government at Madrid and by return came instructions which he no doubt expected. Apart from the four government spies, the whole party should be executed immediately.

Today, thousands of tourists throng the extensive sands of the beach at Málaga. But almost 180 years ago these same sands were witness to a grim scene. Chained to a post at the convent and unable to sleep through the night before the executions, Robert Boyd wrote his last anguished letters. 'The preparation for death is going on,' he wrote, 'and in two short hours life's "fitful fever" will be terminated. The clashing of chains is ringing in my ears, and those harbingers of disaster, beings clad in the hosiery of the grave, are flittering before me.'

At half past ten on the morning of Sunday 11 December, as the bell of the convent began to toll, the men were dragged out to the beach, bound, blindfolded and ordered to kneel in a line. Their last shout for 'the Constitution and for Liberty' was choked off by the volley of the firing squad. Most, including Torrijos, who was shot through the eye, fell dying or dead. But as the echoes of the crashing volley died away, it was clear that Robert Boyd's personal Calvary was not over. Boyd survived the first volley, partially or completely uninjured, and slowly staggered to his feet again. The soldiers reloaded their muskets and a second volley rang out. Every one was aimed at Boyd and this time he did not rise again. Málaga was a poor village and soon a crowd of villagers, accustomed to scavenging on the beach, moved in to plunder the still-warm bodies. After their work was done the bodies of the dead liberals were flung into rubbish carts and left to rot in a ditch.

Boyd's body was recovered by William Mark, the British consul, and buried in the English cemetery where it lies to this day in a handsome tomb. More than a thousand English people are buried there today, including many expatriates and several airmen who died during the Second World War. Robert Boyd was only the second to be interred. The cemetery records give the single word 'shot' as his cause of death.

The families were traumatised by this news and John Sterling especially felt the agony of guilt. He had been responsible for introducing Robert to Torrijos and firing his enthusiasm for Spanish liberal revolution. Unlike Robert he had evaded any personal danger. He had lived and Robert had died. For the rest of his life, Sterling refused ever to discuss the affair.

The news reached Malta early in 1832. John Boyd wrote to Fitzjames 'with a bleeding heart and an aching sight' to give him the terrible news of 'poor Robert's tragedy'. It is not clear whether the two men were serving together at the time or whether one was on the *Hind* and the other on the *St Vincent*. Boyd gave Fitzjames copies of Robert's last letters, although 'you will scarcely be able to read them'. He himself had 'hurried them over, not intending to the mind dwell on what might appear a dream, but the horrible disastrous reality'. Boyd wanted Fitzjames to have these letters because 'you knew him, felt for him and will cherish his memory … and preserve it from soil or contamination, and there is always something pleasing and great, tying us [to] the solicitude of the manly and the generous'.

Fitzjames kept these letters for the rest of his life.

The poem Robert Boyd wrote during his final agonising night, with its second verse horribly prophetic of Fitzjames' own fate, read:

Let pitying zeal, his name from censure save
And truth to Heaven in judgement see his grave
What were crimes? Come let the Spaniard tell,
The first – he loved their native land too well
The next, the blackest, darkest. let us see
He burned, he tried to make that country free.

He failed. His valiant life the forfeit paid
But still the proud experiment was made,
His worth the same, his glory not the less
Save that it lacked the sanction of success
Let sympathising friends with me combine
While Britain's loss I mournfully repine.

Fitzjames and John Boyd's life on the *St Vincent* in harbour at Malta must have seemed secure compared to these tragedies. Robert Boyd was the first of Fitzjames' close friends to die tragically and young.

In the summer of 1832, still based at Malta, Fitzjames started on an adventure of an entirely different type. On 30 August he was entered as a midshipman passenger and as 'Supernumerary, HM ship *St Vincent*, lent and doing duty by order of the Commander in Chief' on HMS *Madagascar*.

The *Madagascar* was assigned to convey the future King of Greece to his new kingdom. After the years of fighting and civil war in Greece, the great powers were attempting to broker a peace and it had been decided to establish a hereditary monarchy there. After a brief search failed to locate anyone who could claim descent from the last of the Byzantine emperors, the 17-year-old Prince Otto of Bavaria was selected as a suitable candidate.

Fitzjames was transferred from *St Vincent* to form one of a party of well-connected young naval and military officers, including Midshipman Lord Clarence Paget, to accompany Prince Otto of Bavaria on the *Madagascar* from Trieste to Nauplia in Greece, which was then its capital. Unlike the others Fitzjames was not an aristocrat or well connected, although he may have met Paget before as Paget was related to the Earl of Essex. Fitzjames' lively intelligence and attractive personality, combined also with his exceptional language skills, presumably won him this privileged appointment.

Although Fitzjames was not overawed by the vastly superior social standing of the young grandees with whom he mixed, financially it was a strain. He wrote of 'so many temptations in one way or the other in spending money that it is quite a bore, still one does not like to be behind hand in joining the others in any party that may be furnished'.

At first he was intimidated by the ceremony and, rather unkindly, referred to Otto as 'this little beggar of a king', although later he grew to like Otto. He was apprehensive at being 'obliged to be in uniform all day long and on our best behaviour', especially as 'I suspect I shall get into a little row with skipper Lyons [Captain Lyons of the *Madagascar*] as I believe I told you the Greeks at Corinth when I was there took a fancy to my sword and borrowed it, i.e. stole it'. He was able to obtain a new sword before joining the *Madagascar*.

Everything to do with Otto was carried out with great panache and ceremony and Fitzjames was soon able to enjoy the opportunities it presented. He described the ship as 'like a fair all day' and said that the young midshipmen had seen 'everything that was to be seen in the shape of Palaces, Paintings, Statues, Gondolas and co.' He visited many of the antiquities in the region, including the huge Roman amphitheatre at Pola. By December he was able to write that he had 'got up a weekly newspaper on board, of which I am the editor, and which causes a deal of fun'. Again, his combination of personal wit and high standard of education served him well.

Fitzjames kept a personal journal which, after he departed on the Franklin Expedition, remained in William Coningham's possession. This was passed down the Coningham family to William's granddaughter Hester, who donated one volume of it to the National Maritime Museum in 1969. This single volume covers the period from February 1833 to October 1834 and is like a ray of sunlight suddenly shining in and bringing the young man to light. It opens with the day Otto of Bavaria came ashore to his new kingdom at Nauplia on Wednesday 5 February 1833:

This being the day fixed for the landing of the King of Greece, all the ships at the anchorage except the Madagascar draped colours at daylight. A stage had been erected about 2 miles from Napoli, and all the Bavarian troops drawn up along the Higos road. He shoved off from the ship at noon in our barge, pulled by twelve Mids of the Madagascar, draped in white shirts and trowsers without braces, uniform cloth caps and a blue silk scarf over the shoulder with a white knot on the hip. A white O worked on the breast part of each scarf. I was one of the pullers. The First Lieutenant in full uniform steered and the standard of Greece in the bow supported by a Mid in full uniform surrounded by three youngsters holding an English, French and Russian ensign and all in silk. On our shoving off the Madagascar hauled the Standard down and dipped in Colours. We then pulled into the centre of the Squadrons and the procession formed in the following order – first, seven Greek boats with their Admirals, Captains and co. Next our barge containing his Majesty and Aide de Camps, the four regents and Captain Lyons, the English Admiral (Sir Henry Hotham) followed close astern leading all the boats of the English squadron. The Russian Admiral Ricord on our starboard quarter with all the Russian boats – and the French Admiral Hugon on the larboard quarter with all the French boats. There were English boats, French and Russian amounting with Greeks and those of the Neapolitans to 67 boats all with their respective Ensigns and Pendants flying. On our putting our oars up, the whole of the ships saluted and manned yards – there were nineteen men of war with the Greeks. The procession then pulled to the landing places where the King landed and was received by the Greek deputation and members of the Government who read him a congratulatory address, to which he replied through an interpreter. Admiral Miaounlis handed him out of the boat – the three distinct lines kept by the boats of the different nations astern of the barge was most beautiful and the whole scene was splendid, the day lovely and everybody in good humour. Having landed our passengers we took in the ladies … who had accompanied us in the jolly boats and pulled them to Napoli, where we accompanied them in our pulling drapes to their house which is close to the Gate of the town, from whence we saw him enter the town. First came a body of guards, the Greek deputation, members of the Government and several Chiefs amongst which were Colocotroni and Grivas with their followers all on horseback, his two Aide de Camps Counts Sapata and Baron Arch immediately preceded him. He was dressed in a handsome light blue uniform coat with silver facings and epaulettes, cocked hat and feathers and large boots over white breeches. He looked extremely well. After him came the Regents, Admirals and Captains of the Allied Squadrons, and the whole of the Bavarian troops. A triumphal arch had been erected out-side the gates very tastefully decorated, with olive branches, Colours and the Greek Standard surmounting the whole. The crowd of Greeks was immense, and he was most vehemently cheered as he entered the town. He went direct to the church (the troops remaining outside the town) where the Archbishop of Corinth performed service and I believe the King swore some oaths, and he then marched on foot to the palace, where he shewed himself at the balcony and was cheered. After partaking of some light refreshment at the Countess's house, we went on board and the King came afterwards, incog., and dined. In the evening, the town being illuminated, he went ashore accompanied by the Captain and a dozen of us with swords on, and walked through most of the streets of Napoli. The crowd was immense, and we had to surround him, and by main force make a passage for him and the Regents. Captain Lyons held his right arm under one of his Aide-de-Camps. He left on arriving at the square called the Platana. We halted and some blue lights were burned by some of our men. The mob to see him was now immense and it was with the utmost diffi-culty we prevented him from being crushed. The air was rent with acclamations and cries of Zitou which answers to the Spanish bravo. On his return to the palace he shewed himself at the balcony three times by the light of blue lights and putting on his plain clothes again went on board. We all followed with the Countesses who had borne the squeeze with great forgiveness. Thus ends the 6th February, 1833, which will certainly be a day to be remembered by me. I trust that the little King will have a happy night of it, but he has a difficult task and I am afraid he will often wish himself on board the Madagascar.

The magnificent painting by Peter von Hess, 'The Entry of King Otto to Nauplia', which today hangs at the Kunstareal in Munich, depicts the scene. It shows the royal barge conveying King Otto to the city and the young midship-men 'pullers' are clearly visible. One, a tiny white spot, is our first illustration of Fitzjames (see plate 11).

But pageantry alone was not enough to secure good governance and Fitzjames' judgement was right: King Otto's reign was a failure and ended ignominiously in 1867.

After the ceremonies were over, the *Madagascar* sailed back to Malta and Fitzjames rejoined the *St Vincent*. The homecoming was not smooth though, as on 24 February 1833, 'in consequence of a row I had at Trieste with the caterer of the birth, the Captain to whom it had been much misrepresented, abused me on the quarter deck, and confined me in a cabin on the main deck'. The entry for Monday in its entirety reads 'all day in the cabin' with a 'ditto' for Tuesday and Wednesday. But on Thursday the 'Captain wrote me a note saying he would forget everything and that I might mess in the starboard birth [sic]. Answered him accordingly.' This was the end of the matter.

Fitzjames always cultivated good relations with his senior officers and their families and was clearly fond of Admiral Sir Henry Hotham. When Hotham died suddenly on 20 April 1833, Fitzjames wrote: 'this news spreads a gloom over everything. In fact I can hardly believe it to be true.' Hotham's funeral was a major event and Captain Sir John Franklin of HMS *Rainbow* was with Fitzjames among many other mourners. This is one early occasion where they may have met.

Fitzjames frequently visited the opera and on one occasion appeared on stage himself in an amateur dramatic performance. He enjoyed opera and recorded his impressions of the different performances of *Barbiere di Seviglia* (9 March 1833), *Rob Roy* (12 March 1833), *Siege of Corinth* (19 March 1833) and so on. Music was not the only attraction of the opera. His journal is one of several places where we find evidence of his relations with the opposite sex. On some days ashore, there is a clearly defined and unexplained 'X' which presumably signifies sex. This X appears on nine occasions while Fitzjames was in Malta from 21 February to 21 July 1833. In most cases it coincides with the opera or a social event ashore and presumably records visits to prostitutes or lower-class girls in taverns rather than a serious relationship or affair. Especially since an X later rounds off the day in Portsmouth on which he was handed his lieutenant's passing certificate, which does rather suggest celebration.

But Fitzjames was interested in more than just socialising and assignments in the Maltese demi-monde. His journal records a keen interest in the countryside and history. He liked to ride and would take long rides or hikes when he could. He shows a countryman's keen awareness of good agricultural land and the pleasant sight of growing crops. Wherever he was he appreciated the archaeology, topography and history of the area, which is hardly surprising given the eclectic intellectual interests of the Coningham circle.

On 19 July 1833 Fitzjames visited the site of the ancient city of Troy. His classical education was good enough that senior officers asked him to come with them when they explored these ruins.

Another adventure started on Monday 12 November 1833, when:

Captain Marsham, having asked me to go with him to Magnesia, started on horseback at 3.10 a.m., five in number, and two guides. We rode to the end of the plain, crossed the mountains to the northward and at about 9 arrived at a small village, where we cooked a good supper of ham, eggs and tea in a sort of summer house, and spreading our cloaks on the floor, went to sleep in a heap.

Tuesday 13th: Started at ¼ past 1 in the morning and rode through the mountains. At daylight we descended into an immense plain bounded every way by mountains and at about 5 arrived at Magnesia situated at the southern extremity of it. A very remarkable and lofty rock overlooks the town, and immediately, at the back of it (the town) a hill on which are the remains of a castle.

Magnesia is certainly the cleanest of Turkish towns I have seen. It … is said to contain 70,000 to 80,000 inhabitants. The streets are tolerably wide towards the suburbs. At the southern side of the town are the remains of a palace and seraglio of one of the first Sultans – nothing very curious. We saw a place for lunatics – a small yard in the centre of which is a fountain and all round small cells, in which the unfortunate creatures are left chained to a wall by the neck like dogs!

We ascended the hill at the back of the town which is tolerably high and very steep and saw the ruins of an old castle with some Cyclopean walls. But the view is splendid, commanding the whole of the fertile plain through which runs a river. The mountains in the distance and the town with its Minarets and Domes, interspersed with trees as one's feet. Our quarters were at a Khan or Caravanserai, a square yard, two sides of which are stables for camels and horses, and the other two divided into small stone cells, where the traveller is at liberty to spread his cloak. The people in this country never undress, and carry their beds with them when they travel. Before starting we had a capital breakfast of fruit and milk, and on our return from our walk a dinner of capital stewed mutton and eggs. We set out on our return at 3 p.m. and arrived at the summer house at 7, where we put up for the night. The road from Magnesia is beautifully wild and picturesque, and the view from the top of the mountains looking back at the plain is splendid.

The party arrived back on board the following morning at 8 a.m., having started back at 4 a.m., and Fitzjames was pleased to note that it 'only cost us 3½ Spanish dollars'.

At 10 a.m. that same day, the Governor of Smyrna visited and 'after having been shown round the ship we exercised boarding & co. for his amusement'. Many other people visited and the ship was 'crowded with people of all sorts lounging about the decks. Some old Turks came in the morning, spread their mats between the guns – sit all day smoking and eating their provisions, cry Inshallah! and depart at night.'

It is notable that his journal, indeed all his writing, betrays absolutely no prejudice against or intolerance of any other religions. Unlike the letters of so many of his contemporaries, there is never any preaching or overt Christian grandstanding.

Fitzjames was now approaching the time when he would be eligible for promotion to lieutenant, once he had six complete years of service. He would need to pass examinations and provide the Examiners' Board with proof of his age. Admiralty regulations were explicit that any candidate producing false information to a Board would automatically be barred from ever being commissioned as an officer and subject to summary dismissal if the irregularity subsequently came to light. There were risks in this.

Fitzjames had already written to Robert Coningham asking him to forward his baptismal certificate. He would need to produce this document to the Examiners'

Board, knowing that it was fraudulent. The mother and father given on it were people who did not and had never existed, and he had not been born in London.

On 8 August 1833, the date marked on his passing certificate in the Admiralty's records, he was examined at Malta by Captains Senhouse, Marsham and Sir George Young of HMS *Rover*. Senhouse and Marsham were sympathetic, but it seems Sir George was not. Fitzjames had to answer questions about seamanship, navigation and discipline.

He was not passed. As he later retook both seamanship and navigation, it looks likely that he failed both these exams. But that was not the only problem. One of the three captains, presumably Young, objected 'about my time as Midshipman', possibly realising that Fitzjames had not been entitled to that appointment at all. The three captains could not agree what to do and referred his case to the admiral. Fitzjames' heart must have sunk when the admiral, in turn, referred his case back to the Admiralty in London for a definitive statement of what time Fitzjames could actually be allowed towards his promotion. But the bureaucratic wheels of the Admiralty misinterpreted the question, and when their answer eventually came back it stated that his time as a volunteer of the second class on the *St Vincent* should not be allowed towards his lieutenancy. This was simply a repetition of what Sir John Barrow had written on Fitzjames' letter to the Admiralty in January 1831 and was of course *not* the answer to the question the three captains had asked. Senhouse was put in an embarrassing position by his protégé's cavalier disregard for the rules, and all three captains ran the risk of embarrassing their admiral also. Perhaps not fully understanding the background to the Admiralty's somewhat Delphic reply, the three captains seem to have let the objection to his time drop. They accepted his paternity. The three captains also noted 'Party's [that is, Fitzjames'] father' against his certificate in the relevant book. Fitzjames had presumably shown them his baptismal certificate and Captain Senhouse would have been able to identify Fitzjames' true father informally to the other two members of the panel.

Captain Senhouse told him off the record that 'nothing had better be said about it [his irregular promotion to midshipman] and that most likely it would be passed over unnoticed'. Senhouse suggested that Fitzjames arrange for Robert Coningham to test the water by calling in innocently at the Admiralty to collect Fitzjames' passing certificates, 'but to say nothing about the time unless they mention it first'. Fitzjames quoted Senhouse as saying that 'there would be some trouble if they were to say anything, but says he should lose no endeavours to get it settled, so that I trust I shall not have to serve three years once again for nothing'. In this visit, Coningham was not successful, but that seems to have been more because Fitzjames had not at that stage passed his seamanship and navigation exams than because anyone at the Admiralty understood the whole story.

Fitzjames seems to have been more confident of beating the system this time than in 1831, as he cheerily ended his letter to Robert Coningham with a 'love to all hands under the roof of dear old Rose Hill'.

Fitzjames threw himself into the social life of Malta while he waited to find out whether he would be promoted. In October 1833 he went to the opera no less than seven times, seeing *Don Giovanni* on four separate occasions. Only one of these visits coincided with the X of sex, so clearly the music and the drama attracted him also.

He took a leading role in amateur dramatics, attending several rehearsals before, on 28 October 1833, he starred in a burlesque with his friend John Boyd and 'some army chaps'. It is not surprising that a flamboyant character like Fitzjames, who was a natural mimic, would be attracted to the world of greasepaint. The play was called *Chrononhotonthologos, the most tragical tragedy that ever was tragedized by any company of tragedians*. It is an extraordinary play which must be overdue revival. In 1833 it was already about 100 years old, having been written by Henry Carey allegedly as a satire at the expense of Queen Caroline and Robert Walpole. John Boyd was cast as captain of the guard and Fitzjames was cast, in drag, in the lead role as Fadladinida, Queen of Queerummania.

Fitzjames spent the whole day 'getting rigged for the Queen … in women's clothes all bediamonded and bepearled'. The large athletic officer must have made a fine sight as he ostentatiously sat through the first amateur performance of *The Heir at Law* by officers of the garrison, which he watched from a box among the audience. Then it was his turn to go backstage to prepare for his role in *Chrononhotonthologos*.

The play opens with two courtiers discussing their sleeping king, exhausted by the rigours of war. Around him his army, having just been paid, are 'all as drunk as so many swabbers'. They are afraid the noise will wake the king so resolve that 'the baths be fill'd with seas of coffee to stupefy their souls into sobriety'. The king awakes in a bad temper, so the courtiers put on a pantomime to humour him. While this is playing, the captain of the guard enters to announce that the kingdom is about to be invaded by the army of the Antipodeans, a people from the other side of the world who do everything upside down, including walking on their hands.

John Boyd's dramatic entrée was rather spoiled because he 'entered with such energy and vehemence that he stuck his sword so deep in the boards as not to be able without some trouble to get it out', Fitzjames wrote, so that when he finally freed it 'the recoil nearly [sent] him into the pit'. The scene ended with the courtiers agreeing that the king would lead his forces to victory over the Antipodeans.

Barely recovered from his laughter at John Boyd's faux pas, Fitzjames entered in the next scene as a gigantic drag queen in the role of Queen Fadladinida with her favourite and two ladies. The scene opens with the queen having ordered tea in a strange pastiche of the elegant tea parties of Lady Senhouse and Lady Lyons, which Fitzjames was wont to attend:

Tatlanthe: Your majesty was pleas'd to order tea.

Queen: My mind is alter'd, bring some ratifia.
[They are served round with a dram]
I have a famous Fidler sent from France,
Bid him come in. What think ye of a dance?

[Enter Fidler].

Fidler: Thus to your Majesty, says the suppliant muse,
Wou'd you a solo or sonata chuse;
Or bold concerto, or soft Sicilinia,
Alla Francese overo in Gusto Romano?
When you command, 'tis done as soon as spoke.

After this skit on high culture, Fitzjames' inappropriate line in the role of the queen must have brought the house down:

A civil fellow! – play us the Black Foke.

The plot continued with the inevitable defeat of the Antipodeans and the queen falling in love with the captive Antipodean king, enabling Fitzjames to deliver the memorable lines:

Oh! my Tatlanthe! have you seen his face,
His air, his shape, his mein, his ev'ry grace?
In what a charming attitude he stands,
How prettily he foots it with his hands!
Well, to his arms, no to his legs I fly,
For I must have him, if I live or die.

The bawdy plot continues with the death of the king, after which it transpires that the queen's marriage to him has never been consummated. She ends up deciding to live in sin with both of the late king's courtiers, once the king's 'dead and bloody' corpse has been dragged away. This was not a play that could have been performed in the high Victorian era and it would raise a few eyebrows today. It closed with Fitzjames as the queen addressing her two courtiers, shortly to become lovers, with the lines:

Make preparation for our wedding-day.
Instead of sad solemnity, and black
Our hearts should swim in claret, and in Sack.

Fitzjames said that he had 'never laughed so much in my life'.

After this risqué performance, it must have been difficult for the three captains to envisage failing to pass for lieutenant this popular young officer, who must have been the talk of the garrison and the ships at Malta. Two weeks later he was examined again for seamanship and it seems that this time he passed as he was awarded his Mate's Warrant the following day.

HMS *St Vincent*'s commission was coming to an end. On 5 February 1834, Fitzjames and the other junior officers gave a dinner to mark Captain Marsham's departure from the ship to take up his new position as captain of HMS *Malabar*. The mess president was John Boyd and he presented Captain Marsham with a fine snuff box as a farewell token.

But less than a week later, the *St Vincent* was almost wrecked in harbour when a violent squall broke her moorings and she was blown across the harbour onto a mudbank, fortunately without foundering. It took a week's hard work for the ship to be stripped and lightened. All her 120 guns, her masts, spars and stores had to be landed ashore before she could be refloated. Then the whole process had to be repeated to bring her back to her operational state. There seems to have been a release of tension after the hard work. On 17 February Fitzjames went ashore to a ball at the Governor of Malta's residence, but he was sorely disappointed as it was a children's ball and clearly a much more sedate affair than he had anticipated. There is no doubt that young officers led a fairly energetic social life. Only a few days later, Fitzjames recorded that he had been 'skylarking with Boyd in the Gunroom at 10.00 p.m.' and almost choked to death. Who knows what the skylarking involved!

HMS *St Vincent* finally sailed for England on 3 April 1834 at 8 a.m., when the ships' boats of the squadron towed her out. The wind was so light that *St Vincent* remained in sight of the town of Valetta all day. The voyage home was leisurely, delayed either by light winds or very bad weather. She anchored off Gibraltar on 18 April and remained there for six days. Fitzjames went ashore and had dinner with yet another Campbell relative of the Coninghams who was serving in the 92nd Regiment in the garrison.

There was also a more sombre meeting. Fitzjames recorded in his journal that, on 24 April 1834, as *St Vincent* sailed from Gibraltar, she took on board two passengers. These were a Mr William Mark and his daughter. Mark was a half-pay Royal Naval officer who had served under Nelson. But his significance for Fitzjames, and even more for the Boyd family, was that he was the British consul at Málaga. It was he who had been powerless to save Robert Boyd from the vengeful Spanish government, who had witnessed his execution and then buried him in the British cemetery there. There must have been some quiet tears shed on board *St Vincent* as she sailed through the Bay of Biscay.

St Vincent finally arrived back at Portsmouth on Friday 9 May 1834. On the following Monday Fitzjames was 'working Navigation at the Royal Naval

College', which at that time was situated in Portsmouth. The next day he was 'examined by old Narrien about sextants & co., and at half past two got passing certificate from Admiral Maitland'. This was a huge achievement even though technically, again, he was not entitled to it. He celebrated with the discreet X mark in his journal.

On 23 May 1834 the ship and its 20-year-old mate, James Fitzjames, paid off.

The following evening, after staying overnight at the Star and Garter in London 'with Boyd and a few more Vincent's', he arrived home at Rose Hill to be reunited with the Coninghams. John Boyd followed him to Hertfordshire and the two men relaxed with their extended family and their old friends at and around Rose Hill.

Only two weeks later, Fitzjames was offered a position on HMS *Rose* by its captain, Commander William Barrow, with whom Fitzjames had served on the Experimental Squadron in 1826, and who was now commissioning the *Rose* to sail for the Far East. William Barrow was a son of Sir John Barrow. This was an excellent opportunity, so the next day Fitzjames and Robert Coningham left Rose Hill and went to the Admiralty so that Fitzjames could sign on to the *Rose*.

There, by chance, they met Admiral Sir Bladon Capel, son of their wealthy neighbour, the Earl of Essex. When Capel heard that Fitzjames was planning to join the *Rose*, on the spot he offered him a vacancy on HMS *Winchester*, the new flagship for Capel's commission in the Far East. This was clearly a better posting than HMS *Rose*, so Fitzjames declined the *Rose* and accepted the *Winchester* instead. He was enrolled and immediately sent to Portsmouth 'to try and get some men'. In those days sailors had to be signed separately on each commission of each ship. Capel evidently felt he could trust Fitzjames sufficiently to give him the responsibility of recruiting sailors for his ship in Britain's largest naval port. Before doing so, Fitzjames went to Chatham to see his new ship and the man who would be her captain, Edward Sparshott.

He arrived at Portsmouth on Friday 13 June and stayed there until September. Initially he lodged at the Ship and Castle, a pub which stills stands today just outside the main gate to the historic dockyard at Portsmouth. Later he took rooms nearby. Towards the end of August, Robert Coningham came to stay with him and the two men moved into better accommodation at nearby Southsea. In the evenings Fitzjames socialised a great deal with fellow officers, including several who had served with him on HMS *St Vincent* and others who were also recruiting for their own ships in competition with him. He worked hard and kept up a frequent correspondence with Sparshott, who was fully engaged commissioning his ship at Chatham. It can well be imagined that Fitzjames was a very persuasive recruiter. He spent lavishly, but gained results and recruited almost eighty men for HMS *Winchester*. Once the men were signed up, they were not trusted to go cross-country to Chatham themselves, but were, in Fitzjames' words, 'draughted

round to Chatham in steamers and lighters'. Sparshott was pleased with the
results and wrote to the Admiralty to commend Fitzjames and make sure his
expenses were repaid.

Robert Coningham and Fitzjames spent time meeting friends and relatives, including Coningham's brother-in-law John Sterling, who had just been
ordained as curate of the parish of Herstmonceux, 70 miles along the coast to
the east. Sterling had recently acknowledged the tuberculosis that would eventually kill him and his clerical career was not a success, being dogged by his
theological differences with the orthodoxy of the Church of England. The vicar
of Herstmonceux was the Reverend Julius Hare, like Coningham, Cambridge
educated, clerical and another leading intellectual of the day.

Coningham and Fitzjames also socialised with the Campbell family, including Major-General Sir Colin Campbell KCB, the officer who, four years earlier,
had helped Fitzjames obtain his position on HMS *Asia* as a midshipman, and his
namesake Colin Campbell, the future Lord Clyde. When they refer in their letters or journals to 'Colin Campbell', it is not always clear which man they meant.
One Colin Campbell, presumably the lieutenant-governor, had a boat and in it
Coningham and Fitzjames enjoyed sailing with the Campbells in the Solent and
to Cowes on the Isle of Wight. Both Campbells were friends of the Coninghams
and also of John and William Barrow, the sons of Sir John Barrow.

Commander William Barrow, the man Fitzjames had turned down to enter
HMS *Winchester*, was there preparing his ship HMS *Rose* for service in the Far
East. When the *Rose* sailed, Fitzjames, Robert Coningham and a Colin Campbell
accompanied her as far as Yarmouth on the Isle of Wight in Campbell's boat
before finally waving goodbye.

This vignette shows just how varied Fitzjames' life was and how adept he was
at mixing with people at all levels in society. By day he was busy selling the attractions of HMS *Winchester* to the hardened matelots who milled around the naval
base, weeding out the malingerers, deserters and fantasists and closing the deals
with the men he wanted. All this took place in competition with other recruiting officers. At the same time he was mixing with the intellectual and ascetic
members of his foster family. As well as sailing with Colin Campbell, he enthusiastically caroused with his own circle of young naval officers, recording that he
had 'some good larks with several old Vincent's'. One of these was the incident
which Admiral Sir Edward Gennys Fanshawe, GCB, remembered at the end of
his long life when 'Lieutenant Fitzjames ... a humorous fellow and noted for his
physical strength and agility ... broke a chair'. Admiral Fanshawe remembered
the landlady's comment, when informed of the damage, that 'that there young
gen'leman is as strong as a rhinoceros'.

It was during this busy time, in fact precisely at midnight on 20 August 1834,
that Fitzjames wrote the poem that appears in Appendix II, delighted to have
signed up seven men that day.

Early in September, with HMS *Winchester* now fully manned, Captain Sparshott wrote to congratulate him on his excellent recruitment and granted him three weeks' leave. After a final dinner with the Campbells, he packed and travelled overnight to London, arriving at Rose Hill the following morning.

After two weeks at 'home', as he called Rose Hill, Colin Campbell came to stay. Presumably this was the more junior Campbell, the future Lord Clyde. Whichever Campbell it was, he brought Fitzjames a proposal that captured his imagination totally and was to change completely the direction and length of his life. Campbell had heard that an artillery officer called Captain Chesney, who had been commissioned to set up a new fast line of communication by steamship between Britain and India, was looking for naval officers to man them. Steamers were already used to convey mails from London to the Mediterranean. The Honourable East India Company was introducing steamships capable of sailing from India to the Persian Gulf. Chesney's fast steam route along the Euphrates would link the two together and thus establish a continuous fast steam mail route from London to Bombay.

Fitzjames was enraptured by Chesney's ingenious vision as Campbell outlined it to him, calling it 'a plan ... which entirely altered all my views'. He decided there and then to volunteer. The quest for a faster route between England and India was the one which Colonel Capper, Fitzjames' foster-grandfather, had struggled to complete in 1778. This expedition was a great opportunity for an ambitious naval officer – to set up and be a key part in an important new imperial link. But it was much, much more. It was a way for Fitzjames to prove his value to the Royal Navy not just for being an able seaman, but also a technocrat, exploiting the vital new power of steam. And emotionally, this was surely a link with Colonel Capper. Fitzjames would be able to complete the work of the most senior officer in his foster-family's ancestry and win for himself a place in the family that had been so generous to him by merit alone. When one understands the emotional pull of the Euphrates on Fitzjames, one can see why he accepted with such alacrity.

The following day, Campbell and James Fitzjames travelled to London and Campbell introduced Fitzjames to Captain Chesney. Chesney was looking not just for officers who could form the cadre of his new shipping line, but also men who could carry out the extensive surveying and mapping which would be needed to prove the route. He was a stickler for high standards. He accepted Fitzjames subject to his being passed as competent in surveying by Professor Narrien, the professor of Mathematics at Sandhurst College, who had earlier passed Fitzjames for the navigation test of his lieutenant's examination.

Chesney would not waive these tests and he would not confirm his offer to Fitzjames until they had been completed. The problem was that Fitzjames only had a week of his leave remaining which left very little time to complete them. He rushed to Sandhurst and 'set to work with Professor Narrien, took lunars and attitudes every night, and worked during the day at the Observatory in the

College grounds'. Whether he could complete the tests in the remaining time of his leave depended entirely on the weather – without clear skies he could not take shots of the moon, stars and sun to prove his navigational skills. Luckily the weather was good and Fitzjames got on well with Narrien and his wife, who he described as 'very kind'.

Fitzjames needed more time before his leave ended to arrange his resignation from HMS *Winchester*. Robert Coningham, therefore, wrote to Captain Sparshott asking for an extension to Fitzjames' leave, but without explaining why. Sparshott declined to extend his leave, so Fitzjames had to rush from Sandhurst to Chatham in order to return to his ship in time – to be absent without leave would make his release from HMS *Winchester* more difficult.

Breaking his journey from Sandhurst overnight in London, he stayed at the Regent Street house of the Gledstanes', the Coningham family merchants. It was a strange coincidence that Colonel Chesney had served under a General Gledstanes during the Napoleonic Wars. Robert Coningham was staying at the Gledstanes' too as he had gone to London to meet William Coningham, who had just returned from Germany. William had matriculated from Trinity College, Cambridge, in 1833 and purchased a commission as a cornet in the fashionable First Light Dragoons. The four men had dinner and early on the following morning, Saturday 20 September, Fitzjames set off for Chatham to break the news to Captain Sparshott that he wished to resign his commission.

Fitzjames explained his wish to Sparshott and, fortunately, found him to be 'very civil'. Sparshott agreed to release him if the Admiralty would accept it. For the moment, Fitzjames remained on board the *Winchester*. His journal makes it clear that he liked the *Winchester*, which he called 'a very fine 52 gun frigate with a poop and round stern'. He liked Sparshott and the officers and had recruited a fair proportion of the ship's company. He was 'almost sorry I am not going out in the *Winchester*', but 'determined to go to Euphrates'. The newly commissioned ship sailed from Chatham and made a slow voyage to Portsmouth, where on 8 October he was discharged 'to Captain Chesney's Experiment'.

Leaving the *Winchester*, he seems to have been at something of a loose end for the next few weeks. He dallied in Portsmouth and then returned to Rose Hill, waiting to complete further 'observations' with Professor Narrien. Narrien seems to have realised there was little point to this as Fitzjames' appointment to the Chesney Expedition had already been confirmed. He took a few more observations under Narrien and perhaps it was then that he met some of the other officers who would be coming with him to the Euphrates.

On 27 October he again stayed with the Gledstanes' in Regent Street. This time the Gledstanes' other dinner guest was Captain Chesney himself. Fitzjames returned to Rose Hill the following day to wait until the Chesney Expedition was ready for his services.

Fitzjames was becoming an explorer.

Four

COLONEL CHESNEY:
'A MOST DETERMINED MAN'

The Chesney Expedition was a complete departure from anything Fitzjames had done before and has many parallels with the Franklin Expedition. Both expeditions confused scientific, adventurous and political objectives. Both relied on relatively untried and, for the time, advanced technology. Both paid scant regard to the feelings and knowledge of the local inhabitants. Both had high casualty rates. But while the Franklin Expedition continues to attract huge interest in the twenty-first century, the Chesney Expedition has been almost completely forgotten.

The unorthodoxy of Fitzjames' career so far had mainly been forced on him by his illegitimacy. But joining the Chesney Expedition was a highly eccentric move. A letter exists from Robert Gambier to him from this time. Clearly the older man was surprised and perhaps rather upset by Fitzjames' impetuosity in turning down the *Winchester* and signing up for this expedition without discussing it with the Gambier family. Fitzjames presumably felt he owed them very little. But, overall, the letter has a gently avuncular tone. Gambier offers Fitzjames advice on the necessity of good record-keeping and the need to 'do all things to the glory of God'. The letter, which Gambier signed as 'ever your affectionate friend', is clear evidence of the concern the Gambier family continued to maintain for their illegitimate relative.

The expedition was named for its leader, Francis Rawdon Chesney, who was promoted to colonel especially for it (see plate 12). Like Robert Coningham and Francis Crozier, Chesney was an Irishman of Scottish descent. He was 45 at the time of the expedition. He had joined the Royal Artillery in 1805 having been a cadet at the Royal Military Academy at Woolwich, which, in the days of purchased commissions, was the nearest a British army officer came to having professional training. He was only 5ft 1in and had originally been turned down for admission to the Royal Military Academy on the humiliating grounds that he was too short. He overcame this by reapplying with the benefit of false cork heels, which he wore inside his stockings.

He married three times in all and his first wife was a niece of Sir Albert Gledstanes. This made him very tenuously related to the extended Campbell clan to which the Coninghams belonged. After the death of his first wife in 1825, he became something of a traveller and was almost sent to West Africa by Sir John Barrow as an explorer. He went to Constantinople in 1829 to assist the Turkish army in introducing Congreve rockets into its armoury and to observe the short war with Russia. From there, he made a survey of the Balkans and the Middle East. It was here that he conceived the idea of a fast steam route between India and England.

He travelled extensively in Syria and the Euphrates valley, including rafting down the Euphrates and surveying the Suez area. Napoleon's engineers had earlier concluded that a Suez ship canal would be impossible as the level of the Red Sea was up to 10 metres higher than the Mediterranean. Chesney's survey determined that this was an error and that the two seas were actually almost exactly the same height, thus making a ship canal practical. As well as this survey work, Chesney was covertly monitoring the fragile political situation between Egypt and the Ottoman Empire and the extent of any Russian infiltration into the region. He was one of the first, albeit peripheral, players in the 'Great Game' and, through him, Fitzjames came to have a 'walk-on' part in this 'Game' too.

Directly and indirectly, Chesney had a huge influence on Fitzjames' life, and his character is critical to understanding what was to follow. He was extremely energetic and forceful. Once, when the objection 'won't there be difficulties with the Arabs?' was raised in connection with the expedition, Chesney had snapped: 'Difficulties, Sir! Difficulties! Do you think I would have had anything to do with it if there had been no difficulties?' After he died his family published this not altogether flattering pen-portrait of him:

> He was a small, wiry man, with very small hands and feet, and had the look
> of being capable of enduring great fatigue. Few could beat him in walking,
> mountaineering, riding, or swimming … His eyes were blue, small, and par-
> ticularly bright; when amused, or in a mischievous mood, they would twinkle
> with a fun which was irresistible. His hair was dark brown, and very fine and
> soft; as a young man he used to wear it brushed straight up, perhaps under
> the idea that it would give him height; latterly he wore it brushed back from
> his forehead, which was very white and well formed. He always said that his
> beauty had been spoilt by his nose being broken when he was thrown from
> the top of a coach on Salisbury Plain; but the accident left the nose sufficiently
> large and prominent. He had a mobile mouth, showing his teeth a good deal
> when laughing and talking. It was not a handsome face, but it was so intelligent,
> so genial, and so instinct with life and humour, that it never failed to make a
> pleasant impression. He was very courteous, with the polished manners of
> the old school. He would insinuate himself quietly into a room, dressed in his

unvarying evening attire of blue swallow-tail with gilt buttons, white choker and waistcoat, make his bow, and sit down. It was only after some conversation that you discovered the talent and knowledge that underlay his unpretending manner. He talked a great deal, in spite of a slight hesitation in his speech, with a certain amount of nervous excitement when much interested, and with a good deal of gesture; what he said was always worth listening to, but he was over-argumentative and apt to wax warm in discussion. His opinions on all subjects were very decided and not readily modified even by proof. Displeasure with him was evinced more by silence and a certain cold demeanour than by any strong expressions. He was extremely observant: nothing escaped him. He would come home from a party and describe the minutiae of a lady's dress which pleased him, or any other detail, so as to bring it clearly before the eye of his listener. He noticed dress very much: as a young man he had been very particular about his clothes, and he dressed well at all ages, though in a somewhat old-fashioned style. He had a keen eye for harmony in colour he hated yellow and disliked anything gaudy, or too much jewellery, and would take a great deal of trouble to select what he thought becoming for his wife and daughter, making many suggestions to their milliner. He was very neat and natty, and could not tolerate anything out of a straight line; and he would invent various contrivances suited to his occupations and wants, which always answered their purpose admirably. Above all things methodical, he was also full of resource, and great at expedients. No one could organize a party, a pic-nic, or festivity of any kind better than he. He took great pleasure in such social amusements, and was especially fond of the games of skill which ended the day. Of his passion for billiards as a youth we have already said enough; whist was his lifelong delight, and, with all his charity, he never could forgive a partner for trumping his best card. Chess was another natural taste of a mind like his; but he could not endure being beaten, and finally gave up the game after finding himself rolling on the floor in rage and despair, because he had overlooked his adversary's triumphant move. He was very simple in all his tastes. He took but little wine himself, finding his head easily affected by it, but he was very particular to have the best at his always hospitable table. His sense of humour was very strong, and he had a terrible habit of banter, and of giving nicknames to everyone, which were generally ridiculously suitable; but although his banter was sometimes disagreeable by drawing everyone's attention to his victim, it was never really unkind.

He was, at the very least, something of a flawed character and there were many occasions when his autocratic nature seriously jeopardised the whole expedition.

The Duke of Clarence, later King William IV, had taken a shine to Chesney and his career benefited from this royal patronage, although his star was to wane under Queen Victoria. Private correspondence in the old India Office archives makes it clear that his superiors in Bombay and London did not share the king's confidence in Chesney.

The political backdrop to the Chesney or Euphrates Expedition stemmed from the consequences of Napoleon's invasion of Egypt in 1798. Napoleon destroyed the power of the Mameluks, who had ruled Egypt as part of the Ottoman Empire for two and a half centuries, but after Nelson destroyed Napoleon's fleet at the Battle of the Nile, Egypt was wrested back from the French by a joint British-Ottoman army. The second in command of the Albanian contingent of this army was Mehmet Ali and, after the French left, Ali seized power in Egypt. He was appointed Governor of Egypt in 1805 and recognised as such under the notional sovereignty of the Ottoman emperor in Constantinople. He embarked on a rapid modernisation programme and Egypt became regionally powerful. It had been Egypt's modern fleet that was sunk in 1827 by Codrington at the Battle of Navarino. Mehmet Ali had sent the fleet in response to desperate pleas from his notional overlord, the Ottoman emperor, for assistance in putting down the Greek rebellion.

In 1831 Mehmet Ali finally rebelled against the Ottoman Empire and invaded Syria. His forces defeated the Ottomans and left unchecked he would probably have advanced to Constantinople and taken over the seat of power there. The great powers of the Concert of Europe wanted to prevent this, so a Russian-brokered peace, known as the Agreement of Kutahya, was agreed in 1833. Under this the Egyptians held back and it was agreed that Rashid Ali, an Ottoman general, would rule Syria as its governor under the Ottoman Empire. This fragile stand-off between Ottomans and Egyptians was the territory into which the Euphrates Expedition would venture.

While a ship canal at Suez was the logical solution, politically it would not serve British interests. Its effect would be to strengthen and enrich Egypt at the expense of the Ottoman Empire. British control of a canal in a modernising and wealthy Egypt would be uncertain. It would weaken the Ottoman Empire and increase the chance of its collapse, perhaps aiding Russia to infiltrate closer to Constantinople, Persia or even the Gulf. British suspicions about Russian expansion were growing and would lead to the disastrous First Afghan War, the Crimean War and, of course, the 'Great Game' itself. In a sense, this assessment of the proposed canal was right, as it was British failure to control a resurgent Egypt which ultimately led to the failed Suez Campaign of 1956. The seeds of that disaster were sown unwittingly in the 1820s and 1830s.

Chesney came up with a solution which he believed would offer most of the advantages of the canal, but without its political problems. At its closest, the River Euphrates comes to within 125 miles of the Mediterranean coast. He recommended that a canal be dug, later replaced in his proposals by a railway, from the Mediterranean coast to the Euphrates. British steamers could convey passengers, mail and urgent goods across the Mediterranean to the Orontes estuary, whence they would be whisked up the Orontes valley by canal or railway and across the Syrian plain to the Euphrates. Here, fast steam river boats would shuttle them down the river to Basra, where waiting steamers from the Honourable East India Company would run the final leg of the journey to India. It sounded sensible. The political advantage was that the route would run almost entirely through Ottoman territory. The line would act as a British *cordon sanitaire* to bolster friendly Ottoman rule and limit Russian infiltration. The shorter legs of the journey were within the range of contemporary steamers. A further advantage was that it took account of the British 'carve up' of the world at that time. The Mediterranean was a Royal Naval sea where the political lead came from London. From Basra to the Indian Ocean, British political leadership came from the Honourable East India Company in Bombay. Such independence was important then, when mails between Britain and the Far East could take three months to travel. Chesney's scheme neatly reflected this split.

But motives were very mixed. In the same way that the Franklin Expedition was charged with not only locating a North West Passage but also transiting it, so the Euphrates Expedition was intended both to demonstrate this concept and instigate it. The steamers were not supposed to be experimental; they were intended to be the first two ships to operate the line.

Chesney's secret weapon was his relationship with the king. William IV was not the most intelligent of British monarchs and there were many errors and misconceptions in Chesney's plan, but the king had confidence in Chesney and gave his protégé's scheme his enthusiastic backing. Chesney's reputation was good and he was thought to understand 'the Arab mind'. With the King on his side, Chesney was able to persuade the British powers in both London and Bombay to support and underwrite his venture.

Although Chesney was issued with a commission by the king and promoted to colonel, the Euphrates Expedition was not strictly either a naval or a military expedition. It was a quasi-commercial venture with the backing of the British government and the East India Company. King William IV was the largest commercial backer, investing in a personal capacity, and Parliament voted £20,000 to support the costs. The India Board chipped in an additional £5,000. With the king's support, Chesney was free to recruit serving officers and men from the Royal Navy, the army and the forces of the Honourable East India Company for the expedition. Although technically commercial, Chesney ran it on military lines, with expedition members expected to adhere to military discipline and wear uniform on formal occasions.

The Honourable East India Company commissioned the firm of Laird & Co. in Birkenhead to construct two iron river steamers. Laird's pioneered both steamships and the use of iron in ship-building, but at the time the 'Euphrates boats' were laid down they had only constructed one previous paddle steamer, the *Lady Lansdowne*. The 'Euphrates boats' were allocated the builders' numbers

4 and 5. Both followed the same general arrangement, being constructed from iron and with a shallow draught, flat bottom and no keel. The decks were wooden. Number 4 was the larger vessel, being 105ft long and 19ft wide but drawing just 4ft 6in of water. She was a substantial vessel of 179 tons, powered by a two-cylinder steam engine rated at 50hp, driving a paddle on either side of the ship. Number 5 was 15ft shorter and 3ft narrower, with a tonnage of 109 and a 20hp engine. She drew just 4ft. The ships were named *Euphrates* and *Tigris* respectively. Aft of the engines there was a map room at the stern, a large saloon with fitted bookcases and cabins for the officers. The massive engines were amidships and accessed from hatches through the deck. Forward were the stores and the men's accommodation, where they slept in hammocks. The interiors of the ships were lit with plate-glass windows 2ft across, just 1ft above the waterline. Laird's charged £4,808, but Chesney refused to pay their 'incidental expenses' of £268, so the bill for the two ships was settled at £4,540.

Most remarkably, these substantial ships were designed to be taken in pieces overland from the Mediterranean coast and then assembled on the banks of the Euphrates. They were manned by mixed companies drawn from the Honourable East India Company and the Royal Navy, with experienced steam engineers provided by Laird's. They were heavily armed and carried regular soldiers. This armed force would have the covert intelligence role of monitoring and, if necessary, limiting Russian penetration into Mesopotamia.

Like the Franklin Expedition, the Euphrates Expedition would not neglect science and learning. The expedition carried out magnetic observations and also archaeological and Biblical historical studies. Included on its staff was William Francis Ainsworth, president of the Royal Physical Society of Edinburgh and former president of the Plinian Society of Edinburgh. Like Goodsir, the surgeon-scientist on the Franklin Expedition, Ainsworth trained in medicine at the University of Edinburgh, although he never practised. Like Sir John Barrow, he was a founder member of the Royal Geographical Society in London. He carried out extensive antiquarian, geological and natural history research, which he published voluminously; so much that on the expedition he earned the nickname 'Young Strabo'. His writings are still of interest today. As a geologist he was an acute observer, but he continued to use the Old Testament as the basis for dating what he saw so, for example, he attempted to distinguish between flood depositions of the 'Noachian deluge' and subsequent, localised depositions. He found the reconciliation impossible and concluded, rather sadly, that 'it is to be regretted that, in the most careful manner in which abstracts can be made on questions in history, they always entail more diffusiveness than questions of science'.

At the same time that Colin Campbell had visited Rose Hill, the Royal Navy had asked for volunteers, mates or lieutenants to officer the two boats. One of the volunteers was a Staffordshire man called Edward Charlewood. He had asked his captain to put him forward, but assumed he had been rejected as he heard nothing more. About a month later, Charlewood noticed several visitors 'looking at our wonderful steam man-of-war vessel, then a novelty in the navy' while he was serving as officer of the watch. One of them, 'a plain but intelligent-looking man', questioned Charlewood about the ship and he answered the stranger 'somewhat conceitedly'. The conversation continued until the stranger asked after Mr Charlewood at which Charlewood replied, 'with some astonishment, that I was the person for whom he enquired'. The plain-looking stranger turned out to be Colonel Chesney. Chesney gave nothing away in the conversation and it was not until several weeks later, when Charlewood received a letter from the colonel telling him to go to Sandhurst College to sit the same exams Fitzjames had passed under Professor Narrien, that he realised Chesney was prepared to take him. After two weeks of tests, Professor Narrien passed him and he was appointed as acting lieutenant to the Euphrates Expedition.

The most senior naval officer was Lieutenant Lynch of the Honourable East India Company Navy, with Lieutenant Richard Cleaveland, RN, as second in command. Lynch and Cleaveland were accompanied by three mates: Edward Charlewood, Henry Eden and Fitzjames. Other regular and Honourable East India Company army officers were attached, including Captain Estcourt of the 43rd Light Infantry.

Both ships had a complement of thirty-one. Cleaveland was captain of the *Euphrates*, with Charlewood and Fitzjames as his junior officers. The ship had a crew of fifteen seamen and also carried two army officers, Captain Estcourt and Lieutenant Murphy, fourteen soldiers under Sergeant-Major Quin, two interpreters, Engineer Thomas Hurst and William Ainsworth, the scientist-surgeon. The smaller *Tigris* had a similar complement under the command of Lieutenant Lynch.

The reporting lines for the expedition were confused. They would land on the Mediterranean coast, take their ships overland to the Euphrates, and then sail them down to the head of the Persian Gulf under Chesney's commission from the king. There they would come under the control of the Bombay government and start a regular steamboat service up and down the Euphrates carrying the mails. All the officers were told that their service on the expedition would count as a continuation of their military and naval service. Fitzjames understood that it would not jeopardise his promotion to lieutenant, which obviously he would have received had he remained on HMS *Winchester*.

As well as political confusion, the expedition suffered time and again from Chesney's refusal to take a realistic view of the difficulties they faced. Instead he relied on brute determination to win through.

The first example of this was the difficulty of finding a cargo ship large enough to take the whole expedition. The components of the *Tigris* and the *Euphrates* alone weighed over 300 tons and the expedition took a vast amount of supporting equipment including rafts, wagons, harnesses and provisions, including tinned meats. Chesney even included a diving bell. Despite saying that he was determined 'never to fire a shot except in the last extremities of self-defence', the expedition was heavily armed. Chesney boasted:

> the larger steamer is to have two light nine pound carronades on revolving car-riages, six one pound half swivels with locks and finally a six pounder and three pounder Congreve rocket tube. The smaller steamer is to have but one nine pounder on a pivot carriage, with six one pounder swivels, also a six pounder and three pounder Congreve Rocket tube. In addition to the guns, swivels and rockets, there are five wale-pieces for each steamer with a fair supply of muskets, carbines, pistols, pikes and boarding nets; also sky rockets, blue lights, musket, grape and other ammunition.

His own estimate was that with this massive armament he could probably take on an Arab army of 1,000 men. So much for self defence!

They took magnetic and gravitational instruments and were advised by Colonel Sabine, who also was to advise the Franklin Expedition and many of the other polar expeditions of the period.

Fitzjames was sent to Birkenhead to get to know the ships as Laird's con-structed them, and to be instructed in how to assemble and sail them. He had never worked with an iron ship before and had no experience of steam, so he must have had a lot to learn. He moved into rooms rented for him by Laird's at Church Street, about half a mile from the Laird Yard. Church Street was, and is, a pleasant residential street looking down over the Mersey estuary towards Liverpool, although the house he lived in has now been demolished.

Also living there were Edward Charlewood and Henry Eden. Charlewood and Fitzjames became lifelong friends, being referred to later as 'the Euphrates twins'. Charlewood was six months younger than Fitzjames, but at that time was a month senior to him in the Royal Navy. He came from solid, respectable Staffordshire yeomanry, having been born in Cheadle, and was a diligent officer. He was a great contrast to the more raffish Fitzjames. Several times in his memoirs Charlewood says of Fitzjames that he was not hardworking, but that his flair and good humour more than made up for this. It seems both men learned a lot from the other.

They had a fairly wild social life at Church Street. On one occasion they acci-dentally burst in on their landlord and landlady asleep in bed, in the middle of a nocturnal pillow fight. Much later, Charlewood remembered what 'a noisy pair we were, as the following anecdote will show. Mr Laird one day wished to invite us for dinner, and sent for his confidential old servant, when the following took place:

> Mr Laird: 'William! Go down to the young gentlemen's lodging, and find out if they are at home: if they are, ask them to come and dine.'
>
> William departed, and in a quarter of a minute returned to the room, and informed Mr Laird that the young gentlemen were at home.

Mr Laird: 'Why, William! How on earth can you know they are at home? You have only just left the room!'
William: 'Oh, Sir, there was no occasion for me to go to their lodgings: I just listened at the front door, and heard them a-larking at their lodgings!'

They were joined by the sappers and engineers of the expedition, who gained experience of steam by 'working the engines of the ferry-boats between Birkenhead and Liverpool'.

Liverpool was a very different place from Malta, Constantinople or Nauplia. Fitzjames was awestruck by the scale of the industrialisation taking place in the north-west. He wrote that 'Liverpool is a most extraordinary place. Really one is quite astonished at the enormous number of splendid warehouses'. Liverpool and Manchester were the first cities in the world to be connected by railway, the famous Stephenson-constructed line. Fitzjames added to this letter: 'I have not seen the Railway but fully intend going to Manchester before I go.' Meanwhile, in an eery presentiment of the future, on 22 November Fitzjames' commanding officer, the not yet promoted Captain Chesney, breakfasted with Fitzjames' future final commander, Captain Sir John Franklin. The two men discussed the magnetic instruments Chesney would be taking, as Franklin would, on his expedition.

With the material of the expedition assembling at Liverpool and Birkenhead, the transport ship *George Canning* was selected as being large enough to carry the whole expedition, and loading began at Liverpool. Work was punctuated by sudden descents of Colonel Chesney, who 'would appear in Mr Laird's yard full of reproaches for the slow progress the steamers seemed to be making'.

By February 1835 the *George Canning* was ready to sail from Liverpool Docks. Fitzjames was optimistic, writing that 'we are all in good health and spirits at the prospect of embarking in an undertaking which, if it succeeds according to our expectations, will be the most useful as well as the most delightful and interesting expedition ever sent from the shores of England'. The last material to be taken on board was the substantial stock of gunpowder. On 1 February 1835, while the dockyard workers and the ship's company were loading this dangerous cargo, Fitzjames distinguished himself with almost wanton bravery.

The gunpowder was brought to the *George Canning* on a steamer tied up next to the ship. A tidewaiter, or customs official, called James Dickinson, slipped on the wooden gangplank between the two ships and fell into the fast-moving and filthy waters of the Mersey. Charlewood claimed the tide was running at 6 knots, and in a few seconds the man would be swept out of sight. Given that the customs official could not swim his fate seemed sealed, especially as the weather was cold and there was a strong wind blowing. Without pausing for a second, Fitzjames dived overboard into the Mersey after the man, not even stopping to take off his heavy greatcoat. Despite being encumbered by his clothing and boots, he was able to swim after the floundering man and reach him before he drowned. He seized him by the hair and trod water, holding the man's head above water and preventing him from drowning. Fitzjames' life, and that of the man he had committed himself to, now depended on the steamer tied up to the *George Canning* casting off and reaching the two men in the water before exposure overcame Fitzjames. It did not reach them until the tide had swept them at least half a mile along the Mersey estuary. Charlewood said that 'never have I seen anything done so nobly' and he 'never felt so happy as when we saw him, once more safe on board'.

Fitzjames' clothing was ruined, as was the very expensive pocket watch that he had been carrying. In recognition of his bravery he was granted the Freedom of the City of Liverpool at a dinner in his honour and presented with a silver cup by the Corporation of Liverpool (see plate 13).

Fitzjames seems to have been genuinely taken aback by the overwhelming response to his bravery. He wrote modestly that 'it was quite extraordinary to see the kindly feelings that everybody entertained towards me after the affair in the Mersey. I was on shore all day afterwards and was stared at most tremendously; everybody I heard wanted to see me. The feat is I think said rather too much about it in the papers.'

After the dinner, he brought the cup back to the *George Canning*, where 'we filled it with mulled Port on board and the chaps drank my health'. Fitzjames cannot have been entirely sober as he had already been toasted at the dinner. The drinking of his health on board the *George Canning* was a high-spirited affair and 'by the by it [the cup] got a slight [sic] knock at the bottom in drowning and leaks a little there'. He asked Robert Coningham to look after it while he was away, and arranged for Mr Laird to send it to Rose Hill. He suggested Coningham might be able to mend the damage as 'a little bit of solder would fill it up'.

174 years later the cup is in the collection of the National Maritime Museum at Greenwich. I wrote to the museum to recount this story and Barbara Tomlinson, curator, wrote back to say: 'This is most interesting. The cup is on display, I had a look inside (with a mirror) and there is indeed a small soldered patch in the bottom.'

Fitzjames asked Robert Coningham to take the certificate and cup to the Admiralty. His fellow officers thought he might be rewarded by promotion to lieutenant for this feat, but Fitzjames' bruising and high-risk encounters with the Admiralty made him more realistic: 'I know them too well to hope for anything of the sort,' he concluded, although 'it may do good, particularly if backed up by any other applications.' In this he was prophetically right, although he cannot have known that an even more protracted battle over his next promotion would lie ahead. Chesney wrote a private letter to the king describing Fitzjames' bravery.

Five

STEAMING ON
THE GREAT RIVERS

The expedition sailed on 10 February 1835 and arrived at Malta on 12 March. Just like the Franklin Expedition ten years later, its passage through the Atlantic was extremely stormy. Fitzjames wrote that 'never was I in a vessel that knocked about so much; nearly all our breakfast and dinner things got broken, and the table in the after-cabin got unshipped one morning and smashed the lamps'. At Malta, the expedition bought two flat-bottomed boats, engaged interpreters and seamen and chartered the steamship *Columbine* to tow the *George Canning* to the Syrian coast.

By 2 April the expedition was approaching the Syrian coast at the estuary of the Orontes. Charlewood recalled:

> all hands were naturally looking out most anxiously for the mouth of the Orontes, where we expected to land. At last we were rather startled by noticing what appeared to be a regiment of soldiers in their red coats, drawn up on the shore close to the point for which we were making. Various were the surmises as to what this could be, when the whole regiment, evidently by command of their colonel, rose up together into the air, and proved to be a flock of flamingos. It was a beautiful sight, and, strange to say, these birds were never seen again during the whole time we were encamped at the mouth of the Orontes.

There was no port and the ship drew so much water it could not get closer than half a mile to the shore. Chesney selected a campsite which could be easily defended, being surrounded on three sides by the Orontes estuary, the sea and a creek. Fitzjames' very first task of the expedition ashore was to clear mud from the creek, set up three tents and build up the defences of the site using some of Chesney's impressive collection of artillery pieces. Like the tents, which years later the Franklin Expedition would set up on King William Island, the larger tent was made from the *Columbine*'s awning. A sketch by Fitzjames survives showing the camp, the shore and the mountains behind (see plate 14).

A 1,200-yard continuous rope was strung from the ship to this camp, which was named Amelia Depot. Everything had to be ferried ashore via this rope in lighters. The boilers of the *Tigris* and the *Euphrates* were so large that they were floated in the water with lighters lashed either side. The work had only proceeded for a week when the first setback occurred. The valves of both engines had been packed in a cask, which fell off its lighter and rolled to the bottom of the river. Charlewood was given the task of retrieving this cask from the 'exceedingly turbid' water. A diver using the diving bell was able to feel his way to the cask and Charlewood ingeniously used a large clamp, which the expedition had brought with it to haul rocks from the river bed, to lift it. Fortunately the valves were undamaged, as without them the expedition would have ended there and then.

Four days later Captain Henderson, skipper of the *Columbine*, was almost drowned. He was rescued by Fitzjames, making him the second man to be saved by Fitzjames from a watery death that year. The expedition was shaken by this second near-disaster and it was plain that tough times lay ahead.

It took two solid weeks of dangerous work, wrestling heavy loads through the pounding surf, simply to land all the stores at Amelia Depot. The *Malta Gazette* reported that 'the people of the surrounding places constantly visited the camp, and viewed with wonder and amazement the operations of our sailors and mechanics'. The correspondent also noted that 'the beautiful scenery, with the crest of Mount Cassius towering above to the height of 5,618 feet in the back-ground, formed altogether a striking picture on the ancient coast of Syria'. Chesney had earlier claimed that the land from the sea to the Euphrates was flat and easy to transit with heavy loads, so Fitzjames and the other officers must already have started privately to question their leader's judgement, and wondered just how big an effort it was going to take to reach the river with their heavy ships and supplies across this forbidding terrain.

The sheer scale of their labour was not the only problem. It was clear that the local political authorities, who reported ultimately to Mehmet Ali in Egypt, had not granted the expedition permission to land or operate. Local people were prevented from trading with them; Chesney attempted to negotiate, but in vain. Ignoring the fact that permission had specifically been refused, Chesney ordered his men to survey the best route from Amelia Depot to the river – a distance of 140 miles. At least their location, an encampment by the sea benefiting from cool coastal breezes, was healthy. There was one unpleasantness which lay behind a typical joke of Fitzjames. The site was infested with snakes. One morning Charlewood had to leave the camp early, but could hardly mount his horse as his leg was very sore and stiff. After a few days it began to recover. He then received a letter, presumably from Fitzjames, which enclosed a bottle of spirits containing a small hairy snake and a note saying: 'We are anxious to hear whether you are all right, for on making up your bed the morning you left, the accompanying snake was found comfortably stowed away in it.'

Chesney's surveying had outlined the route and a location at Bir, on the banks of the Euphrates, which was selected for the assembly of the ships. Chesney sycophantically renamed it Port William. But permission for the expedition to set out was still withheld. At a standstill, Chesney instructed his men to start to assemble the *Tigris* at Amelia Depot, telling them that it might be sailed up the Orontes and used to ship supplies directly to the River Euphrates. In fact, Charlewood and Cleaveland had already surveyed the river and told Chesney that it was completely impassable to either steamer. The colonel ignored them as his assembly of the *Tigris* was simply a way to occupy his men. At the same time he also opened negotiation with Ottoman officials in Diyarbakir to try to get permission from them for the expedition. So hopeless was Chesney's perception of the political situation that he armed the men and prepared to fight it out.

The *Tigris* was launched into the Orontes estuary as a shell on 22 May, having taken only sixteen days to assemble. A week later she was loaded with a cargo consisting of components from her larger sister ship, the *Euphrates*, and the pointless attempt to force her up the Orontes was made. This having failed, she returned to the camp and was partially stripped down. Chesney chose to break her up into eight large components. This proved to be a mistake as the pieces were too large to be easily transported over land. Later it became clear that it would have been better to break her down fully.

Chesney's poor decisions and the magnitude of the task must have daunted Fitzjames. Good news at last came on 26 June when Captain Estcourt returned from Diyarbakir with authorisation from the Ottoman authorities to carry on with the expedition. This was of questionable value but it was the 'fig leaf' Chesney needed to start to move again.

What followed was nine solid months of backbreaking work by the whole expedition before the steamers were floating on the Euphrates. Murphy, Cockburn and Thompson carried out a major survey from the coast to the Euphrates, which made it quite clear that with the technology of the day a railway, let alone a canal, was completely out of the question. Although this showed that one of the basic premises of the entire expedition was impossible, Chesney was not deterred and the work of moving the expedition from the coast to the river started. It was a massive undertaking. Roads had to be constructed over rocky and, in some places, mountainous terrain. Special wagons had to be constructed to carry the boilers, some weighing over 5 tons each, over the very rough landscape. Hundreds of men and draught oxen were needed to haul them. Charlewood claimed that 'this work fell almost entirely on the naval officers and men' and that 'the practical habits acquired by each individual officer ... were put to the very severest test'.

In some places the ground was rough and roads non-existent. Sometimes the boilers were dismounted from their trucks and rolled up or let down hills on ropes. In other places the huge boilers had to be dragged up hillsides by sinking anchors into the ground at the peak and winching them up bodily using block and tackle. The terrain was too rough in some places even to run ropes, so there the boilers had to be literally inched up using screw-jacks. It was gruelling, disheartening and agonisingly slow work. It is difficult to credit that these men set out on such a massive task in such hostile terrain, but they were determined.

The expedition was divided into four teams. Each was commanded by one of the naval officers, who were given responsibility for their part of the route. Components or loads passed from one team to the next on their way to the Euphrates. Not for nothing was the first team's section called 'the Hill of Difficulty'. This was given to Charlewood, Cleaveland and the two Staunton brothers. The second team, crossing Lake Antioch from Guzel Burj to Murad Pacha, was given to Fitzjames. Materials were punted across the lake on pontoons and Fitzjames was nicknamed 'the Admiral'. It is worth noting that Lake Antioch was such a massive source of malaria that, from the 1950s, it was progressively drained. Its bed is today the site of Hatay Airport.

The final and easiest section of the route was given to a third team under Captain Estcourt. A fourth team was given a train of camels and tasked with taking lighter loads directly to 'Port William' by a more northerly route.

Fitzjames had spent a long time in the malarial environment of Lake Antioch and, not surprisingly, he was taken ill. He described this as 'a severe headache, which terminated in a sort of brain fever and left me in bed in the tent. Just one month after which I had shivering fits and ague, being cold with the thermometer at 90 degrees, and just as I was getting well I had one night and eleven hours attack of cholera, which nearly finished me.'

Some components were so large that work right across the whole project had to be halted and all the manpower of the entire expedition concentrated on a single load. For example, each boiler in turn had to be mounted on a sledge and pulled up the Hill of Difficulty by a train of no less than eighty oxen and 100 labourers. The heaviest of the *Euphrates'* boilers weighed 7 tons (see plate 15).

Although he did not tell his men this, Chesney was already under financial pressure. This forced him into the serious error of refusing to purchase pack animals. Instead, he insisted his officers hire them locally as and when they were required. As a result, the teams frequently found themselves short of animal and human capacity just when they needed it most. It also meant that the political authorities could easily withdraw support at short notice. And it saved no money. Charlewood recalled one crisis which occurred while he was trying to haul one of the boilers, so heavy it required sixty bullocks and sixty labourers to pull it, up a hill:

After some days of hard labour, we had succeeded in getting two of the heaviest boilers (one I think weighing four and a half tons) to the summit of the most difficult hill, and here the Syrians, being heartily sick of their work, deserted me with their oxen. It was about eighteen days before a sufficient number of men and oxen could again be collected to proceed with these two boilers, when I again took charge of them, and we made glorious progress in one forenoon. We now arrived at a narrow defile, where the road was little better than a very rough water-course, and had not proceeded any great distance in it when one of the fore trucks of the foremost boiler waggon struck against a boulder, the huge guiding pole knocking over the English sailors who were holding it, and striking against a rock, became hopelessly smashed. Here was a pretty dilemma! We were miles away from our camp, and apparently no succour to be obtained elsewhere. Moreover it was quite impossible to get the sound waggon to the front. It had taken eighteen days to assemble the men and oxen, and now they would assuredly disperse again after only one forenoon's work if we could not proceed. One thing however was clear – it was dinner-time, and they would remain until they had eaten that meal. So the oxen were unyoked, and all hands sat down to refresh themselves. The heat of the sun was intolerable, and nothing in the shape of trees to be found in the vicinity. There was a small shepherd's house, or rather hovel, upon the plain some little distance off: to this I repaired for shelter. The good people were sitting round their dish of pillau, and invited me to put my fingers into the dirty-looking pile. After going through the form of eating for the sake of politeness, I threw myself down upon a mat, crest-fallen and full of vexation. As I lay upon my back trying to hit upon some plan for overcoming this difficulty, my eyes gradually rested upon something which, although not King Bruce's spider, urged me on to perseverance, was certainly quite as efficacious. I noticed that the roof of the hovel was supported from end to end by one large beam, double the size of my smashed pole. Excited as this discovery made me, I took care to proceed cautiously, quietly asking my host, in my broken Arabic, if he would sell his house. He laughed at me at first, but when I took him to one side and showed him a few gold gazi, his cupidity was excited. At last I made my bargain, stipulating that his whole family and their traps should be out instanter, and ran out in high spirits to call my sailors. Before the family were fairly cleared out, my men were on the roof, delighted with their job of clearing away for the beam. The poor Syrians evidently thought they were in the hands of a parcel of madmen. The beam was quickly brought down, and by the time the Syrian waggoners had finished their dinners, my English crew had fitted a new pole, double the size of the old one, and we had no more trouble with the waggon.

It took weeks for the expedition to clear the first section of the journey to the lake. Although extremely dangerous to his health, Fitzjames was able to convey everything which made it over the Hill of Difficulty smoothly across the lake and on to the third team. Chesney moved his headquarters to Port William, which he had sent Lynch and Cockburn ahead to construct. Aware that he had spent most of the expedition's budget, Chesney reacted violently when he arrived and found that they had laboured hard to construct a large earthen fort with a ditch, three substantial two-roomed stone buildings, a shed, a cookhouse, storerooms and workshops. They must have expected his approval. Instead, Chesney berated them for extravagance and was so furious that he refused at first to occupy the room they had prepared for him, living in a bell-tent instead. To set an example of frugality, he ordered them to stop. The buildings were left unroofed so that in the autumn, when the rains set in, the men were soaked and many stores ruined. It was a typically autocratic diktat and not a rational response to the exhaustion of the expedition's budget, knowledge of which he kept to himself.

Though the Hill of Difficulty was the worst single obstacle, an immense amount of labour was still required to complete the journey. The situation was eased by the British government's intervention with the Egyptian government, which at last and somewhat belatedly permitted the expedition to pass through its territory. The work of assembling the ships started. But again, in an echo of the Franklin Expedition, disease started to affect their ability to continue. Port William, on the banks of the Euphrates, was not a healthy location. Two men died and Chesney was taken extremely ill. The men stopped riveting to try to help him recover, but even in his delirious state he insisted they continue as 'the sound of eight hammers hard at work gave me immediate relief'.

Surveyors started to explore downriver to plan the route the steamers would take, identify sources of coal and establish fuel depots ahead. To add to their problems the rains started. But despite this all the major components of the *Euphrates* had reached Port William by September.

The hull of the *Euphrates* was launched onto the river on 20 September 1835 in front of a large crowd of several thousand curious local people. Many had doubted that an iron ship could float. For the occasion, the *Euphrates* flew no less than five different flags – the Union Jack on her bowsprit, the Blue Peter over her bow, the 'Arab flag' at her foremast, the Turkish Crescent on her mainmast and the White Ensign at the stern. The launch was another near-disaster and the ship was almost lost before she even reached the water. She had been assembled on the river bank parallel to the river and 25ft above its level. The 150-ton steamer had to be launched sideways down three makeshift slips. This was a recipe for disaster. The men attempted to lower the ship down the slips using chains, but after she had descended only about a quarter of the way, Cleaveland realised that one chain was about to break. He ordered the other chains to be released and the ship plunged uncontrollably sideways into the Euphrates. Fortunately it survived and the men celebrated with what Chesney describes as 'moderate conviviality'.

Although the hull was afloat, much work remained to complete the *Euphrates*. Some components, including two parts of her boilers, were still on the road between the coast and Port William. At this point, possibly because they had heard of the successful launch, the Egyptian authorities became extremely obstructive again and prevented Chesney from hiring draught animals and casual labour. Chesney later blamed this on Russian agents. The first violence flared when Lieutenant Lynch and some men were ambushed by Arabs and one man was seriously wounded.

Enough pieces of the *Tigris* had now arrived for work on assembling the second ship to start. But problems remained. Estcourt's health collapsed completely and so many men had died or been repatriated that Chesney no longer had enough manpower to sail both ships. Many components were still strung out along the route from Lake Antioch to Port William and the torrential autumn rains had now soaked the land. Conditions became so muddy that plankways had to be laid in front of each wagon or sledge and then taken up after it had passed. Yet Chesney could not abandon the work until the spring, even if he had wanted to, as the engineers he had hired to assemble the ships were on fixed contracts and wanted to get back to Birkenhead.

Responsibilities for the remaining parts of the road were reallocated and Fitzjames was given a land section from Azaz to Gindareez. Chesney reported that 'he [Fitzjames] was specially entrusted to open the road near Antioch, of which the last portion completed was that down to the camp, which displayed when running (to our surprise) a finger post, having on it in large letters "The Road to India"'.

By the end of the year, nine months after the expedition had sailed from Liverpool, practically all the components had finally reached Port William. But Chesney had now managed to alienate both the Egyptian and Ottoman authorities. Even had it been led by a tactful man, an armed British military expedition, operating in a virtual war zone, would have attracted suspicion. Once again, supplies were withheld and accusations made, which rumours of the completed, well-armed steamships must have exacerbated. Chesney contemplated either blowing up the ships to prevent them being seized or sailing downriver in the completed *Euphrates* and leaving the *Tigris* to follow on. He decided against the latter course only when new sailors arrived to replace those who had died or been repatriated, enabling him to crew both ships.

All the stops were pulled out to try to drag the last remaining components of the *Tigris* to the banks of the Euphrates. Its last boiler did not reach Port William until 27 February 1836, drawn by no less than 104 oxen, 52 locally hired labourers and many members of the expedition.

On 9 March 1836, the *Malta Gazette* was able to report to readers, who will have remembered the expedition passing through Malta almost a year previously, 'that almost every individual in the party had been, at one time or other, attacked with fever and ague, and nineteen of the men were dead. Colonel Chesney was on a tour to Aden, Marrash, and Orfa, in search of coal and other supplies.' Chesney's mission was to try to remedy another of his errors. Bizarrely, he had earlier claimed that coal outcropped in the Syrian plain and that 'coal of a greyish-white colour' could be dug out from the banks of the Euphrates. Relying on this erroneous geology, they had not brought enough coal to complete the voyage. When it ran out they would have to fell wood for fuel as they progressed.

The expedition had already taken on its first passengers. Dr and Frau Helfer were a young married couple who had decided to travel in Asia Minor and Mesopotamia for their honeymoon. He was a German homeopath and naturalist and she was a flighty, partly French and German aristocrat. She was nine years older than her husband. The couple had met and fallen instantly in love on a stagecoach between Hamburg and Prague. After marrying they had embarked on a quasi-scientific wandering journey to Greece and the Middle East. Their story is so bizarre it is irresistible to mention a little more. Initially they had been accompanied by Frau Helfer's faithful maid Lottie, but she had fallen in love with a German boot-maker on the Syrian coast, married him and settled there.

Helfer's medicine was based on the use of natural plant remedies. He wrote that 'when the natives saw me digging up plants and I told them in answer to their questions that it was for medicine, they laughed, dug some up themselves and ate them, saying "that is not medicine, it produces neither vomiting nor purging"'. Local remedies, like those of the Royal Navy, were more brutal than the doctor's homeopathy.

Their first acquaintance with the Royal Navy came when the Helfers were collecting butterflies on the beach at Hierapolis in Syria. Moored nearby was a Royal Navy sloop. Pauline Helfer recounted with glee how the officers of this ship had trained their telescopes on her and gaped open-mouthed as she cavorted with a large net on the beach, helping her husband collect his specimens. These officers were used to seeing the local women demurely covered up and dressed in black.

One of them, overcome with curiosity at this exotic sight, even took a boat ashore and attempted to introduce himself to the Helfers on the beach. He strolled up and down near them, but under the prevailing code of gentlemanly behaviour was unable to step forward to introduce himself. Teasingly, the Helfers refused to engineer an introduction and were amused by his acute discomfort. In the end, etiquette demanded that he return to his ship without speaking to them. The next day, under more conventional social circumstances, the Helfers were introduced to this officer and took a liking to him. Pauline Helfer said that he 'took an interest in other things beside his profession (not often the case with Englishmen)' and was 'as highly educated as he was amiable'. His name was Owen Stanley and the peculiar workings of fate would determine that ten years later he would be one of the last Englishmen to see Fitzjames off on the Franklin Expedition.

Continuing their peregrinations, both Helfers adopted male 'Mameluk' clothes. In the Bir region they fell in with two English-speaking Indian men who claimed to be princes travelling back from London overland to India. It was at Aleppo that the Helfers and their Indian friends first encountered Lieutenant Lynch and other members of the Euphrates Expedition. Frau Helfer recalled that Lynch had 'a taste for Asiatic hospitality and Oriental luxury, which, however, it is necessary to indulge in there to a certain extent for the sake of keeping up your dignity … Like ourselves he had adopted the Mameluk dress, only his was richly embroidered.' After the British officers and the Indian princes had overcome their initial mutual distrust, the two parties joined forces.

At times, at least, the officers wore local dress, which would have been a lot more comfortable than their uniforms. Fitzjames had written to the Coninghams to say that if he were to alight at Rose Hill from the 9 p.m. coach from London, he doubted they would recognise him due to the extensive beard and moustache he had grown.

Given the levels of sickness on the expedition, it is not surprising that Chesney immediately recruited Dr Helfer as an additional medical attendant. He offered the Helfers and their Indian friends passage to Basra on his ships. The Helfers jumped at the chance to share in his exotic experiment, although their Indian friends were wary of the British officers. Frau Helfer described the camp and its organisation:

> It was surrounded by earthworks surmounted by a few guns. The commander lived in a flat-roofed house built of stamped mud, which barely kept out the sun, and with nothing but openings for windows; besides a few small rooms, it had a good sized mess room for the officers … The next day being Sunday we were invited to attend Divine service, which in the absence of a clergyman was performed by Dr Staunton, the physician … I then understood but little English, and nothing of the sermon that was read; still, the seriousness displayed by the officers and men did not fail to induce an elevated frame of mind. Although there may be more of outward form and usage than inward devotion in the English Church service, it has a greater and more salutary influence than many will allow. In the most remote quarters of the globe, and under circumstances the most various, it is a bond of union between every member of the English nation.

The officers' initial suspicions about the 'Indian princes' proved to be justified when they, and all the Helfers' money, disappeared. The two 'princes' turned out to be clerks from Bombay who were ultimately identified and forced to pay the Helfers back.

Charlewood described Pauline Helfer as 'a kind-hearted amiable woman, rather romantic'. She joined in whatever activity was going on although she was 'rather out of place'. He felt she 'had a great deal of hardship to undergo, and bore it exceedingly well'. One wonders what stories might lie behind his observation that 'I never was very attentive to her, but she had plenty of attention from others'. She certainly had a warm relationship with Fitzjames, remaining in touch with him later and writing to him informally as 'Dear James', which is certainly evidence of a close relationship.

By 16 March 1836, over a year after the expedition had left Birkenhead, the *Euphrates* was finally ready for her maiden voyage. Dr Helfer described the great day:

> The Mutsellim and chief magistrate of Birjick were invited to the solemn com-
> mencement of the voyage. They came, with their numerous suits, a great deal
> too early, and were in the way as we were still packing. I undertook to entertain
> them by showing them the splendid edition of 'Parry's North Pole Expedition',
> the plates in which really interested them. When they saw the Eskimo they
> laughed and said they were Arabs in winter costume.

While Helfer entertained the guests with prints of Inuit, the crew wrestled with the steam engines. Aware of Chesney's Irish roots, Fitzjames quipped that the engines would refuse to work until St Patrick's Day, which, of course, was the following day. After repairs, and true to his prediction, the successful maiden voyage took place on 17 March.

It was a triumph. There were doubts as to how handy the huge ship would prove on the river. Before sailing, Fitzjames and several men were landed on an island with a hawser in case the ship had to be hauled through the narrow opening between the island and the river bank. But all was well and Chesney steamed up to the town of Bir at full speed – he later claimed 14 knots – firing a twenty-one gun salute, which was returned 'by such artillery as the place afforded'. It is hardly surprising that this attracted a lot of interest. Not only was steam power novel, but so was the use of iron.

The expedition started to plan the descent of the river and roles were allocated. Lieutenant Murray was responsible for plotting their longitude and latitude. Captain Estcourt, now fully recovered, was charged with triangulation and mapping. Fitzjames was responsible for convoying coal, which Chesney had purchased, downriver on flat rafts or pack horses to establish fuel dumps ahead pending the discovery of a local source of fuel. This was also necessary because with full bunkers the *Euphrates* drew too much water to sail on the river.

The *Euphrates* started the descent. Chesney set a daily routine. Everyone was woken at daybreak for breakfast. Dinner was served at 5.30 p.m., with lights out at 7.30 p.m. The food was prepared by 'an American negro', presumably an escaped slave who Chesney had engaged, although Dr Helfer reported that he was 'unfortunately not skilled in his art, or the conversation might have been more lively'.

Each morning the surveying parties moved downriver along the banks, as did Fitzjames with the coal. Sailing stopped every Sunday when the men were permitted shore leave.

Even with limited coal on board, the large ship frequently grounded, but Pauline Helfer cheerily observed that 'on the days we are stuck, we occupy ourselves with reading, and the ship's classical library provides a good selection'. Carrying a classical library is not quite as eccentric as it sounds; the ship was supposed to be the prototype passenger and mail steamer and was therefore fitted out with a saloon and a library.

Pauline Helfer was the butt of a typical example of Charlewood and Fitzjames' rather heavy humour. Charlewood related that:

> Mrs Helfer's failing was evidently her stomach. Our fare was generally speaking rather ordinary, but occasionally we managed to buy a sheep from the Arabs, and then Mrs Helfer made little arrangements with Mr Rassam, our interpreter &co., a most excellent fellow, who had a similar weakness. These two individuals managed to get the liver, and have a good tuck out together. Rassam had at one time made a delicious pudding, which he carefully concealed, and (as he considered) safely deposited it in his cabin; he then went off to Mrs Helfer, who was walking about on shore, the steamer being alongside the bank. Unfortunately for them, Rassam's movements had been watched by one of the officers, who quickly discovered the pudding hidden in the cabin. Fitzjames and myself were called, and in three minutes every atom of the pudding had vanished down our throats, and we stowed away our persons in convenient places to watch the result. Mrs Helfer and Rassam were sadly taken aback when they found their pudding was gone; the former seemed to make up her mind at once that a trick had been played upon them, and quietly sneaked away. Not so Rassam, who grew very angry, and at last finding Fitzjames' hiding place, gave full vent to his wrath, and declared he was a thief, & co. This pudding story soon got wind, and was a joke against the two for a considerable time.

The descent was not easy, although at this stage relations with the local people were not excessively hostile, despite the astonishment that an iron, steam-powered ship caused. Some local Arabs even raced the ship along the banks on their horses. Chesney was amused that when men on shore hailed for a boat to return to the ship, calling 'If you please! Send a boat', the local people misheard this as the Arabic '*eblis*', which means devil. They asked him why all his men bore the name of Satan. Chesney corrected this misapprehension and tried to teach them the correct names. According to him, his name could be pronounced without difficulty, but the nearest the local people could manage to Fitzjames was 'Fissajimmis'.

From 30 March until 17 April the *Euphrates* remained held fast on a sandbank, while the *Tigris* was still not ready to sail. While the crew laboured to free the steamer, Pauline Helfer curled up in the saloon and improved her English by reading Addison, Johnson, Shakespeare, Gibbon and a few humorists. While stuck, the expedition became caught up in a feud between two adjoining Arab tribes, and at one stage a hostile mob had to be driven off by firing blanks from the vessel's 9-pounders. Fitzjames was able to interpret and explain to Chesney the nature of the feud between the tribesmen, which suggests that he had acquired some Arabic and understanding of the local people while ashore or detached with his coal barge.

No sooner had the *Euphrates* been refloated than Fitzjames' barge was upended when it hit what he thought was a submerged bridge pile. He lost all his clothes and 15 tons of the precious coal. That evening, as the *Euphrates* lay tied up at Kara Bambuge, the smaller *Tigris* at last steamed into view. There were now two steamers on the river. The *Tigris* brought with it several more rafts, including one bearing the expedition's diving bell, which Chesney had refused to abandon. The expedition had now covered just over 100 miles from Port William. Perhaps it might succeed after all the sacrifices? They maintained communications with Port William by horse and the surveying and mapping met all Chesney's expectations.

At Beles, Chesney halted the expedition so the steamers could be repainted and serviced. He hoped to interest the local merchants in establishing a port there for his fast steamer service, but unfortunately relations with the locals took a turn for the worse. Corporal Greenhill, while assisting a surveyor, was suddenly seized by three mounted Arabs, who jumped from their horses, put their lances to his throat and cut off his brass coat buttons, which they apparently thought were gold. Greenhill at least had not adopted local dress.

Greenhill escaped and Fitzjames, having raised the alarm, marshalled a few men and rushed to rescue him. Unfortunately, while returning to the steamer Fitzjames slipped – some said larking about – and broke his leg. This was a serious injury, although Fitzjames made light of it. Helfer remembered that Fitzjames was 'of such a cheerful temperament that when he was hardly come to himself, and only just informed of what had happened, he began to arrange his toilet, even while his leg was being set, in order, as he said, that he might be fit to receive visitors'. Charlewood added the revealing detail that shortly after this accident Fitzjames was again attacked by ague (malaria) and his shivering was so intense that for a time it prevented the break from mending. He would cry out in agony as the uncontrollable shivering which wracked his body jarred the broken edges of his fracture. This story throws light on the terrible disease experienced by the expedition. There was no treatment for malaria and, living at water level on the *Euphrates*, everyone was exposed to all sorts of water- and insect-borne illnesses. At one point or another, every member of the expedition suffered from fever or ague and quite a number died.

The tribesmen who had attacked Corporal Greenhill remained in a threatening position on high ground overlooking the steamer. Chesney opened negotiations with their chief to try to come to an amicable relationship. After three days, his interpreter Rassam invited the three chiefs and their eight attendants to visit the steamers. Dr Helfer described with fascination the 'arrival of the "Princes of the Desert"'. The chiefs first camped by the ships and prepared their own feast of rice and mutton. Helfer was impressed by the quantity, commenting that 'the viands prepared for us would scarcely have satisfied their keen appetites' and was amazed that for them 'to pitch their camp, kill the sheep, skin and tear them in pieces, and make an excellent pillau, was but the work of a few minutes'.

The chiefs were then invited on board the steamers. They were greeted, with all the formality that he could muster, by the colonel and his officers in the grand saloon of the *Euphrates*. At nightfall Chesney arranged a demonstration firing of the Congreve rockets which the expedition carried. Deterrence was a concept that came readily to Chesney and he never lost an opportunity to lay on a demonstration of firepower. The chiefs were impressed and asked 'if the stars went beyond the moon and remained suspended there'.

The following morning, the three chiefs were shown demonstrations of bayonet drill, musketry and the firing of grapeshot and shell from the ships' 9-pounders into the water. Chesney wryly commented that the 'discharge of canister from the 9-pounders, as well as from some of our smaller brass guns ... produced such an effect on the surface of the noble river as would be very striking even to those well acquainted to the effects of artillery'. The chiefs were duly impressed and asked Chesney: 'Who can resist you? You kill a thousand men with one shot!' Taken down into the interior of the ship, they were shown the engine and were astonished by the size and precision of the castings. 'How', they asked, 'can you work iron like that? It is cut as fine as cheese.'

They were introduced to Fitzjames, confined to his couch, and expressed 'polite regrets' at his fracture. They recommended eating lamb as the best means of curing a broken bone.

Passing into the library, which Frau Helfer had praised, they were struck by the lettering on the books' spines, which was picked out in gold. 'See,' said one, 'that is where they get their wisdom from! How costly these books must be; they are even gold outside.'

Next it was time for dinner in the grand saloon of this iron ship, constructed in Birkenhead and moored on the banks of the Euphrates. Helfer was amazed by the dignity of the three chiefs:

> Our guests ... had never before sat on chairs at a table, but dexterously took the places assigned to them. Having never handled spoons, knives, or forks, they watched their neighbours, and imitated them so well that one might have thought they had often been guests at European tables. They made their remarks with dignity and without constraint. 'What do you want these instruments for?' they asked, pointing to the forks; 'has not God given you fingers?' When pork was put on the table, a delicacy to us, after the everlasting mutton, they did not touch it, but made the sensible remark that 'everyone must obey his precepts.' They took no wine, but were not surprised that we drank what was forbidden to them. The transparency of glass was new to them; they wished to pour out water for themselves, but could not tell whether the glasses were full or empty.

Chesney's mixture of blandishments and threats worked and a treaty of friendship was signed that evening between King William IV, represented by his colonel, and Aniza Jedaan, the chief of the tribe. Jedaan told Chesney: 'we are friends to the English; I have made you my father, you must take care of me'. Chesney followed this, one of his very few diplomatic triumphs, by forcing Aniza to sign a treaty of friendship with their sworn enemies, the Shamar. This was cemented with a marriage for which Chesney provided a 'limited donation' from the British government. Chesney lectured the wedding party on the attractions of peace. He was listened to with respect, although it is questionable how long the treaty remained in force, as when he had finished the eldest Arab replied: 'Peace is good, but there must be war too; without it there would be no men. Our fathers and forefathers made war with the Shamars and we must and will do the same.'

The expedition set off again on 4 May with the smaller *Tigris* leading. By now, with their coal severely limited and no local supplies, the expedition was forced to cut wood from the river banks to feed its voracious boilers. This practice would soon dramatically worsen relations with the local people. At Amram, Chesney secured an assurance of friendship 'on his head and beard' from Rassam, chief of the Weldah, and tried to barter goods for wood. Unfortunately, one of the ships' guns was accidentally discharged and the Arabs fled. Later Rassam returned, evidently trusting his new friend Colonel Chesney. Friendly relations were restored, goods were bartered and the expedition stayed an extra day while all hands were employed in cutting down and stockpiling as much wood as possible. The flat-bottomed rafts were sent south to depot wood for fuel and the ships then sailed a further 45 miles.

It was at this point that Chesney received an unwelcome message from Sir John Hobhouse, chairman of the Board of Control of the Honourable East India Company, telling him that the expedition was to be terminated due to its heavy expenditure. This is hardly surprising. The British authorities had concluded, correctly, that the premise underlying the expedition was completely wrong; it had also done nothing for British relations with either Egypt or the Ottoman Empire. Yet Chesney was not a man to give up, under any circumstances. We have seen his widow's comment that 'his opinions on all subjects were very decided and not readily modified even by proof'. This was one such occasion. Chesney ignored this order and wrote back that he was going to 'continue the service with, if possible, such increased exertions, as might, by their success, secure not only the support of the country, but also the approbation of His Majesty's Government also'.

In an age of slow communications, this was not quite as insubordinate as it looks today, especially as Chesney had reason to suspect that the authorities in Bombay would continue to underwrite the venture. Yet Chesney was now risking his reputation on a very uncertain outcome. Worse was to come.

On the afternoon of 21 May, both steamers were caught in a very strong squall. Fitzjames was acting as officer of the watch on the *Euphrates* and was the only officer to observe the whole disaster. He described what happened:

> A squall was observed on the right hand, which it was thought would not reach us; but just as we were going through the rocky passage of Is-Geria (which, however, we did not see, as there were three feet of water over the rocks), the squall was observed coming in our direction from the WSW, with great rapidity, and looking like a large cloud of black mud. As soon as the rocks were passed, the 'Tigris' made signal to pick up our berth, and she rounded by us to the left bank. As our broadside came to the stream, we were taken with the violence too of the hurricane, which made us heel considerably; but being too near the Tigris, it became necessary to back our paddles, to avoid a fatal collision. It was blowing tremendously, and the air so thick with sand we could scarcely see. On our bow touching the bank, Charlewood and a number of the crew jumped on shore, and by the greatest exertions got an anchor out, which, with the full power of steam, held her till two chain-cables were got out, and secured by means of jumpers driven into the ground; but with all this she dragged, and would have gone down at her anchor had the storm continued – for the waves were then four feet above the bank of the river. When at its height, we saw the poor 'Tigris' fall off the shore, and drift past us at a fearful rate, broadside to the wind, and heeling over considerably. She soon disappeared in a cloud of sand, but on looking astern, soon after, I saw her in a sinking state, with her bow already under the water – in fact, going down, and it is believed that, on reaching the bottom, she turned keel upwards.

Within twenty minutes, twenty men were dead or, as the *Morning Post* reported it, 'fifteen men with five natives in addition'. The expedition had been dealt a mortal blow. It was extremely bad luck that the ships were hit by the storm at a point where the banks were too shallow to permit them to tie up. Had that been possible, they would have survived.

During the next few days of bad weather, the expedition salvaged what it could from the wreck of the *Tigris*. A few days later, on 24 May, the *Euphrates* was hit by a further storm, during which, according to Chesney, hailstones of 1½in diameter fell. Over the next few days, some of the bodies of the dead were recovered from the river and buried.

Colonel Chesney convened an ad hoc court martial over the loss of the *Tigris* with Lieutenant Cleaveland as president and Charlewood and Fitzjames as members. They concluded that nothing more could have been done to save the ship and that all the survivors had behaved in an exemplary manner.

Six

THE RIVERS OF BABYLON

By the rivers of Babylon, there we sat down, yea, we wept, when we remembered
Zion.
We hanged our harps upon the willows in the midst thereof.
For there they that carried us away captive required of us a song; and they that
wasted us required of us mirth, saying, Sing us one of the songs of Zion.
How shall we sing the LORD's song in a strange land?

Psalm 137, 1–4, King James Bible

The expedition had depended on the shallow-draft *Tigris* to find deeper channels
for the *Euphrates* to use to sail down the shallow and meandering river. As if its
loss was not enough, Colonel Chesney released two more bombshells. First, the
Tigris had been carrying the expedition's treasury, every penny of which was now
lost. The diving bell, their one possible way to salvage material from the wreck,
was at the bottom of the river with the *Tigris*. Then he told them that he had
been ordered to wind up the expedition. Chesney is the only eyewitness to have
left an account of how this was received and he claimed that at this news 'one and
all, officers and men, at once expressed themselves not only ready, but anxious to
second me in every way, and volunteered to forgo their Expedition pay, in order
to lessen our expenses as much as possible'. He is not always an entirely trustwor-
thy witness to events and without another contemporary account it is difficult to
say what really happened.

Chesney reported the disaster to London and requested additional funds so
he could complete the voyage to Bushier and hand over the *Euphrates* to the
Honourable East India Company. He sent the survivors of the *Tigris* back home.

On 1 June 1836, the Board of Control of the Honourable East India Company
replied, authorising the completion of the voyage to Basra. The determining
factor seems to have been the influence of the king. Chesney was given new
orders to take the vessel down to the Gulf, collect the Indian mails from a steamer
at Basra, bring them back up to Port William and then wind up the expedition

there. The surviving steamer would remain the property of the Honourable East India Company. From Port William the mails could be sent overland from the coast to Alexandretta on the Mediterranean coast, where the Admiralty would arrange for a steamer, the *Tartarus*, to be waiting to rush them to London. If this shortened the time it took to bring the mail from India to England, then the expedition might still be classed as a success. Perhaps, after all, the *Euphrates* could become the first of a class of fast mail steamers sailing on the river of its name? Chesney could hope.

The *Euphrates* raised steam on 31 May 1836 and headed south. Chesney anticipated reaching the Gulf in a week and then making a rapid voyage back north using depots of coal which he had left on his way south. On the first day's steaming, they made 67 miles. Bizarrely, when the colonel knocked on Ainsworth's cabin door to invite him to dinner, he realised that they had left 'the young Strabo' behind inspecting the ruins at Anah. Chesney halted the ship and remarkably Ainsworth appeared the following day. Once he realised that he had 'missed the boat', Ainsworth had simply walked south down the river bank until he came across her. He said that every time he asked a local how far ahead the ship was, he had been assured that he would find the steamer around the next bend of the Euphrates 'whither she had come with the swiftness of a bird'.

For a while progress was smooth. The crew were experienced and the course of the river was deeper and wider. Chesney identified a better source of fuel for the steamer at Hit in the 'celebrated and inexhaustible [sic] bitumen fountains of this place'. He fuelled the steamer with bitumen because he found that 'when sufficiently consolidated by an admixture of earth … [it] answered every purpose of coal'. Chesney had made a solid fuel out of naturally bubbling crude oil, meaning that Fitzjames was one of the very few Royal Naval officers of his generation to sail an oil-fuelled ship (see plate 21).

Passing the site of Babylon, they stopped so that everyone, 'even the men', could visit it. This was the first of three visits which Fitzjames was to make to the famous city.

But from now on the steamer encountered much more overt hostility from the peoples through whose territories it passed. Partly this was because of their assertive Shia faith, and perhaps also because of the aggressive way that Chesney's men depredated their woods for fuel.

The first violence occurred at Hillah. The river meandered so much, with so many different channels, that the expedition was dependent on a local man acting as a pilot. The people of Hillah were extremely hostile, so this pilot was kept hidden on board. Before they sailed he was required to meet the Ottoman Governor of Hillah, and as soon as he ventured ashore one of the locals attacked him and cut him down with a 'war-hatchet'.

Chesney, whose temper was never far from the surface, saw red, especially as the pilot was a trusted friend of his who had helped him on his earlier rafting survey of the Euphrates. It was obvious that the people of the town were arming to attack the ship, which could be rushed while tied up to the bank. Fortunately, steam had already been raised, so Chesney cast off and steamed downriver. As the ship passed downstream, several thousand armed tribesmen came out of their hiding places and lined the banks of the river. They jeered at what they thought was the ignominious departure of the steamer, not realising that its engine enabled it to travel upriver as easily as down.

The colonel placed the steamer in a position where it could threaten the town. 'There are a good many of them', said the peaceable Ainsworth to Chesney, to which the colonel replied: 'the more we shall have to kill!'

As the black 'Devil-ship' approached, her brass guns manned, the crowd started to melt away. Fortunately not a shot was fired; otherwise Chesney would definitely have attacked with all his armaments. The ship steamed slowly to the castle, where the governor was based, and Estcourt, with the interpreter Rassam, was landed to speak to him. The governor assured Estcourt that the wounded pilot would be compensated for his injuries and that his near-assassin would be tried in Baghdad, where the British agent could monitor proceedings and ensure that he was not simply freed. Chesney was satisfied and the ship sailed south from Hillah.

They were now entering the marshes of the south of modern-day Iraq, which were much more extensive then.

Around Diwaniya the river meandered tortuously and the principal channel narrowed. The marsh plants were so luxuriant that the bed of the river was almost entirely covered by reeds. Only the levees, built up over millennia, held the river in its course. Everyone was acutely conscious that if the heavy and clumsy steamer rammed one it would penetrate it. The river would drain into the surrounding marshes until it found a new channel, leaving the steamer, as Ainsworth put it, 'embedded like a large fish amidst reeds and sedges'.

On 10 June they moored for the evening at Lemlun, a village built entirely from the reeds of the marshes on a narrow tongue of land where the river branched with a mud-brick fort sited at the promontory, and inhabited by the aggressively Shia and hostile Khazail tribe. Ainsworth described them as 'unquestionably the most wild, cunning and untrustworthy of all'.

The Khazail's first attempt to shake off the expedition was to direct them down a dead-end channel rather than the main river. They steamed about a mile up this backwater before becoming stuck in a mudbank 'enveloped in a cloud of mosquitoes which added greatly to the darkness of the night'. Even burning fires to generate smoke was no protection against the swarms of mosquitoes. The seamen had taken to slinging their hammocks as high as they could in the ship's rigging to try to avoid the worst of the insects, but there was no real defence against them.

The expedition spent a night in this ghastly and unhealthy location. Ainsworth waxed lyrical about the extraordinary scene beyond the channel they were stuck in:

calm, glassy, and diversified by flowering plants, we could distinguish from the deck that all around us was water, out of which grew plants of the reed, rush, and flag kind, and tall grasses, which in these latitudes assume the port and bearing of reeds, while the reeds themselves became bamboos. Amid this dense vegetation were meres or lakelets, interspersed with great white lilies and other large and beautiful flowering plants, amid which stately pelicans sailed. Sunset cast a red glare of splendour over this extraordinary scene. Birds began to wing their … flights with prolonged screeches, and the far off villages were obscurely illumined by the early night fires, becoming so many beacons to the Khazailees, who now paddled away in their canoes along the golden flood, rising up giant like out of the surrounding reeds and rushes, and wending their way home with songs and choruses, till the savage sounds were lost in the distance and everything was enveloped in the stillness of night.

They eventually freed the steamer by paying out an anchor and hawser and backing her paddles, while the men hauled the anchor in with a windlass. They returned to Lemlun and tied up for the night.

Here Fitzjames lost another watch in sinister circumstances. On another stifling night tormented by mosquitoes, the officers tried to sleep in blankets or rugs on the deck, while the men slung their hammocks in the rigging again. Ainsworth, Chesney, Helfer and Charlewood all left slightly different accounts of what happened, but Charlewood's has the ring of truth:

The Arabs were intent on plundering us, and we were therefore obliged to keep strict watch all night, expecting an attack every moment. One party kept watch on shore, alongside the vessel, and a few walked the deck, whilst the remainder lay down upon the deck, Dr & Mrs Helfer among the latter. In the middle of the night, Captain Estcourt, who was keeping watch outside, came on board to report that the Arabs were advancing. This alarmed a rascally Arab, who had adroitly dropped, or rather floated, down the stream alongside our vessel, and had entered the after-cabin through one of the windows, which were close to the water's edge. In the cabin he set to work, plundering everything he could get hold of, amongst other things a silver chronometer, and he also tried to wrench off the gold fingers from the other chronometers. Estcourt coming on board alarmed him; he rushed on deck, seized Mrs Helfer, or the cloak she was lying in, and dragged her to the stern, Dr Helfer holding on by her legs, and another man holding Dr Helfer by his legs. The Arab must have been a strong fellow, for he dragged all three to the stern, and then leaping over, still holding and dragging poor Mrs Helfer. At last Estcourt came to the rescue, ran to the stern, and fired his pistol at the man, who let go his hold, and dropped silently into the water. We did not discover whether he was wounded. Of course, when the affair was over, Dr Helfer gave it out that the Arab wanted to steal his wife's cloak, and it was tacitly agreed that such was the fact; but some of us wicked youngsters could not help remember[ing] the leering look with which a number of the Arabs treated Mrs Helfer during the evening, and we came to the conclusion amongst ourselves that it was Mrs Helfer herself, and not her cloak, that the Arab was trying to walk off with.

The only loss to the expedition was the 'silver chronometer', which turned out to be Fitzjames' and was presumably a replacement for the one ruined when he jumped into the Mersey to save the customs man's life.

As news of the dramatic event spread, the town rose up in defiance. Chesney refused to sail away without attempting to extract satisfaction. More bloodshed was avoided because, Ainsworth said, 'the sight of our guns acted as a charm, and they found a safety valve to their hostility in dances and songs'. The following day Chesney demanded the return of Fitzjames' watch from the Sheikh. But the Sheikh replied: 'Where am I to seek for it? Surely, if you, who are so well armed, cannot take care of your things, how can I be expected to do so?'

Chesney admitted defeat and eventually the *Euphrates* steamed off. Ainsworth concluded his account by saying that 'the Sheikh had decidedly the best of the argument. We had unquestionably been outwitted, and we had to quit this strange place.'

There was further hostility at El-Khudr, where Chesney had high-handedly dragooned the inhabitants into cutting down their own wood to fuel his ship. The following morning these villagers attacked the ship with musket fire. Chesney was affronted. Having got everyone on board, he brought the ship close in to where the tribesmen were gathering and 'discharged a broadside of grape and canister'. The Arabs continued their fire, but a second broadside 'cleared the wood at once, after some consultation on their part'.

Steaming over to the other bank, Chesney observed fire on the steamer from a 'castellated building', but 'the discharge of a Congreve rocket and two or three Cohorn shells caused its immediate evacuation'. That the ship now had literally to fight its way south shows yet another miscalculation by the man who knew 'the Arab mind'.

The *Euphrates* steamed south through the low-lying marshes. The land was so waterlogged that one of the men, seeing the vast sheet of water, mistakenly thought the vessel had already entered the Persian Gulf. Chesney described it as 'the country of pelicans and quite unsuited to man'. There was no remaining source of wood or coal. Only by burning everything combustible which could be spared was the *Euphrates* able to enter the Shatt el-Arab, the confluence where the two great rivers meet, and finally to tie up at Basra. Fitzjames and his shipmates had sailed their ship almost 1,200 miles down the river after which she was named. At Basra, two East Indiamen were at anchor. They had linked with India.

Here they said goodbye to their passengers, the Helfers, who embarked on the East Indiaman *George Bentinck* bound for Calcutta. Pauline Helfer was struck by the formality of Chesney and his officers. There was no display of emotion, just 'a shake of the hand, and a laconic "good bye" which, with the monosyllabic English, expresses all that other nations use many words for', and they were gone. In India, Charlewood recalled, the Helfers 'were feted to a considerable extent. Dr Helfer afterwards went with a party to the Andaman Islands, and was killed by natives.' That sad event concluded the Helfers' extraordinary honeymoon. Frau Helfer later remarried and eventually came to live in London as Countess Nostitz. She stayed in touch with Fitzjames and in old age occasionally met Colonel Chesney, by then a general, and Charlewood, by then an admiral.

The steamer needed a complete refit. The only place this could be achieved was across the Persian Gulf at Bushire, but to get there would require the ship to sail across the open sea, which was something she had never been designed to do. The ship had no protection from corrosion. The engines took up their boiler water from outside the hull and they were not designed to run on salt water. Even more seriously, her hull was built only for calm river waters and was not stressed to resist the bending forces imposed by even shallow waves. She was flat-bottomed with no keel and would roll badly in open water. Lastly, she had large rows of plate glass picture-windows, each 2ft square, set only 1ft above the water line. And if all that was not enough the ship, being made of iron, did not have a working compass. Contemporary navigational instruments were designed for wooden ships.

All of this was pointed out to Chesney and there was clearly a huge argument about what to do next. Chesney's own widow and daughter recorded that 'the naval officers entered a strong protest, representing to their commander a fact he was as well aware of as they, that a vessel built solely for river navigation was utterly unfit to contend with swelling seas, and stating that the proceeding would be extremely hazardous'. Chesney, having the king's commission, simply over-ruled all their objections.

The officers were in a very difficult position, as Chesney fully knew, in that they were dependent upon his goodwill for their promotion. Chesney was not a man to be held back by what Fitzjames said he called 'details'. He ordered them to prepare the battered river steamer for the open sea. The cabin windows were planked over and the heaviest moveable weights, which were the ship's brass cannon, stowed away below. The *Euphrates* raised steam and sailed down the Shatt el-Arab to the open sea of the Persian Gulf. They made good progress until they lost sight of land. Then their only clue to navigation was the position of the blazing sun in the sky. Their compasses were useless.

At one point, Charlewood happened to be walking on deck and was puzzled that the water looked 'very thick' with the waves breaking ominously. He dropped a lead over the side to measure the depth of the water and found that the seabed was only just over 6ft deep. Although out of sight of land and with no idea of their position, they were in just 18in of water.

He shouted a warning and the coxswain immediately put the helm over to prevent the ship grounding. The ship rolled as she turned and a wave burst the planking over one of the windows in the side of the ship. She started to take on water. Charlewood rushed the crew down to the gaping hole and plugged it by forcing hammocks into the window frame. With the flow of water stemmed, the ship could be pumped out and a more seaworthy repair made. They worked the ship back into deeper water, but it had been a close-run thing and 'the vessel was nearly wrecked'. With night falling, they started again in the direction of Bushire, navigating by the stars. Conditions below were terrible and there seems to have been a near mutiny. Charlewood says that 'the stoke-hole was so intensely hot; the men could not be induced to remain in it. I, with others, had occasionally to go down and put coals on the fire.' It was, as he said, with 'no small relief' that when the sun came up they were able to make out an island in the distance. This turned out to be Karack, which they knew to be close to Bushire, and from it they were able to steer for the harbour. The unheralded appearance of a squat, black, iron steamer with no sails caused consternation at Bushire, but when the *Euphrates* was recognised the crews of the Honourable East India Company's warships at anchor manned their yards and gave her three cheers.

Chesney's rash voyage had virtually wrecked the vessel. Her structure had flexed while at sea, allowing cracks to open behind the paddle boxes and spread. This sounds very similar to the near-catastrophic failure which afflicted her famous sister ship *Nemesis* off the east coast of southern Africa on 16 July 1840. The *Nemesis* was struck on the port quarter by a heavy wave, after which a crack appeared in the structure on both sides of the ship at the aft corner of the paddle boxes. By the time the *Nemesis* made it to Delagoa Bay, the nearest port, these cracks had extended from 2ft 6in to 7ft. In addition, there was much water damage from the broken window.

The *Euphrates* had reached Bushire just in time.

It is unlikely the shipyard at Bushire had ever received an iron ship, being geared to service wooden sailing ships. The *Euphrates* was taken to the yard and Fitzjames was put in charge of the refurbishment. The damage to the *Nemesis* was repaired by fitting long wooden stringers inside the frames on each side, with the cracked plates then being stripped out and new ones riveted in. Perhaps Fitzjames employed the same process. He organised the dockyard workers and started the task of refurbishing the ship and making good the damage while the rest of the expedition waited for the Honourable East India Company steamer *Hugh Lindsey*.

Meanwhile, Chesney had yet another crisis on his hands. Most of the ship's company claimed their discharge, as did three of the soldiers on the expedition. They were perfectly within their rights and Chesney could not stop them, although in pique he refused to advance them their due pay. Even this did not persuade any to rejoin so, perhaps recognising his high-handedness, Chesney offered them passage back to the river on the ship which would tow the *Euphrates* rather than the riverboat itself. The ship's company were not mollified and most still insisted on their discharge. This loss of most of the ship's company at the earliest possible opportunity makes the huge enthusiasm for the voyage claimed earlier by Chesney sound rather hollow.

In the end, Chesney succeeded in signing up some replacements from the companies of the Honourable East India Company ships at Bushire and Basra. Apparently, at one point, he even tried to buy slaves as stokers and was only thwarted by their owners' concern that they would run away! It seemed Chesney had been willing to ignore the 'difficulty' of slavery being illegal under British law.

Fitzjames was fully occupied refurbishing the ship. Chesney praised him, though he said 'the assistance given by the native smiths and carpenters had been very inefficient'. There was considerable unease among the officers, however, as Cleaveland, the most senior Royal Naval officer, had received advice from the Admiralty to leave the expedition immediately and resume his career. He was told that his service on the expedition would *not* count towards his seniority. This had serious implications for the other naval officers. In this uneasy atmosphere, Fitzjames continued to lead the teams in refitting the ship.

On 5 July, the East Indiaman *Shannon* arrived and brought news that the mails would shortly arrive on the *Hugh Lindsey*. The *Euphrates* could then start the journey upriver and take these mails on the next stage of their journey to England, provided they could get her safely across the Persian Gulf again.

Chesney had failed to persuade enough sailors to voluntarily sign up as crew, so the Honourable East India Company commodore in charge of the Persian Gulf was forced to draft seamen into the ship. Many must have viewed the journey as hazardous.

It was clear even to Colonel Chesney that the steamer would be wrecked by another voyage across the open sea, so she was completely stripped of her heavy top-burden of weight, including the huge funnel and her guns, and the windows were properly sealed. Chains were lashed around the hull to prevent the joints opening up again under the stress of the waves. The East Indiaman *Elphinstone* was used to tow the *Euphrates*. The journey was taken extremely carefully with frequent stops, sailing only in the lightest of winds and calmest of conditions. The *Elphinstone* was a sailing ship so the steamer was dragged behind it each time the latter tacked, and on one occasion the two ships collided during a tack.

The expedition did not reach the mouth of the Euphrates until 1 August. The *Euphrates* was ready for its ascent of the river, but the mails had not yet arrived from Bombay. In the stifling heat of the summer, they waited at Mohammerah, the modern Khorramshahr, where Lieutenant Murphy died and Corporal Greenhill was taken dangerously ill with fever. After the arrival of yet another East Indiaman, the *Cyrene*, still without the mails and with no news of the *Hugh Lindsey*, Chesney decided to test the *Euphrates* again on the Rivers Karun and

Bah-a-Mishir. He was clearly keen to show that his ship was now a practical way of transiting the rivers of Mesopotamia.

Starting on 7 August, they started the ascent of the Karun but turned back to avoid shallows and returned to Mohammerah. They then explored the Bah-a-Mishir, returning in time to meet the East Indiaman *Shannon*, which at last brought some mail. However, the principal batch of mail on the *Hugh Lindsey* had still not arrived. Chesney now faced a dilemma. Every day he waited for the *Hugh Lindsey*, he was now delaying the *Shannon's* mails. But he had no idea when the *Hugh Lindsey* was due. He discussed this with Fitzjames and the other officers and they arrived at a compromise. They decided to take the *Shannon's* mails up the Tigris as far as Baghdad, from where they could be sent across country to the Mediterranean, then steam downriver again to meet the *Hugh Lindsey* and bring her mails up the Euphrates as planned. They knew that the later in the season they sailed, the lower the level of the river would be.

They steamed up the Shatt el-Arab, but had only got as far as Basra when Calder, the last trained engineer on the expedition, fell ill and died. Chesney allocated responsibility for running the engines to Sgt Black, an army engineer whose only previous experience of running a steam engine had been when he took a turn on the Mersey ferries with Laird's engineers back in Birkenhead.

At Basra they engaged a local pilot, took on the French consul as a passenger and started their ascent of the Tigris on 15 August. It seems remarkable that Chesney was apparently so keen to take passengers, but he was presumably trying to demonstrate that he was running the prototype of a shipping line. They made 30–60 miles each day, proceeding relatively cautiously. Knowledge of the ship spread before them. Chesney said that people came from miles to see the ship which moved 'without sails or oars, and roaring like an elephant' and were so 'struck with the English as handsome men' that they asked 'what must their wives and sisters be?'

North of Kut-el-Amarna, the scene of a memorable British defeat in the First World War some ninety years later, the river widened and became much shallower. Navigation became difficult. They engaged a second pilot and could only move forward by having their pilots wade or swim ahead, sounding the river and marking the deepest sections with poles. They had been promised that coal would be sent upriver from Basra to keep the furnaces supplied. But the coal did not arrive and the limited supply and poor quality of the wood available slowed them further. They halted briefly to inspect the Sassanian ruins at Ctesiphon, where Charlewood succeeded in climbing right across the great arch. It's tempting to imagine that Fitzjames, the other half of the 'Euphrates twins', crossed it too. They continued upriver and arrived at Baghdad on the afternoon of 30 August, 'into the midst of the wondering population'.

Already their position was perilous because the level of the river was falling and the promised coal from Basra had still not arrived. But at least they had delivered the first batch of India mails. They tied up opposite the British Residency and were entertained by Colonel Taylor, the British Resident. Fitzjames described Taylor's household: 'The Residency is a large building, with courts, a harim, &c. Ross (the doctor) and the dragomans' houses near it, all facing the river, which in the high season rises up to the lower windows. Colonel Taylor keeps a capital table and lives in a fine style; he has some good horses, and an ostrich, a lion, and a leopard.'

Fitzjames was pleased that Mrs Taylor visited the ship and brought 'an immense swarm of ladies to see the vessel, who all unveiled, and some of whom were good-looking'. There was great excitement as a large crowd of these ladies, Christian Armenians, were entertained on board the steamer. The arrival of the Pasha, a Muslim, meant that the Armenian ladies were forced to spend hours below decks in the stifling heat, unveiled, in the company of the young officers. They seem to have been as excited by this as Fitzjames and his shipmates were to mix with them. One of Fitzjames' most beautiful drawings was done at this time of the river and the Bridge of Boats just upstream of Colonel Taylor's Residency (see plate 20).

After sourcing as much wood for fuel as possible in Baghdad, the ship started its descent of the river on 5 September. They grounded only 22 miles downriver from Baghdad and were stranded on a mudbank. After refloating, they made 54 miles that same day and 60 on the day following. Passing through Kut-el-Amarna, the promised coal had still not arrived and the wood available burnt so badly that they had to steam on reduced power. Again they grounded. This time it took two days to work the ship free and resume the voyage. Clearly the Tigris was too shallow for a vessel of this size.

Arriving back they found that the *Hugh Lindsey* had been waiting for several weeks. Her captain was extremely nervous as his long stay was seen as threatening by the local populace. The Marsh Arabs were already unsettled by the continuing presence of a large and well-armed British steamer on their river and this enforced stay by the *Hugh Lindsey* seemed to them like the start of a more permanent English presence.

Bad relations had been exacerbated by Jacob Samuel, who had arrived as a passenger on board the *Hugh Lindsey*. He was a Prussian Jew who had converted to Protestantism and had already been expelled from Baghdad after starting a riot in the bazaar by distributing anti-Islamic tracts. This time, in Basra, his zeal had initially been directed towards converting the local Jewish community to Christianity. After that he had been unable to resist the temptation to try his luck in the bazaar, where he attempted to convert the local people. Although the inevitable riot had died down, it had inflamed local feeling and raised a great deal of suspicion in local eyes about the long-term intentions of the British.

This concern was well-founded, for English influence would have greatly increased had the steamer route been practical. The ship's company of the *Hugh Lindsey* had been prevented from landing to obtain fresh food and water. They were interrogated by a deputation of local elders who had asked them their business. 'Was it dates or corn? If so, they should be loaded; if not, let them go away.' The Sheikh of the Montefik Arabs was said to have given orders to attack the *Hugh Lindsey* and burn the *Euphrates* if she attempted to ascend the river again. According to Ainsworth, 'it was represented to the Sheikh that the English were quiet people, friends and allies, and paid for whatever they got'. 'The English', replied the Sheikh, 'are like ants; if one finds a bit of meat, a hundred follow.'

Colonel Chesney, following his usual approach to any challenge, manned and loaded the *Euphrates*' guns and took up a position in the river alongside the town. He threatened to bombard it unless amicable relations were re-established. When the expedition was able to land and discuss this in a less fraught way, it became clear that the ham-fisted missionary had exacerbated the tensions Chesney had already caused. It was also clear now why no coal had transited up the Tigris: the Sheikh had prevented the barges from sailing.

Chesney secured supplies and coal from Basra and from the *Hugh Lindsey* and loaded the sixteen boxes of the vital India mails – 3,600 letters in sixteen boxes, plus an important parcel. Less welcome were two British army officers as passengers, Messrs Stewart and Anderson, with 'cumbrous baggage'. Chesney wrote to inform the Sheikh that he intended to ascend the Euphrates 'if possible on a friendly footing', but was 'quite prepared to resist and signally punish anything like hostility on their part'. According to him, his 'knowledge of the Arab character led me to believe that we should accomplish this much more effectually by pursuing a decided rather than a timid course'.

This delayed the departure of the *Euphrates* until 20 October 1836. On the first day, they steamed 68 miles upriver, passing innumerable traditional reed boats. But all the time the water was receding. On a mudflat Charlewood saw a huge carp which had been beached, 'at least 4 feet thick at the shoulders and 15 feet long … much longer than any shark I have seen, being more like a young whale than anything else'.

The consequences of Chesney's threats and bluster became clear the first evening, although resistance was restricted to 'people … pelting the vessel with sticks and hard mud [and] the women also showed their anger by exposing their persons in a very indecent manner'. Steaming between these lines of exposed female buttocks, the officers and men tied the vessel up at the town of Sheikh-el-Shuyukh. Major Estcourt tried to visit the Sheikh to make peace, but 'was met with the usual excuse, that the Sheikh was in his harem, and could not be disturbed'. Chesney was refused access to the Sheikh also, but seems to have been allowed to proceed by promising to 'punish' the rival tribe of the Montefiks. With this, the Sheikh provided him with a pilot and 'one of the most influential men of the … tribe' to accompany the ship.

Two days later they arrived at El-Khudr, which the populace had completely evacuated. Evidently they had heard that the ship was hostile and taken up defensive positions in two castles. Chesney went back on his hostile undertaking and told the town elders 'that we proposed to leave the settlement of our grievances to the great Sheikh and his delegates'.

Approaching the Lemlun marshes the following day, the river became so shallow that the steamer would no longer answer to her helm, presumably because she was sliding along the riverbed. Cleaveland and the other officers tried to persuade Chesney to abandon the ascent, but he ordered them to continue the plainly impossible task. Chesney engaged local men as labourers to help drag the ship through the shallows, and eighty were employed. Their job was to haul the ship from either side of the river with ropes.

Fitzjames described the death throes of the expedition. On 26 October the ship, with its trackers, made 500 yards. To everyone except Colonel Chesney it was obvious that the effort was pointless. On the 29th, 'in cleaning the engines [it was] found that the cross-head of the air pump of the larboard engine was broken, which stops us'. This breakdown, caused by mud and sand being sucked into one of the cylinders, halted the ship.

In this desperate situation, Fitzjames volunteered to take the vital India mails upriver himself and then across country to Scanderoon on the Mediterranean coast, where they believed a steamer was waiting. He would then convey the mails to London as quickly as possible. This was an astute move if he succeeded, as he could perhaps earn some favour again in London and Bombay. Stranded in his disabled flagship in the Marshes, like Charlewood's gigantic carp, Chesney agreed to let him go.

But the journey was a desperate epic for a virtually unarmed man carrying vital mails. It is a travesty that an echo of this brave act was remembered in Dan Simmons' book *The Terror* as a raid on some Bedouin during which Fitzjames was imprisoned. The reality was that it was a huge achievement. The distance to be covered was the best part of 1,000 miles, upriver and then across the desert and mountains. Fitzjames intended to travel light with just the trusted interpreter Seyd Ali and the mails. But Colonel Chesney forced him to take Stewart, Anderson and two additional servants. These inexperienced travellers brought with them their entire luggage. It was yet another misjudgement by Chesney.

Fitzjames and his companions started on the evening of 30 October in a small boat, which they intended to sail upriver to Hillah before cutting across country. The following day they made it as far as Lemlun, the town where Frau Helfer had almost been abducted. Their reception was civil, and Kamur el Abbas, Sheikh of the Ghazuel, entertained them at dinner. But the following morning, as they prepared to sail upriver, they were surrounded by more than thirty armed men and held at gunpoint while their boat was systematically plundered. There was little they could do especially as the Sheikh, their host of the previous evening, was calmly 'performing his devotions on the shore' while watching the whole thing.

Fitzjames later established that the Sheikh had been told by one of their boatmen that the boxes on the boat contained gold. Realising that the heavily armed

Euphrates was too far away to intervene, he had decided to avail himself of the 'gold'. Fitzjames and his companions were held prisoner for two days. The robbers pillaged Stewart and Anderson's luggage and stole goods, which Fitzjames valued at £400. The Sheikh was convinced there was more and even took Fitzjames aside, offering to split the 'gold' half and half with him if he would say where it was. Fitzjames coolly declined this offer.

There was no immediate way out of this stand-off. The party was cornered in an 'Arab hut' until 8 November. They had managed to retain their personal weapons and were not overwhelmed, and the mails were safe, but they had no money. Eventually, when the Sheikh accepted there was no more booty, he permitted them to pawn some of their clothes to raise enough money to hire a boat.

After this narrowest of scrapes, they resumed their voyage up the river and reached Diwaniya on 9 November. Here they were received civilly by the Sheikh, but unfortunately he was weak and his rule did not extend beyond the town's walls. The town then came under siege by the hostile Agra tribe, so Fitzjames, his companions and the India mails were again trapped. They abandoned the boat and waited until 16/17 November.

With a small guard of armed men they crept out in the dead of the night. By sunrise they had evaded the besieging tribesmen and, following the river upcountry, they reached Hillah after a two-day forced march. Here they intended to hire dromedaries and make their way across the desert and the mountains to Scanderoon via Aleppo. But there were no dromedaries for hire.

Fitzjames left the mails with the rest of the party the following day and made an epic forced march 50 miles across country to Baghdad, which he reached that evening. Not for nothing did he later describe himself to John Barrow junior as 'the best walker in the Service'. Here he conferred with the British agent, Colonel Taylor, who he had met previously when the *Euphrates* had sailed there up the Tigris to Baghdad. Taylor gave him the unwelcome news that the steamer waiting for the mails at Scanderoon had given up and left. Instead, he suggested Fitzjames head via Damascus for Beirut, where he was more likely to find a ship. Taylor also seems to have relieved Fitzjames of his unwelcome passengers, Stuart and Armstrong, as we hear no more of them.

Fitzjames returned to Hillah and with four camels, sent by Taylor, the party set off for Damascus on 24 November. This was a journey of at least 500 miles across country. Fitzjames rode so hard and the camel was so uncomfortable for him that, when they called a halt the first evening, he was unable to dismount and had to be carried off its back, whereupon he fainted. In the days that followed they made good progress towards Damascus, although the pace was punishing and, given that he was personally responsible for the India mails, the strain on Fitzjames must have been tremendous. During the journey their two guides appear to have made a further attempt to rob the packages, which they were convinced contained gold. The guides gave false directions and caused the party to wander. They were presumably waiting for the opportunity to overwhelm Fitzjames and Seyd Ali. They were thwarted in a most unlikely way by the sudden appearance of a caravan of 400 camels led by men of their own tribe, heading to market at Damascus. This seems to have provided a measure of security, possibly because the guides did not want to share the 'treasure' with so many of their countrymen. But as part of a caravan, progress was agonisingly slow. With the coming of the rains, the caravan did not reach the Euphrates until 4 December. After four days, with the whole party still not across the river, Fitzjames' patience snapped. Splitting from the caravan overnight on 8 December, he forced a march directly for Damascus via Tadma (Palmyra), reaching the city finally on 18 December.

Once at Damascus Fitzjames knew that he and the mails were safe. He was able to confirm that a steamer was expected to depart Beirut for Malta on either 27 or 28 December, so he had the luxury of three days' rest before making the final leg of his journey to Beirut, arriving on 26 December. The final indignity was that the steamer itself was delayed, so Fitzjames and the mails did not leave Beirut until 4 January 1837. He was clearly extremely nervous of being blamed for any delays to the mails and wrote a long and carefully constructed letter to the chairman of the Board of Control in an attempt to clear his name. In this he was successful. The mails reached London before Fitzjames.

He seems to have recovered quickly. He was still wearing 'Turkish' clothes, presumably also with a beard of a couple of years' growth. Bronzed and fit, he did not immediately look like a 24-year-old mate in the Royal Navy. On the way home, the ship carrying him called in at Cádiz, where he found the Royal Navy frigate HMS *Pique* riding at anchor. A friend of his was a lieutenant on the *Pique* and Fitzjames, still dressed in his 'Turkish' gear, called on him. The friend arranged for a midshipman to show the important foreigner around the ship. Fitzjames pretended he spoke no English, but communicated in a few words of muttered Arabic and sign language. The unsuspecting midshipman took Fitzjames on an extended tour of the ship until finally he spent some time trying to impress his Turkish visitor with the height of the deck. 'Look,' said the midshipman, 'high, very high', pointing to the beam carrying the deck above them. Fitzjames, who was very athletic, suddenly aimed a huge kick at the beam, managing to touch it with his toe, before agreeing with the innocent midshipman. 'Yes, very high indeed', in what was described as 'very hearty English'. Fitzjames seems to have found it impossible to resist practical jokes.

Having been delayed by his quarantine at Malta, Fitzjames did not arrive in England until March 1837. Presumably shortly after leaving Cádiz, he finally shaved and changed into naval uniform again.

Back on the great river, the remaining members of the expedition patched up the *Euphrates* and sailed the battered steamer downriver to Basra. It was clear that the expedition would be wound up. His family thought it was characteristic of Chesney that, once the steamer reached Basra, he wrote to a neighbour in Ireland, who he had heard 'had a fine strain of Irish red setters, to have two dogs ready for him on his approaching return'.

The repopulation of his kennels under way, Chesney went to India for further orders while Estcourt and the team surveyed the southerly rivers and then steamed up the Tigris to Baghdad. There, the sailors drafted from the Honourable East India Company insisted on their discharge. Baghdad being about as unsuitable a spot as anywhere on earth in which to attempt to recruit sailors for an iron steamer, Estcourt had no choice but to lay up the ship and, with the rest of the expedition, make his way back to London. It had been politically inexpedient and a costly failure.

Chesney, Charlewood and Cleaveland did not know what had happened to Fitzjames or whether he had succeeded in delivering the mails. Charlewood said:

> we all felt very anxious about him, especially when news arrived, some weeks after, to the effect that he had been robbed at Lemlun, and the mail boxes opened to ascertain their contents, but that the Arabs, having discovered that the boxes only contained letters, had allowed Fitzjames to pack them up again and proceed with them on his journey. Beyond this we heard nothing of him for a full year, and our anxiety was very great. At last, upon our arrival at Palmyra, on our journey across the desert homewards, I went into one of the towers which had been used for burial places. (The inhabitants of Palmyra, instead of being buried under ground, were placed in niches arranged up the inner sides of high towers.) After examining it for some time, the thought flashed across my mind that if Fitzjames had succeeded in reaching Palmyra he would certainly have visited this largest tower, and very probably (Englishman-like) have written his name in one of the niches. Accordingly, I hunted about and there to my delight I actually discovered his name in his well-known handwriting, and Said Alli's name underneath, with the date. This gave me great joy, for we now had reasonable hope that he had long since arrived safely in England.

The graffiti on the towers lasted until recently, when it was cleaned away.

To round off the story, it should be recorded that a further attempt was made to run a British steamer service on the great rivers of Mesopotamia. Lynch re-commissioned the *Euphrates* in 1838 and by 1839 the ship had been joined by three smaller sister ships, the *Nimrod*, the *Nitocris* and the *Assyria*. Learning from Chesney's many mistakes, further exploration of the concept continued until 1842, when the *Euphrates*, *Nimrod* and *Assyria* were towed to Bombay. The *Euphrates* remained in commission with the navy of the Honourable East India Company until she was scrapped in 1847. By then, following the death of Sir John Franklin, her one-time junior officer James Fitzjames had become captain of HMS *Erebus*, irrevocably locked in the ice off King William Island.

Seven

'A HUGE GINGHAM UMBRELLA'

The very next morning they met in the church,
And foolish Alphonso was left in the lurch,
And they said, 'In the future you'll know how to tell a
Great lord from a loon, by his gingham umbrella.'

From *The Gingham Umbrella*, or *A Lesson in Politeness*, by Laura Elizabeth Richards

Fitzjames was officially signed off from the Euphrates Expedition on 9 March 1837. The limited success of the expedition was not immediately apparent to the wider world, and Fitzjames was now a seasoned explorer. Little more than half of the original expedition made it back. Nine of the forty-five original members, or 20 per cent of them, had died on it and sixteen more had insisted on an early discharge. Three more were still in the Middle East. Fitzjames was one of only six of the original band to return at that time. Much had changed while he was away and it must have been a struggle for Fitzjames to realign himself with the new era, which would come to be known as 'Victorian'.

At home, his foster family was sadly depleted. At some point while he was away, Fitzjames had learned that Robert Coningham, the foster father who had cared for him with the love of a true father, had died. This news may have reached him as early as Basra on the Euphrates Expedition, or perhaps it only caught up with him on his journey back home from Beirut.

Robert Coningham's death almost a year ago, at the age of 52, had been completely unexpected. William and Louisa Coningham had both written to Fitzjames in May 1836 to tell him the tragic news. Wherever these letters reached him, the news must have affected him hugely. A massive emotional prop in his life had been kicked away. He had always been very close to Robert, as when the two men had conspired to try to swing Fitzjames' appointment as midshipman on HMS *St Vincent*, or when Coningham came to stay in Fitzjames' lodgings at Portsmouth in 1834. His correspondence with Robert Coningham is much more affectionate than his limited correspondence with the Gambiers.

Louisa wrote a very moving letter to tell him of Robert's death in which she addressed Fitzjames as her 'dear afflicted child' and told him that Robert and she had considered him as their own son. Her description of Robert as one who 'fostered you from your earliest childhood and whom you mourn with a sorrow not to be exceeded' is very powerful evidence that Fitzjames had been fostered from shortly after his baptism at the age of 1½ and not from the age of 7, as Robert Coningham had once claimed. She signed this short, dignified and intensely touching letter as 'ever dear James your affectionate friend, L. Coningham'.

William Coningham wrote at the same time addressing Fitzjames as 'my dear, dear fellow'. In his letter, he made a revealing slip of the pen, referring to Robert Coningham as 'our father'. He called Fitzjames 'the friend of my earliest childhood', which again does not suggest the fostering started at age 7. The two men thought of each other as brothers.

Rose Hill, the beautiful estate which Fitzjames considered his home, had been sold. William Coningham's cousin, the intellectual Rev. John Sterling, was ill with worsening tuberculosis. He was also in trouble, having resigned his living because of his increasing acrimonious theological disputes with the Church of England. William Coningham had sold his commission after the failure of his abortive military career in the First Light Dragoons. There must have been a huge contrast between the fit and deeply tanned Fitzjames, the ailing Louisa Coningham, the dying John Sterling and the sickly William Coningham. William had now developed strong aesthetic and intellectual views and connections among London's intelligentsia. Thomas Carlyle, who had a great liking for William, described him at the age of 24 as 'a young, very tall, very lean, dyspeptical, gentlehearted, rich and melancholic man; the son of a man we liked well, and lamented for the Death of'.

On the other hand, William was lonely; this tragedy was the first of several events which enriched him, as more and more of his family's wealth devolved upon him. During the late 1830s he, with John Sterling and another cousin, inherited the proceeds of a slave plantation on St Vincent, which had been owned by his great-uncle Walter. The ironies, and perhaps the guilt, of inherited wealth based on the slave trade were not lost on any of them.

With Rose Hill gone, Fitzjames had no real home and seems to have spent most of his time in London living with the other survivors of the expedition. They were lucky to be alive and Fitzjames, like all of them, must have been overjoyed to return home. Edward Charlewood remembered, when they reached Beirut, 'the delight of seeing the Mediterranean once more, and bathing in it, and lodging too in a clean house, and sleeping on clean mats; and then putting on clean clothes, entirely free from vermin! Day after day I used to walk out to the promontory, and sit upon one particular stone, watching for the steamer which was coming to take us to England.'

Fitzjames was reunited with Charlewood and Cleaveland in London, as the rest of the expedition straggled home. The three men were now lifelong friends. Charlewood remembered they were 'feted in all directions':

> The Duke of Sussex invited us to a conversatzione, and Lord Lansdowne to dine with him, & co. ... An evening spent at the Duke of Sussex was rather amusing. Fitzjames, A. Staunton (a young Artillery Doctor) and myself arrive at Kensington Palace in a cab. Upon alighting, we ascended some steps leading up to a long corridor, along which, powdered footmen were posted, to call out the names of the guests as they arrived. Fitzjames led the way, and the lackey at the head of the steps demanded his name & co. Fitzjames replied, in a very modest tone, 'Lieutenant Fitzjames'; upon which the servant roared out, in a stentorian voice, 'Captain Fitzjames'; and so along the corridor right up to the Duke, 'Captain Fitzjames' name was passed. Staunton's turn now came, and to prevent any mistake, he presented his card to the servant, on which was inscribed the name: 'A. Staunton, R.A.' The fellow, I am sure, had a spice of fun in him, for on looking at the card, he roared out 'Rear Admiral Staunton', and away the newly dubbed Admiral – a red-headed boy without a beard, and perspiring with nervousness, as if he had just been dipped in a bath – had to march up to the Duke. The Duke received the 'Admiral' with a merry wink in his eye, talked to him a moment and then passed him along. I was more fortunate; I gave my name and rank distinctly, and then passed the Duke, after the usual common-place civilities. We three youngsters, however, behaved very ill at this reception, for after strolling about for some little time, we got into a small ante-room by ourselves, and were surprised, in a bolstering match with red velvet cushions in which we were engaged, by a solemn-looking old Bishop, who looked at us as if he would eat us up, and then left in disgust.

Some of their experience would be valuable to the Royal Navy in the right position. Fitzjames now had some exposure to steam power and iron ships, both then highly innovative and very controversial. He also seems to have been reasonably fluent in vernacular Arabic as well as Portuguese and French. But would he ever have another position in the Royal Navy? The rest of 1837 was to be a deeply troubling year for Fitzjames.

For the third time in his career he faced a titanic struggle for promotion and this time he was not at fault. The expedition appeared to have effectively destroyed his career in the Royal Navy and he was almost certainly out of pocket. He had received no pay from the Royal Navy as he was supposed to have been paid by the expedition, but it seems unlikely that he was given any money since the *Tigris* sank a year previously with the expedition's entire treasury on board.

Worse, the promotion to lieutenant, which he believed he had been promised, was refused. A letter dated 26 April 1837 from the Admiralty to the India Board confirmed it would not 'allow seatime to these officers' and would not be promoting Fitzjames, Cleaveland or Charlewood. All Fitzjames' sacrifice and risk had been in vain – none of it would count towards his naval career. In fact, in career terms, it had put him back, as the last service the Admiralty would take account of in promoting him had ended on 8 October 1834, almost four years ago.

Although Fitzjames was an experienced 24-year-old officer who had entered the Royal Navy at the age of 12, as things stood he only had about seven and a half years allowable service, and of that only eleven months had transpired since he had passed for lieutenant in November 1833. What really grated with Charlewood, Cleaveland and him was that Eden, the officer they had not liked and who had left the expedition early after the sinking of the *Tigris*, had already had his promotion and was now serving again in the Royal Navy.

Fitzjames and the other survivors of the expedition seem to have taken lodgings together in south London, while Chesney moved into his more salubrious old townhouse in Down Street, Mayfair. The author of the Chesney family memoir recalled that 'it was natural that those who had shared so much peril and excitement together should like to be in each other's company. A friend met them all one Sunday going to church near Kennington, and remarked that he did not expect to meet the Euphrates Expedition in that part of the world.'

Chesney did not arrive back in England until 8 August 1837 and, to his credit, he immediately redoubled his efforts to obtain promotion for his officers. He was incensed that their service on his expedition, for which he had been commissioned by the king, should not be treated as service towards their promotions. He was acutely aware that he had betrayed the trust of the three officers. His obstinacy, for once, acted in favour of his men as he simply would not accept that the Admiralty's decision was final. He attempted to have them promoted directly by Order in Council, sidestepping the Admiralty, but was denied this by the death of King William IV on 20 June 1837.

Chesney continued to fire off letters demanding promotions for his loyal officers and did not make himself popular. Lord Minto and the Duke of Wellington were just two of the great and the good who had to endure his harangues. Chesney himself never received promotion or pay and had actually incurred debts of £2,000 keeping the expedition going. He was only saved by large personal loans from his first wife's bankers, the Sandmans, and Gledstanes, the banking business of the Coningham family.

Chesney's refusal to admit defeat, plus his very strong sense of honour, meant that he continued to push for what he felt was the right reward for his officers irrespective of the damage to his career. Finally on 18 January 1838, almost a year after Fitzjames returned to England, the India Board made a fresh formal appeal to the Lords of the Admiralty to reconsider the issue. Its submission stated:

I am directed by the Commissioners for the Affairs of India to request you will have the goodness again to call the attention of the Lords Commissioners of the Admiralty to the case of Lieutenant Cleaveland and of Messrs Charlewood and Fitzjames in whose behalf I had the honour of addressing you on 19th April, 1837.

The papers laid before Parliament on the 17th July, 1837 state very fully the satisfactory manner in which those meritorious officers exerted themselves, I beg leave however to transmit to you an extract of a letter subsequently received from Colonel Chesney at this Board in which he more minutely details their valuable services. As Colonel Chesney held the King's Commission to employ officers belonging to the Navy, Army and Ordnance, I hope that this further testimony in favour of Lieutenant Cleaveland and Messrs Charlewood and Fitzjames may strengthen the favourable impression which I trust has been made upon their Lordships by the perusal of the papers submitted to Parliament.

Expectations were certainly held out to all the officers that employment on an Expedition recommended by a Committee of the House of Commons would probably lead to their future promotion, these expectations were in some degree sanctioned by members of the government who took a deep interest in the success of the expedition, and Lord Glenelg in a minute dated 12th December 1834 a few days before he retired stated ... if the other officers and the men give satisfaction during their employment in what must be considered a public service, the time of being employed should be allowed, and those among the officers who may be thought entitled to such a distinction might be recommended to His Majesty for promotion. It was my intention if I had remained in office at the conclusion of the Service to have followed this course.

The Board direct [sic] me in conclusion to express their earnest hope that the Lords Commissioners of the Admiralty will feel themselves justified in granting a favourable reply to this application.

This letter included a fulsome tribute to the three officers written by Chesney, although it had failed to deliver the promised promotion by Order in Council in July 1837. This time Chesney's persistence paid off. A full meeting of the Lords of the Admiralty was convened to reconsider the decision. The minutes read:

My Lords have had again under their consideration the case of the officers of the Royal Navy accommodated in the letter from the India Board of 19th April, 1837 ... after the perusal of the papers laid before Parliament which contain a detailed account of the Euphrates Expedition and of the additional strong testimonials of Col. Chesney in their favour ... these officers displayed great professional skill as well as exceptional zeal and activity throughout the trying circumstances in which they were frequently placed ...

My Lords further find from the letter of the India Board that expectations of promotion in their profession were held out to them as a reward for meretricious conduct ...

Under these circumstances, and anxious to express their sense of the ability and zeal displayed by these officers my Lords are pleased to give to each of them a step in rank.

Therefore Charlewood and Fitzjames having served the necessary time are to promoted [sic] immediately and a Commander's commission is to be prepared for Cleaveland ...

Let commissions be prepared accordingly.

Fitzjames had at last attained the promotion he wanted and on 26 January 1838 he and Charlewood were both appointed to the exalted rank of lieutenant. They had already started courses on HMS *Excellent* as gunnery officers, but at the more junior rank of mate. By the closest of margins, Fitzjames had again rescued his unusual career. Now, with his permanent commission assured, he could resume his career on a more conventional path.

HMS *Excellent* still exists today in the Royal Navy and logically one would expect that she is a ship. It is the long tradition, however, of the Royal Navy to commission shore establishments as 'ships', so today HMS *Excellent* is actually a shore establishment.

Since the victories of the Napoleonic Wars, technological developments meant that the old gunnery techniques, which depended on simply laying one's ship alongside the enemy and blazing away with the highest possible rate of fire, could no longer be relied upon. Accuracy was starting to supersede speed of reloading as the ultimate determinant of victory. In 1830, Commander George Smith had been appointed to set up and head a Naval School of Gunnery, and was provided with the fifth-rate ship HMS *Excellent*, then moored off the north-west corner of the dockyard in Portsmouth, as his base. *Excellent* was moored such that her port broadside faced Fareham Creek, thereby allowing the firing of guns with little chance of injuring civilians. Smith's school soon gained a reputation for professionalism and he was promoted to captain in 1832, to be replaced as commander of HMS *Excellent* by Captain Thomas Hastings. Under Hastings, HMS *Excellent* had a complement of 200 officers and men at any one time, being trained in gunnery. *Excellent* quickly became a scientific experimental station for the Royal Navy, almost an equivalent to Woolwich College which Chesney had attended as a sapper officer.

Fitzjames was one of the very first naval officers to receive proper theoretical tuition in gunnery, which was introduced into the curriculum for the first time in 1838. In later life he showed a keen interest in technology. He approved of the fitting of steam engines to HMS *Erebus* and HMS *Terror*, and in his letters he sometimes refers to inventions of other officers or ideas for technological improvements. It is likely that this, as well as his straightforward sense of adventure, attracted him to the Euphrates Expedition. The training he was now having would equip him for promotion to higher ranks in the Royal Navy and when it was over he would have had a better mathematical and scientific training than many older officers who had not had the opportunity to pass through HMS *Excellent*. As well as training, the social life was excellent too. Fitzjames was the life and soul of his mess and was liked by senior officers as well as his peers. Among the officers on his course were two who were to join him on the Franklin Expedition, notably Henry Le Vesconte and Edward Couch.

Fitzjames was a brilliant mimic as well as a great practical joker. Once, on HMS *Excellent*, Edward Charlewood remembered:

I came down to dinner, and was comfortably enjoying myself, when the sentry came in and announced, with a queer look, that a 'person' wished to see me. I directed him to be shown in, and, to my disgust, in walked a most objectionable looking fellow, with a mean pock-marked face, a dirty white choker, and very seedy clothes. He spoke to me quite familiarly; represented that he was a great friend of my brother George, who had recommended him to come down from London to Portsmouth, for change of air, and was sure I would be glad to see him and be kind to him. There could be no mistake, for he had brought a letter from my brother, in which he spoke most highly of his friend Mr Dent, who was a well-principled and religiously disposed person, whose conversation would be most beneficial to me.

Mr Dent evidently knew the contents of my brother's letter, for he quoted Scripture and talked religion, until I was most thoroughly disgusted. My messmates too began to notice him, and I could hear sly jokes at my expense. I passed a most uncomfortable evening; the fellow ate and drank most heartily, and as the time went on gave no sign whatever of going ashore. At last the sentry came, at 10 p.m., and announced that the last boat was going, so I told my friend that he must depart. Great, however, was my disgust when he announced that he contemplated sleeping on the floor of my cabin. This was more than I could stand. I got up and told him that he must go on shore; so away he went, showering down on my head all sorts of blessings, and prayers for my welfare.

He remained at Portsmouth, at a little pot-shop, for nearly a week, and at last, finding he could get nothing out of me, wrote a pitiable note, saying he had fallen short of money, and asking me to lend him £3 until he got to London. I sent him the money, thankful to be rid of him. A week afterwards a policeman came on board to see me. He brought me a bill from a small tavern in Ryde, amounting to £4 10s, principally for brandy and water, which Mr Dent had obtained on the strength of being 'my friend'. At last he bolted without paying, and stole a silk handkerchief from the chamber-maid. I told the policeman Mr

Dent was no friend of mine; but that I knew where he came from, and would try and get the bill paid.

Charlewood's messmates, including Fitzjames of course, ribbed him mercilessly about his 'Swindler friend'. Then:

About three months after the above occurrence, we had a large party of friends dining with us. After dinner a circle was made round the fire, and we all sat there enjoying our wine and dessert, and a very merry and happy party we were. Presently the sentry appeared and called: 'Mr Charlewood, a person wished to see you'. The 'swindler friend' had by this time apparently been nearly forgotten; so without thinking much about it, I asked if the stranger appeared to be a gentleman. The sentry replied rather doubtfully; but I nevertheless directed him to show the person in. Judge of my horror upon beholding another fellow of evidently the same stamp as my 'swindler friend'. He was dressed in a rusty black suit, dirty white neckerchief, spectacles, hair parted down the middle and plastered with grease, a huge gingham umbrella, and dirty fingernails. I could have sunk through the deck as this fellow approached me, every person maintaining a dead silence. The officer next to me got up to let the visitor sit by me, so there was nothing for it. I asked him to sit down, which he did, holding his gingham out most conspicuously; as if he were proud of it. It was most provoking; no one would speak; all were too evidently waiting to hear the conversation between this new friend and myself. After I was seated, I asked him if he wished to speak to me, when he told me in a sanctified voice that he had just arrived from Manchester, that he was an intimate friend of my brother Harry, who had told him by all means to call upon me as he was going to Portsmouth. He then mentioned various little matters, which fully satisfied me that he really was acquainted with my brother Harry. I then asked him to partake of some dessert and a glass of wine. He declined the wine, and in a disgustingly sanctimonious tone 'trusted I also eschewed all intoxicating liquors'. My misery was extreme; all were now listening intently to our conversation, and someone now called out 'I say, Charlewood, rosin your friend up a little; he doesn't drink wine, for he wants a glass of grog'. Of course my friend professed not to know what grog was, and I had to explain. At last someone called out 'That's all d___ humbug; he knows well enough what grog is!' Upon this my friend exclaimed with a shocked tone 'Oh, my dear friend, I trust you do not follow that wicked example of swearing!'

Whilst this went on my messmates were getting unruly, and showing symptoms of unhandsome joking towards my friend. Some called out 'twig his spectacles!' Others expiated on his handsome umbrella; some flipped nuts at him, and indeed matters looked serious. I begged and implored them to be quiet, first in an undertone, and then angrily. At last the crisis came. Moorman (now a

Captain, RN) had dined after us, and been on watch on deck, and he was sitting by himself on the opposite side of the table, eating his dessert. He now cut an orange in half, and threw it at my friend. This was too much! I sprang up, threw myself across the table, smashing wine glasses, decanters, desert dishes, &co., and seized Moorman by the collar with one hand, and with the other I was about to give him a blow which would never have been forgotten by him had he received it, for there was no mistake, rage had given me the energy and strength of a madman. But my messmates saved me, and Moorman also. Someone leapt upon me, and squeezed me flat down upon the table, my nose being forced tight down, as well as my body; others got hold of my arms and legs; so here I was pinned down, with no end of broken glass under me. It was a mercy I was not seriously hurt. At last I managed to move my head to see who it was so energetically pinned me down to the table to find it was my sanctified friend, and the gingham umbrella was lying on the table by my side. My position now became unbearable; I was nearly stifled, and I roared out 'Let me go or I shall be suffocated!' Upon this my friend slowly and cautiously eased himself off my body, and I was allowed to turn around and sit upon the table, my arms and legs being kept in prison. My friend now stood before me, gave a grin, tore off his dirty white choker, pitched off his black coat, and put on a uniform coat, threw off his spectacles, pushed up his hair, and lo and behold, my hateful, sanctified friend was transformed into my dear old expedition companion, Fitzjames! The roars of laughter at the success of this deception on me may well be imagined. It appeared that this had been planned for weeks before; and I remembered that Fitzjames had latterly been asking me all sorts of questions about my brother Henry, and by this means he had been able to satisfy me as to the fact of the 'sanctified friend' coming from Manchester. I was most truly thankful to find that it all was really a joke, for my shame and misery were intense. My messmates would not let me pay for the breakages, as it was considered a mess joke.

What is interesting about this account is not just Fitzjames' sense of humour, but also what it tells us about his undoubted ability at deception. Clearly he was a great actor as he was able to adopt a disguise which fooled his friend Charlewood completely and maintain it for a long time. But there is also a slightly sinister side to this. Life had forced this man to develop such great self-control that he could conceal his true feelings and keep a secret. These stories indicate that, if he needed to, he was capable of lying and of living with the lie.

Charlewood later recalled how, for Fitzjames and for him, 'this was a happy time, we worked like Trojans, and both passed out with A1 certificates – a most difficult class of certificate to obtain; I think only about six had previously been awarded'. It was not all fun.

There was another benefit to spending time at HMS *Excellent*. Although *Excellent* was a ship, she was permanently moored, conveniently right next to the

Royal Navy's principal port, Portsmouth. Portsmouth is, of course, only 65 miles or so from London. The newly promoted Lieutenant Fitzjames, aged 25 and with the status of a gunnery lieutenant, had ready social access to important people other than those he was serving with. It seems to have been from this time that his friendship with John Barrow junior started.

After passing out from HMS *Excellent* on 17 October 1838, Fitzjames, Cleaveland and Charlewood were in demand.

At this time, another of the voyages of exploration inspired by Sir John Barrow sailed. This was the Trotter Expedition to the Niger, which had some parallels with the Euphrates Expedition. It used three iron paddle steamers especially designed and constructed by Laird's, and it was brought low even more rapidly than the Euphrates Expedition by disease. Trotter asked Charlewood and Fitzjames to join it, but they both declined the invitation. Trotter even tried to have the Admiralty draft them, but this too was turned down.

Fitzjames' opinions on this have not survived, but Charlewood wrote that 'most thankful am I that I had nothing to do with that expedition, mismanaged from first to last'. One who was less lucky was Walter Fairholme, who joined the expedition and was almost killed by tropical fever. He was to die with Fitzjames on the Franklin Expedition. Charlewood remembered 'going in board the principle steamer, when she was just ready to start from Woolwich. The upper deck had a number of placards stuck about it with texts of Scripture, and the sailors were sitting on the forecastle, some of them drunk and singing hymns.' It is notable that many of Fitzjames' jokes parodied preachy, pious types.

Despite turning down Trotter, the two friends were still interested in volunteering for more interesting, and safer, exploration work. Although Fitzjames and Charlewood fought shy of Trotter and the Niger, they both volunteered to sail with Sir James Ross to the Antarctic. Colonel Chesney wrote a reference for them to Ross, saying:

> their good temper, perseverance's and their honourable feelings mixed with that kind of determination which must succeed if it is possible to do have been so prominent and so much tried during the *Euphrates* service, that I cannot suppose for a moment that these qualities can fail even on an ice berg ... the most striking qualities of these officers are cheerful tact in keeping up the spirits of the men to an extent which in trying circumstances tells in the most marked manner; and it is on the latter ground that I venture to predict that you will find them fitted in a peculiar manner to carry through their portion of the adventurous service now contemplated, if you are disposed to select them for it.

Ross asked for them both, but the Admiralty wanted a return from their expensive training on *Excellent* and Fitzjames was appointed gunnery lieutenant to HMS *Ganges*. He never got as far as an interview with Ross.

The *Ganges* was a warship built in India from solid teak. She was an immensely strong 84-gun second-rate ship. She survived until the 1930s, when she was finally broken up, after over a century in service, at Plymouth. Her captain's cabin was salvaged from the breaker's yard and built into the Burgh Island Hotel in Devon, where it can be seen to this day (see plate 23).

Her captain was Barrington Reynolds, an officer who Fitzjames had not previously met. Fitzjames did not rate Reynolds as a captain, saying that he did not 'know his business'. The accident the *Ganges* suffered weighing anchor, and the repeated reports in her log of running aground, suggest that Fitzjames' poor opinion of Reynolds was justified. Standards of seamanship on the *Ganges* seem to have been much lower than Fitzjames had known on the *St Vincent*. In one of Fitzjames' letters from the *St Vincent*, he reported that the great ship had been repeatedly tacked in a strait in the Greek islands within one ship's length of the rocky shores. This shows remarkable seamanship in an engineless wooden ship of 4,600 tons with a crew of well over 1,000. The *Ganges* was a handier ship, but her accident record was much worse. It is no longer possible, though, to pass judgement on Commander William Griffin who Fitzjames said was 'not a gentleman'.

But there is no doubt what the likely mission for this powerful warship would be. Trouble was brewing in Fitzjames' old stamping ground, the Levant, and the *Ganges* was part of a powerful Royal Navy fleet being assembled for the eastern Mediterranean. Fitzjames' experience of this part of the world was in demand, as were his newly acquired skills in gunnery, and HMS *Ganges* was being prepared for war.

There are many parallels between events in the Middle East in 1840 and in recent times. The peace brokered between the resurgent Egypt and the declining Ottoman Empire by Russia in 1833 had broken down again. In 1839, Mehmet Ali of Egypt went to war once more against the sultan's forces and advanced into Ottoman-controlled Syria. As before, the Egyptians were victorious at the Battle of Nezib in June 1839 and again Constantinople looked vulnerable to takeover by the modernised Egyptian forces. The western powers were concerned by the destabilising effects of a powerful regional state. To compound the Ottoman difficulties, the elderly Sultan Mahmud II then died, leaving control in the hands of 16-year-old Sultan Abdülmecid. Dissent broke out in Egypt between those who simply wanted to control Syria and those who wanted to conquer the empire and take over at Constantinople, which would, of course, lead to a breach with the great powers. On 15 July 1840, Britain, Austria, Russia and Prussia signed the Convention of London, which proposed a solution by granting Ali hereditary rule over Egypt and the administration for life of Acre, an important port on the Syrian coast, in exchange for the withdrawal of his troops from the Syrian hinterland and the coastal regions of Mount Lebanon. Ali refused these terms, so the Concert of Europe swung into action and a multilateral European task force was assembled to enforce the convention. The political situation was complex and, as in recent times, there was much jockeying between the great powers, who tended to act through regional proxies. France, for example, was a reluctant participant in the Concert of Europe and pursued an aggressive local policy. Britain too acted through proxies, especially in the Ottoman Empire, where some retired British officers acted as high-ranking mercenary leaders.

This was the crisis for which Fitzjames was selected. The British and Austrian navies blockaded the Nile, shelled Beirut and took over Acre. This was a defeat for Mehmet Ali, who agreed to accept the Convention of London, renouncing his claims over Crete and the Hijaz, and constrained the size of the Egyptian army and navy. On the other hand, he won de-facto independence for Egypt. Though it remained theoretically a vassal state of the Ottoman Empire, the great powers recognised his family as hereditary rulers of Egypt and the Sudan. This was the start of a remarkable dynasty, as Mehmet Ali's family remained in Egypt through all the vicissitudes of the nineteenth and the first half of the twenti-eth century, until King Farouk abdicated and Egypt was declared a republic on 18 June 1953.

HMS *Ganges* sailed from Portsmouth, the port where Fitzjames had been based for over a year, on 10 February 1839, after an accident raising the anchor resulted in fourteen men being injured. Passing Gibraltar and Malta, the *Ganges* formed part of the fleet blockading and threatening Egyptian positions on the coast of what is now Lebanon and Syria. The fleet was based at Besika Bay, at the entrance to the Dardanelles on the Ottoman-controlled Anatolian coast, from which they patrolled the eastern Mediterranean. There was frequent movement of ships throughout the eastern Mediterranean as the political and military situation fluctuated, but as yet there was no shooting war. There were frequent visits to Vourla, Smyrna and other ports to pick up supplies. It is clear from his days on the *Euphrates* that Fitzjames was able to speak at least some Arabic and he also knew the Ottoman Empire well, so he must have been an officer in demand as a negotiator and possibly even as a translator. He was in the right place at the right time and enjoyed the experience. He wrote: 'I like this place much, the country is beautiful, weather fine, sea smooth, mountains blue.'

Fitzjames' friendship with John Barrow, son of Sir John Barrow, seems to have formed before he sailed on the *Ganges*, and it was during this campaign that the first of his surviving letters to John Barrow junior was written, from Vourla Bay on 5 November 1839. While there is no doubt from the gossipy and personal nature of the correspondence that John Barrow and Fitzjames were friends, it was also a useful channel for both men. Fitzjames had an indirect link to Sir John through his son, and Barrow, in turn, working as he did at the Admiralty, also gained useful information about other officers and naval issues through Fitzjames.

Gunnery Lieutenant Fitzjames was one of the most important of the *Ganges'* officers. As in the Dardanelles almost eighty years later, shore bombardment would be the key to success and the ships trained hard. Again and again the log of the *Ganges* describes exercises as the force trained for its forthcoming engagement once the stand-off came to an end. Fitzjames described the work as 'lots of gunnery, firing, soldiery, landing field pieces, etc.' Gunnery from the ships and ashore would be the decisive weapon.

Fitzjames had already visited Constantinople when he sailed there in the *Hind*. He visited again in the autumn of 1839 when some of the ships based at Besika Bay sailed there, but was stranded when the ships sailed back to Smyrna unexpectedly. He made his own way back to the fleet, first crossing the Bosporus to the Asian side and then hiring a horse to trek back to the fleet anchorage at Besika Bay. He seems to have liked riding. He wrote to John Barrow how 'I rode to Bursa where I remained 3 days and then rode past along the south side of the Sea of Marmora crossing the Gramicus. Bursa is the most lovely of spots I ever beheld situated under the Bithynian Olympus [modern Uludag]. It comprises all sorts of lovely scenery – wooded – rocky and fertile gardens. And the cruise cost me £3 10s!'

By April 1840, HMS *Ganges* was flagship of the fleet blockading the Egyptian forces at Beirut. For the whole of that summer, the fleet remained in close blockade. In the days of sailing ships, which could be provisioned for long periods of time, and when guns were short ranged, blockades could be very close and the ships stood close to land. Local people informally traded with them and they kept in touch with events on land.

Another parallel with modern times was the unpleasant act of hostage taking. The 'Damascus Affair' was a particularly disagreeable event which occurred in 1840 as the tension was building up in the Mediterranean. The head of a Franciscan monastery in Damascus disappeared and thirteen Jews, including three rabbis, were accused of murdering the monk to use his blood for ritual purposes. French influence was blamed for importing western anti-Semitic fantasies to fuel the allegation. Whether that is true is difficult to say. Sixty-three Jewish children were also kidnapped, with confessions forced out of them under torture. Public opinion in Europe and America was outraged, and eventually an Anglo-French deputation to Constantinople, led by Sir Moses Montefiore and Adolphe Cremieux, succeeded in negotiating the release of those who had survived their torture. Sir Moses was a prominent member of the Jewish community in Britain and was connected to the Rothschilds. An extremely powerful man, he had made his fortune and retired as early as 1824, devoting the rest of his long life to good causes, especially Jewish philanthropy. He had been knighted in 1838 and, as an early Zionist, was a frequent visitor to the Holy Land.

One day, while HMS *Benbow*, another ship in the blockading fleet, was at anchor off Latakia, she was hailed by a small boat. The boat contained two polite and well-dressed young English gentlemen who, having been invited on board, introduced themselves to the officers of the *Benbow* as missionaries working for

Sir Moses Montefiore. The two young missionaries were of Jewish appearance and both carried copies of the Old Testament. They were 'well made up, with straight black hair divided down the middle'. They were politely entertained by the officers for two hours, until it became clear the two 'missionaries' were actually Fitzjames and Charlewood in disguise. From the perspective of a practical joker, the reference to Sir Moses was masterly. Having the audacity to invoke his name ensured that the 'missionaries' would be treated as honoured guests. This practical joke also shows that Fitzjames and Charlewood were not lacking in nerve.

Fitzjames' personal bravery was put to a much more serious test just before the summer stand-off in the eastern Mediterranean in September. Sir Charles Napier, who had taken effective control of the theatre of war, made an attempt at what is now called 'psy-ops' or psychological warfare. The ships were lined up just off-shore, at ranges of as little as 400 metres. Prints of the time show the sinister black ships, bristling with guns, threatening the soldiers ashore with immediate danger. Napier attempted to forestall the inevitable bloodshed. He issued a proclamation to the soldiers of the Egyptian army, which, with a mixture of stick and carrot, attempted to induce them to desert their officers and disperse. The question was how to get this message to the soldiery without their officers being aware of it. Fitzjames volunteered to take the proclamation ashore, displaying what Napier called 'a lenience of danger'. He would be entirely dependent on his personal presence for survival. He landed in the Egyptian camp, distributed Napier's proclamations to the Egyptian soldiers and made it back to the ships without being captured. When Soliman Pasha, the Egyptian general, heard of this he offered a large personal reward 'for the officer's head who has done so'. But too late. Fitzjames was back on board HMS *Ganges* and this story went down in legend as yet another example of his almost reckless bravery.

His effort was in vain as the Egyptian soldiery did not disperse, so on 12 September the fleet started landing a mixed force of marines and the troops of their Ottoman ally. As the landing was opposed, the fleet opened fire on the Egyptian forces. Edward Charlewood, gunnery lieutenant of HMS *Benbow*, fired the first gun of the entire campaign. By a strange coincidence, the *Benbow* was moored right by the mole at Beirut on which Charlewood had waited day after day for the steamer to England just eighteen months previously.

The gunfire from the ships was well aimed and absolutely devastating. Much of the credit for this was given to the very highly trained gunnery graduates of HMS *Excellent*. Gunnery lieutenants were active onshore. Unlike their successors in the Gallipoli campaign of 1915, they knew that unless their bombardment was immediately followed up by landings to complete the destruction, they would have to face the same fortifications all over again. As well as guns on board ship and ashore, gunnery lieutenants were charged with leading landing parties which would seize and hold the fortifications so that they could be neutralised.

Charlewood's turn to distinguish himself came when an attack on Tortosa by the ships' boats was mistimed. The boats were caught in a withering fire and evacuated with heavy losses and great gallantry.

Acre was captured in November 1840 and by early December, in very bad weather, the signal was received across the fleet that peace with Egypt had been declared. Fitzjames could be satisfied with his role. After irregular service on the Euphrates Expedition, he had now fought in his first war and won a 'mention in dispatches' for his brave conduct at Beirut.

Fitzjames left HMS *Ganges* at Alexandria and sailed home as a passenger on the steamer *Great Liverpool*. He arrived home on 1 June and does not seem to have been well, writing later that 'I have quite recovered my former health by the help of much ale and Port wine – and am now better that I ever was in my life'.

Even the day before the *Great Liverpool* docked, on 29 May 1841, he knew where he would be going next. Good gunnery officers were in demand and a new fleet was being put together for another campaign where shore bombardment would be critical. He was returning to take up his next appointment as gunnery lieutenant on HMS *Cornwallis*.

He spent a few short weeks at the home of William Coningham, now almost the only surviving member of his immediate foster family. William Coningham's life and circumstances had again changed. Although only 26 years old, William was now an extremely wealthy man. His mother Louisa had died just over a year ago in May 1840. William's health and morale was always fragile and these dramatic changes in his situation cannot have helped his stability. Carlyle wrote of him about this time as being 'seemingly quite strong again, even fat; after being, as he says, given up by everybody, even by himself, and having the feeling of death for some days close to his very heart'.

Shortly after his mother had died, William had suddenly married Elizabeth Meyrick. She was three years older than him and was the youngest daughter of the Rev. William Meyrick, yet another wealthy, landowning clergyman. It was at their new home, an elegant townhouse at 11 Cumberland Terrace in Regents Park, that Fitzjames stayed and was caught by the only census he ever featured in.

This was the first time Fitzjames had met William's wife Elizabeth and it is clear that their relationship was fleeting at this stage. Fitzjames later wrote that in 1841 he really knew her 'merely (which to me was much) as the wife of him I love best' rather than 'as yourself'.

With his wealth, and now beyond parental constraint, William had begun almost obsessively to collect art and was starting to be talked about in London's artistic and intellectual circles. By 1844 John Carlyle could write:

[He] has become an immense picture buyer – is said to have pictures the like of which are not to be found in England except in the collection of the Marquis of Stafford!! and so he may for he lays out sums of money on these which it is a perfect shame to hear tell of – a thousand pounds for a small crumpeled sketch by Raphael – eight thousand for a small assortment of rare engravings &c &c – What will this world come to in 'voluptuousness' (as Mr Perry our house agent calls extravagance)! William has only three or four thousand a year of visible means – so that he must be investing great slaps out of his capital in this gratification to his vanity – for I am perfectly certain that he has no genuine passion for Art – only wants to be known as the possessor of valuable pictures – the shortest cut to that notability which his ambitious mind has always thirsted after.

Carlyle may have been unfair in the motives he ascribed to William, but he certainly underestimated his wealth. And as his art collection became more and more extensive, so William's opinions became even more trenchant.

Eight

FITZJAMES' CHINESE PUZZLE

HMS *Cornwallis* was heading for China. China was the next principal theatre of action for the Royal Navy, so this was the obvious posting for an officer like Fitzjames wanting to build his reputation. And since ship to shore bombardment would be a key skill, successful gunnery lieutenants from the Syrian campaign were in demand.

But there is a puzzle about the story of Fitzjames in China which has never before been revealed. He went to China an officer with nothing to distinguish him from thousands, but he returned as Sir John Barrow's favourite to lead the Franklin Expedition and tipped for early promotion to captain. Why? What changed in China? In order to reveal this, we first need to follow the course of the campaign.

Preparations for war started in August 1839 when the Royal Navy seized an outpost on the Chinese coast called Hong Kong. Even though the Chinese population was more than twenty times that of Britain (400 million versus 20 million in 1850), the British were grimly confident hostilities would enable them to impose their will on China.

The British assault on China was triggered by continuing trade and customs disputes, which, by November 1839, had escalated into sporadic fighting both at sea and between British ships and Chinese shore batteries. On 14 January 1840, the Qing emperor asked all foreigners in China to stop helping the British there. Lord Palmerston, the British Prime Minister, had been looking for a *casus belli* and took advantage of this to declare war. Theoretically, Britain's war objective was the enforcement of free trade. But the 'trade' was in drugs. A principal motive for the war was to force the Chinese government to pay compensation for drugs that had been smuggled into China by British traders and, quite rightfully under the laws of the land, seized by the Chinese authorities.

While there is much that is attractive in the activities of the Royal Navy in the early nineteenth century, such as its strenuous efforts to suppress the slave trade, there is nothing attractive about the First Opium War. Royal Naval officers today, fighting with their counterparts in other navies against the drugs trade, will find it strange that in the 1840s a large fleet was mobilised to raid a sovereign nation state in order to enforce the trade in drugs. Yet this was the true purpose of Sir William Parker's task force. Local expatriate British drug smugglers had manipulated the British government and British public opinion so much that the British armed forces were used to coerce the Chinese government to permit opium, produced in industrial quantities, to be traded in exchange for tea.

From a twenty-first-century perspective, there is no question that China had the legal and moral high ground. Some people in Britain at the time thought they had too. A young 30-year-old British MP called William Ewart Gladstone condemned the war in Parliament, thundering that he was 'in dread of the judgement of God upon England for our national iniquity towards China'.

But the die was cast. Palmerston, in conjunction with the Honourable East India Company, had already authorised a British attack on Guangdong in an attempt to force compensation from the Chinese government, the costs being underwritten by the British Exchequer.

None of this could have happened without the very slow communications between Britain and the Far East that prevailed. Letters took up to three months each way. This was how British commercial interests in the Far East managed to manipulate British public opinion in their own interests. Parliamentary or governmental scrutiny would take up to six months to catch up. This time lag is critical for understanding the events which unfolded, and the critical way in which they affected James Fitzjames. A good example of this blatant manipulation of the slow communications channel occurred when the principled and dynamic Chinese scholar Lin Zexu, charged by the Chinese emperor with suppressing the drugs trade, wrote directly to Queen Victoria. This was a sensible approach, although a more tactful man might not have used the word 'barbarian' to describe her subjects. Local British interests were not prepared to take any risks and suppressed the letter, which she never received. Only the very long lines of communication made this possible.

The outcome of the war was defeat for China and victory for Britain. Yet, in the long run, the harm the war did to Chinese society's ability to develop and modernise had catastrophic consequences for China and the whole world in the later nineteenth and twentieth centuries. But this is to look ahead. Fitzjames was typical of his contemporaries in that he does not seem to have taken any great interest in the issues at stake, although he did admire Chinese art and architecture. The Royal Navy would simply do what it had done all over the world: bottle up or sink enemy fleets, closely blockade coastlines, reduce forts and shore installations, land Royal Marines and other land forces and then keep them supplied.

The first wave of British and Indian ships, consisting of fifteen sailing ships with 4,000 Royal Marines and four steam gunboats, was sent from Singapore and reached Guangdong in June 1840. The steamships conferred an important tactical advantage over the Chinese, while the long duration of the sailing ships enabled a close blockade to be maintained. When the compensation payment demanded by the British was refused by the Chinese government, this force blockaded the Pearl River and then moved north to take Zhoushan. Despite British successes in the fighting, by the spring of 1841 there was stalemate. While British casualties in taking Zhoushan had been light, China had not submitted and the action had not ended the war. The British were suffering very badly from disease. Soldiers and sailors lived in cramped quarters ashore or crammed into unhygienic wooden warships, close to and drinking estuarine water. This was a recipe for disaster. Without British reinforcements, the Chinese only had to hold out long enough and the British war effort would be ended, not by daring actions but by microbes which were unknown to both sides. By mid-October, only 800 of the men who had landed in July 1840 remained fit for duty; the others lay dead or dying in pitiful conditions in inadequate field hospitals. Disease had killed 450 men before the end of the year. It was the same story as Fitzjames had seen on the *Euphrates*, but magnified a hundredfold. This was a precursor for the Crimean War, but China was much further from London than the Crimea, so the appallingly unhealthy conditions did not lead to any scandal and conditions for the sick remained dreadful.

The British government decided early in 1841 to send out a second wave of forces, with the naval component under the command of Admiral Sir William Parker, who had just been appointed as commander-in-chief of the Royal Navy's East Indies and China Station. Admiral Sir William Parker was a nephew of the great Admiral John Jervis, Earl St Vincent. His flagship, HMS *Cornwallis*, was recommissioned at Plymouth on 7 April 1841 under her captain, Peter Richards. Parker was under very heavy pressure from both London and Bombay to bring the war to a speedy and successful conclusion. It was to his flagship that Fitzjames was appointed gunnery lieutenant, a key position in a campaign where shore bombardment would be decisive.

HMS *Cornwallis* was another Napoleonic-era sailing vessel. She mounted seventy-four guns and, like the *Ganges*, had been constructed in India. She was almost as old as Fitzjames when he joined her, yet would far outlive him. HMS *Cornwallis* was not finally broken up until 1957. Fitzjames was clearly, professionally, very happy on the *Cornwallis*.

But if his position was favourable, it would only be by his own conduct that he would win the promotion he craved. Fitzjames understood this. He appears to have tried to wangle a posting on one of the iron steamers which he understood would be sent out, although this came to nothing. He recognised that these ships would likely be in the vanguard of the fighting and he mentioned to John Barrow junior in a letter, unfortunately now unclear, that he had experience of these vessels from his service on the Euphrates Expedition.

The task of the fleet Parker was to lead was to threaten Canton and tighten the British stranglehold over Chinese trade by capturing the strategically important

Bogue forts. These controlled access to the Pearl River, the great waterway between Hong Kong and Canton. Doing so would be a dazzling display of Royal Naval might and skill and it is from this perspective that we will consider the mission; the same perspective as that of Lieutenant James Fitzjames.

Fitzjames was in London overnight from 7–8 June, possibly sick as we have seen, as this was when he appears on the 1841 census. By 25 June he was back on board the *Cornwallis* writing that 'we have today taken on board some 80 Marines and heaps of Congreive [sic] rockets & co'. Congreve rockets had been used by the *Euphrates* and the *Tigris* on the Euphrates Expedition. Fitzjames seems to have liked this spectacular and destructive weapon. As disease was such a critical issue on the China station, the *Cornwallis* bore a large contingent of surgeons or, as Fitzjames put it, 'a shoal of saw-bones', making the ship a veritable '*Esculapium*':

HMS *Cornwallis* sailed on 3 July 1841. The passage was fast and she arrived at Madeira only six days after leaving the Lizard. She reached the Cape of Good Hope on 7 September 1841. Arriving at Simon's Town in South Africa, Fitzjames had a sad duty: to visit the grave of his old friend William Barrow, who had died of tuberculosis at the Cape earlier in the year. This would be the first of two momentous encounters with the Barrow family which Fitzjames was to have on this voyage. He visited the grave only two days after the ship docked, describing it in a sensitive letter to John Barrow junior:

> I this day rode up between 12 and 1 and visited the burying ground which is situated about ½ a mile from the town to the SE on the slope of a hill overlooking the Fort and the bay beyond. The grave is in good order, in fact time has worked no change in it except that the flowers now bloom in the low walled enclosure which surrounds it and the trees which have been planted to protect it from the E gales flourish and are nearly my height. I send you a sprig of one of the trees and a couple of the flowers, though perhaps you will not thank me for them, but I did as I felt at the moment. The grave is a black slab of a sort of land slate supported by four square stone pillars is surrounded by a low wall forming an enclosure about 16 ft by 11. And as I before said small trees have been planted on the SE side. The inscription I believe you have.

John Barrow junior used this description in a memoir of his brother which he published privately. William Barrow's gravestone is still there (see plate 24).

HMS *Cornwallis* and the fleet sailed into Singapore harbour on Thursday 11 November 1841. There they found the Royal Navy's brigs HMS *Clio* and HMS *Britomart* in the company of two fine American frigates, the USS *Constellation* and the USS *Boston*. *Cornwallis* remained only five days, sailing on the following Tuesday. During this stay, the officers off duty were free to explore the new British colony of Singapore, although the men would, as usual, have been confined on ship. Here Fitzjames met another son of Sir John Barrow, George Barrow of the

Colonial Office. This encounter is shrouded in mystery and will be discussed later, when its ramifications become apparent.

After a very stormy passage from Singapore, HMS *Cornwallis* entered the northern theatre of operations near Shanghai early in 1842. She arrived at Ningbo on 14 March, just in time to intervene decisively in the campaign. The Chinese had taken the initiative just four days previously, planning a series of assaults at first light on the British-occupied towns of Ningbo (Ningpo), Zhenhai (Chinhae) and Zhoushan (Chushan).

At Ningbo the attackers initially made progress as successive waves of Chinese infantry attacked from several directions, overwhelmed the defenders of the south gate and advanced into the city. After several hours, fierce British counter-attacks drove them back. Simultaneously, Chinese forces on the other bank attempted to provide fire support for the assault while others floated fire-rafts downriver, hoping to disperse the Royal Navy warships. Seeing the fire-rafts drifting downstream towards them, the ships hurriedly launched their boats. The sailors intercepted the fire-rafts before guiding them away from the ships. The Chinese had failed to disperse the British ships, which opened up a steady shore bombardment to suppress Chinese fire from the opposite bank. Such was the technological and tactical disparity that, while many Chinese soldiers were killed, the British did not suffer a single fatality.

At Zhenhai the Chinese opened their assault using similar tactics: infantry assault combined with fire-rafts. Again they were contained by Colonel Schoedde of the 55th Regiment, while boats launched by HMS *Blonde* and HMS *Hyacinth* neutralised the fire-rafts.

At Zhoushan, the British apparently caught wind of the assault, as Admiral Parker sent the Honourable East India Company ship *Nemesis*, a sister ship of the *Euphrates*, to shell the Chinese forces as they concentrated at Taishan. The *Nemesis* dispersed the Chinese infantry before they could attack. Having won this bloodless (for the British) victory, *Nemesis* then attacked and sank several junks for good measure.

The Chinese assaults opened just too late from their perspective, as they found themselves pitted against fresh British reinforcements. The fighting had flared up just as Fitzjames reached China. A Chinese army, led by General Yang, was concentrating at Tsekee, across the river from Ningbo. The morning after HMS *Cornwallis* arrived, 15 March, Admiral Parker personally led an expeditionary force out to attack it. This force contained a naval brigade of sailors and Royal Marines led by Captain Thomas Bourchier. The naval brigade included a Congreve rocket battery led by Fitzjames, meaning he was in action within twenty-four hours of arriving in China.

The combined force was landed 4 miles from Yang's position on the heights of Segaon, behind Tsekee, and advanced. The naval brigade came under gingal fire as they marched across some paddy fields to two large houses, which they intended to use as cover before they attacked.

The 18th Foot and the Rifles were delayed in reaching the starting line they had been assigned for their advance, so the decision was taken to make an immediate advance with the forces already present. This meant that the naval brigade, which was already in position, had to take on a much more significant role in the attack. They were ordered to attack the hill which formed the right of the Chinese line.

Fitzjames, aided by Mr Jackson of the *Cornwallis*, was credited with firing Congreve rockets 'with great precision into the enemy's position'. This action was not decisive itself, but must have boosted British morale and had the reverse effect on the Chinese. This was ironic, given that the use of the rocket in war was originally a Chinese invention.

The fighting was tough, but in the end the naval brigade took its objective through a combination of a frontal assault and an enveloping movement. Two Royal Marine officers and two naval officers were wounded, with three men killed and eleven wounded. In the meantime, the army force had taken its own objective and moved across to support the naval brigade. Many Chinese soldiers were trapped between the two forces 'and the slaughter was unavoidably great'. With the arrival of fresh British forces, the Chinese defeat became a rout.

Chinese casualties were estimated to be at least 450 and this battle was said to have been the most clear-cut British victory of any land battle since the start of the war. It was an impressive demonstration of Parker's determination. A gruesome detail was that many of the Chinese soldiers were armed with matchlock muskets, for which they carried a lit taper. In the dry conditions, when they fell dead or were wounded, their clothing and then their bodies often caught fire. In his extended anonymous poem about the war, Fitzjames grimly described how the locations of the fallen were marked by columns of smoke and how the whole battlefield smelt of roast pork.

The Chinese retired from the action, but with China not prepared to accede to Britain's demands, stalemate ensued. British commanders, like Gough at Ningbo, were reluctant to operate too far inland away from Royal Naval support. The Chinese recognised the importance of this and so on 14 April the Chinese attempted to disperse the ships at anchor at Zhoushan by using fire-rafts. But the ships' boats were launched and it is likely that Fitzjames was one of the officers commanding the boats that thwarted the attack that day.

Chapoo fell to British forces on 18 May 1842, but China continued to resist. Parker decided to blockade the Chang Jiang (Yangtze-Kiang) and occupy Shanghai in an effort to force a capitulation, so on 28 May the *Cornwallis* and the other ships embarked an expeditionary force.

On 13 June 1842, HMS *Cornwallis* and the fleet anchored off Wusong. Parker intended to take this strategic port and from it close the mouths of the rivers Chang Jiang and Suzhou Creek (Wusong River). From Wusong, the British only

1. Commander James Fitzjames. A copy of the sole surviving daguerreotype taken of Fitzjames by Richard Beard. He is seated on the dockside at Greenhithe near HMS *Erebus* and HMS *Terror*. Note the reflections in his cap. Date: 1845. (Scott Polar Research Institute)

2. Commander James Fitzjames. A photograph of the other daguerreotype of Fitzjames. The original has been lost. Date: 1845. (National Maritime Museum)

3. Admiral James Gambier, first Baron Gambier. He was James Fitzjames' first cousin once removed. 'James Lord Gambier, 1st Baron Gambier', by Gaetano Stefano Bartolozzi, published by T. Cadell & W. Davies. (National Portrait Gallery)

4. James Fitzjames. The unfinished chalk and crayon portrait of Fitzjames which William Coningham kept until 1859. It is possibly a sketch by John Linnell for a portrait which was never commissioned. Date: 1844 or 1845. (National Maritime Museum)

5. Mrs Charles Bagot. Date: unknown. (Taken from the frontispiece of her book *Links with the Past*, published in 1901)

6. William Coningham. Date: 1841. Artist: John Linnell.

7. Elizabeth Coningham. Date: 1844. Artist: John Linnell.

8. Rose Hill, Abbots Langley, Hertfordshire, where the family of Robert Coningham lived while Fitzjames was a child. Date: *c.* 1900. (Duncan Ogilvie)

9. HMS *St Vincent* off Graham Island, the volcanic island which appeared off Sicily. Fitzjames was on board *St Vincent* but as he was ill he did not land on the island. Date: 1831. Artist: unknown. (National Maritime Museum)

10. The cutter *Hind* off Graham Island. Date: 1831. Artist: unknown. (National Maritime Museum)

11. 'Entry of King Otto of Greece at Nauplia', 5 February 1833. Inset: Fitzjames was one of the twelve midshipmen rowing the Royal Barge (far right), in which King Otto was landed from HMS *Madagascar*. Artist: Peter von Hess (1792–1871). Location: Kunstareal, Munich.

12. Colonel Francis Rawdon Chesney (1789–1872), shown in later life. He led the Euphrates Expedition and introduced Fitzjames to exploration. Artist: unknown. (National Portrait Gallery)

13. Fitzjames' cup, awarded to Fitzjames by the City and Corporation of Liverpool for his bravery in saving the life of a man who fell into the River Mersey in 1835. Date: 1835. (National Maritime Museum)

14. Landing a boiler at Suedia. The Expedition's camp, Port Amelia, can be seen in the background. Note the mountainous territory over which the Expedition's materials had to be dragged 140 miles to the Euphrates. Date: 1835. (James Fitzjames, RN)

15. 'The Hill of Difficulty'. Chesney made a huge miscalculation in claiming that the terrain between the Mediterranean and the Euphrates would be easy. Date: 1835. (Chesney, 1858)

16. The first boiler fording the Kara-Chai river. Date: 1835. (James Fitzjames, RN)

W NICHOLLS.

17. Crossing the Lake of Antioch. Date: 1835. (Chesney, 1858)

Opposite from top:
18. The *Tigris* and the *Euphrates* steamers, at speed on the River Euphrates. (James Fitzjames, RN)

19. Anah, a town about midway between Port William and Basra and just downstream of the point where the *Tigris* steamer was wrecked. Date: 1836. (James Fitzjames, RN)

20. The Bridge of Boats at Baghdad, showing the old Bridge of Boats across the River Tigris just upriver from the British Residency. Date: 1836. (James Fitzjames, RN)

21. The steamer *Euphrates* tied up at Hit. Date: 1836. (James Fitzjames, RN)

22. The steamer *Euphrates* arriving at Basra on the Shatt el-Arab and exchanging salutes with the Honourable East India Company ship *George Bentinck*. Date: 1836. (Chesney, 1858)

Opposite from top:

23. The captain's cabin of HMS *Ganges*. Fitzjames was gunnery lieutenant of HMS *Ganges* for the Syrian War of 1841. The ship was not broken up until the 1930s and her captain's cabin survives today as part of the Burgh Island Hotel in Devon. Source: The Burgh Island Hotel.

24. William Barrow's grave, at Simon's Town in South Africa. He died there of tuberculosis. Date: 2009. (Susan Alexander)

SACRED
TO THE MEMORY OF
WILLIAM BARROW ESQUIRE
Late Commander of Her Majesty's Ship ROSE
Who fell a Victim to disease
contracted in the East Indies
When zealously employed in the execution of his duty.
This young Officer of great promise
thus cut off in the prime of Life,
yielded it up in pious resignation
to the ALMIGHTY WILL on the
26TH February 1835
Aged 28 Years.

25. 'An incident in the China War'. The sinister-looking ship to the right is the paddle frigate *Nemesis*, sister ship of the *Euphrates*. Date: 1842. (National Maritime Museum)

26. Peace negotiations. Three Chinese commissioners are greeted by Admiral Sir William Parker, General Gough and the British plenipotentiary on HMS *Cornwallis* prior to the signing of the Treaty in August 1842. Date: 1842. (Hulton Archive/Getty Images)

27. The 'Signing of the Treaty of Nanking'. Inset: Detail of James Fitzjames (standing fourth from the left). This is the earliest known detailed portrait of him and he has not previously been identified in it. He had been shot in the arm and back, and his strapped-up left arm is clearly visible under his coat. Date: 1842. Artist: unknown. (National Maritime Museum)

28. 'Opportunity to send letters'. *Erebus* signals to *Terror* to collect letters to be sent back to England. Date: 1845. Artist: Captain Owen Stanley, RN. (National Library of Australia)

29. Commander James Fitzjames' cabin on HMS *Erebus*. Date: 1845. (*Illustrated London News*)

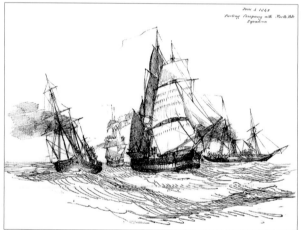

30. 'The steamers cheering the Polar Exploration vessels': the parting of the Franklin Expedition from the steamers, 50 miles west of the island of Rona. Date: 1845. (National Library of Australia)

31. Sketch of the anchorage at the Whale Fish Islands in Disko Bay off Greenland. In the foreground are the prefabricated huts in which Fitzjames conducted his magnetic observations. Date: July 1845. (Scott Polar Research Institute)

needed to advance 12 miles to Shanghai to halt trade on the Chang Jiang. It was hoped this would strangle the flow of tax revenues to Peking and force the Chinese government to capitulate. But the campaign needed to be swift and successful before disease reduced the ships and regiments to impotence. It was also important to force the action before domestic opposition to the war back in Britain could build up.

The first step was for survey ships to sound and buoy the mouth of the river, under the protection of the guns of the fleet. The two officers in charge of this sounding operation were Commanders Richard Collinson and Henry Kellett, both of whom were destined to spend years in the Arctic searching for James Fitzjames and the other lost members of the Franklin Expedition. With the waters charted, the bombardment of Wusong started on 16 June. *Cornwallis* and the other warships closed inshore while the transports, laden with troops, stood 4 miles offshore. As gunnery lieutenant of the flagship, Fitzjames had a key role in this assault. Answering fire from the 3-mile line of Chinese fortifications on the north bank of the river caused casualties initially, but within two hours the superior British gunfire suppressed the Chinese artillery. The ships' boats were then lowered and started to land their Royal Marines and selected detachments of seamen who seized the fortifications, spiked the guns and held their positions until the main land force could be brought up from the transports offshore. The fortifications were captured with the loss of just three killed and twenty wounded. Chinese losses were also light, although they lost some 250–300 artillery guns of varying types. Fitzjames must have taken a leading role in these landings and the seizure of the fortifications.

Wusong was in British hands. By the evening, the advance up the left bank of the Wusong River towards Shanghai began. Modern-day visitors to the region may find it surprising to realise that all of this fighting took place within the urbanised area of what is now Shanghai and Pudong. The soldiers and landed sailors marched along the banks, while others were convoyed in steamers towing small boats. All were covered by the guns of the Royal Navy. The only opposition was from one shore battery, halfway up the river towards Shanghai, which was silenced by gunfire from the supporting warships. Sir William Parker had transferred from HMS *Cornwallis* and, with General Hugh Gough the army commander, accompanied the marching men in HMS *Medusa*.

By 18 June, after silencing another shore battery just downriver from Shanghai, this strong force reached the city. Shanghai in the 1840s was a small walled town. Its only defenders were a few Chinese soldiers armed with matchlock muskets who, after aiming a few shots at the advancing column, abandoned the town. The Chinese authorities had evacuated the city's treasury, which was hastily hauled upriver on junks. Later it transpired that the *Nemesis*, pushing upriver, had come very close to capturing the junks. With no reason to remain in occupation of Shanghai, this British force left the town on 23 June.

With the Chinese still showing no sign of capitulation, Parker and Gough's next objective was to try to halt the flow of trade and the passage of tax revenues on the Grand Canal as well as on the Chang Jiang. This involved advancing around 150 miles into the interior of China, up the Chang Jiang to Zhenjiang (Ching Kiang), which was the junction of the two waterways, and holding them. It was hoped that in combination with the British stranglehold on trade in the south, this would force the Chinese government to accept almost any British terms. The stakes were rising so the force assembled was large, consisting of 9,000 British and Indian troops, 3,000 Royal Marines, 18 Royal Navy warships and 8 paddle steamer warships of the Honourable East India Company. Parker was employing huge resources to force a decision.

The advance began on 9 July led by the steamers, which surveyed and marked out safe channels for the warships. The warships then cleared both banks with their gunfire so the troops could be brought safely upriver on transports. The steamers were fired at from three Chinese batteries sited on a hill at Se-Shan, which HMS *Cornwallis* was tasked with suppressing. A party of Royal Marines and sailors were landed under Commander Charles Richards. Lieutenant Granville Loch describes how:

> at four o'clock we were close to the hill ... It rises abruptly 400 feet from the plain on one side, and from the river on the other, sloping to a valley which divides its centre. At the bottom, and on the face of this hollow, two batteries were erected; a partial fire commenced from each of these upon the steamers and leading sloops. The Modeste was ordered to commence action, which she no sooner did than away the garrison scampered, throwing their uniforms off as the ascent up the hill grew pressing, their movements occasionally accelerated by a few 32-pounders making ricochets after them.
>
> I landed with the storming party sent to take possession, blow up the powder, disable the guns, and destroy the fort. We found a great deal of loose powder lying about covered by temporary sheds and in boxes half buried at the rear of the batteries, besides shot, gingals, matchlocks, bows and arrows, and other munitions of war. In the houses we found some hot messes of rice and vegetables, and several ponies, which the soldiers had left in their haste to effect their escape.
>
> Leaving the work of destruction to proceed, I ascended a narrow ridge leading to the top of the hill – a desperate fag, considering the great heat, and one which I had not anticipated while looking up at the winding path from below.

It must have been a struggle to climb a 400ft hill in hot and humid conditions, wearing nineteenth-century naval dress. When Loch reached the summit he found he 'was not alone. Lieut. James Fitzjames had gained the summit before me, and I found him, when I arrived, sitting upon a granite rock, quite out of breath after his ascent'. Fitzjames was accompanied by his coxswain, who had 'followed him at a slower pace'. The two officers admired the view:

> Inland, towards the S.E., this detached cluster of hills broke into undulating country clothed with verdure, and fir plantations bordered small lakes confined in natural basins. Extending my view across, I saw the windings of the vast river we had ascended; our ships were still scattered over its broad surface, the sternmost divisions coming up under all sail. To the other side I turned with yet more interest; there the land in the foreground continued a low and swampy flat, leaving it difficult at a little distance to determine which of the several broad waters, winding in serpentine channels through the country, was the main the branch. I looked down upon innumerable square sheets of water, separated from each other by narrow mounds of earth; they covered the surface of what we knew to be arable land, but which more closely resembled a vast lake, intersected by many causeways. Willow trees grew along their sides, and here and there small patches, somewhat higher than the common surface, supported cottages and farm sheds. Beyond this, again, towards the west, the pagoda of Chin-kiang-fee was observable; it is built on a slight eminence eight or ten miles in advance, by the river's course, from where I stood. The sun had set some time; the mists rose from the marshes, until it became the only object in the distant view.

Fitzjames and his companions then surprised a Chinese soldier hiding nearby, who they captured and took with them back to the ships.

There was little other Chinese opposition until the fleet anchored off Zhenjiang, which was the terminus of the vital Grand Canal to Beijing. The Chinese defended this vital point at all costs, concentrating on two well-fortified positions on high ground south of the city. Hostilities flared up on 20 July when the Chinese released fire-rafts to float down into the crowded British anchorage. Again the fleet's boats were launched and managed to prevent these rafts catching any ship alight. The next day British land forces were landed unopposed on either side of the city. The weather was so hot, over 90°F, that during the day eighteen men of the attacking force died from dehydration and the effect of the sun. No doubt their stifling uniforms did not help.

As soon as the British had landed, the Chinese defenders came out of concealment and fought vigorously. After three hours' hard fighting, the British breached the Chinese defences on either side of the city and were able to link up in it. Admiral Sir William Parker had landed and marched into battle in a small party with Sir Hugh Gough, Land Forces Commander. Accompanying them was a small naval brigade commanded by the captain of the *Cornwallis*, Peter Richards. This was not the only Royal Naval participation in the assault on the city. Two ship's boats from HMS *Blonde* were rigged to carry four guns of the

Royal Artillery to provide ad hoc gunfire support from the mouth of the Grand Canal. These were commanded by Lieutenant Edward Couch of HMS *Blonde*. Couch, together with twenty-seven men, was wounded by heavy Chinese gunfire from the city wall. The party was forced to abandon their boats and take cover behind masonry on the opposite bank of the Grand Canal. Ships' boats from the *Cornwallis*, under the command of Lieutenant James Stoddart and including Fitzjames, relieved Couch and evacuated the wounded. The uninjured members of Couch's team joined Stoddart's men and together they reinforced Captain Richards and the Royal Naval brigade ashore. Fitzjames again led a team carrying Congreve rockets, which was tasked with assaulting the wall directly.

Fitzjames said that the navy had not been tasked with anything more than landing the soldiers, 'but the Blonde's boats while going down the Canal to land the artillery met with such a warm reception that our boats were sent to support them and our Marines landed (with Modeste's). I accompanied them with a rocket party. I saw some scaling the walls & co.'

Then 'I entered Ching-Kiang [Zhenjiang] over the walls and having lost the scabbard literally "sword in hand". And really mentally repeated "Caesar having crossed the Rubicon & co.", but whilst the sword was in position a marine behind me was shot through the head and effectually knocked all thoughts of Caesar out of mine.' The Marine who was killed was 'the first man up the ladder', so Fitzjames was in the vanguard of the assault and perhaps leading it. Afterwards, while 'resting on the walls we heard some heavy firing in the town which turned out to be an attack on the 49th. We came on the rear of the Tartars down a street which was barricaded and from which we were received with a shower of balls. The rocket which I intended to demolish their defence missed fire twice and the consequence was I received a ball which passed through my arm, entered the body at the armpit and passing round my ribs struck at the backbone.'

Fitzjames walked a few steps and then collapsed. His injury was very similar to the shot which had killed Nelson and, had the ball not lost energy while passing through his arm, it would perhaps have killed him in the same way. He was evacuated to HMS *Cornwallis*. Here he was operated on without any form of anaesthetic or antiseptics and the ball removed from his backbone.

Three months after arriving, his personal war in China was over.

Fitzjames, Couch and another officer, George Hodgson, were all mentioned especially as having distinguished themselves in the hard street fighting on that day. By the end of the day, all Chinese hope of inflicting a decisive defeat on the advancing 'barbarians' was lost and many soldiers, including General Hailing, committed suicide. This fiercely fought battle was the turning point of the war.

Fitzjames was not the only one suffering. He wrote to John Barrow junior that their friend 'Col. Campbell is looking much worn. As his regiment has been subjected to many attacks at night and some sentries killed. The Tartars who were of the Emperor's Guard made a most determined resistance. They fought well and were large fine men. Our loss has been heavy as you will see.' Back on HMS *Cornwallis*, Fitzjames was in the sick quarters. Once the agony of the operation was over, he made a rapid recovery. Only a month later, on 18 August, he was able to write to John Barrow junior about the 'four holes drilled in my body. It is now but a month since I got them and I am already out of the sick-bay. In a fortnight I was walking about and in 3 weeks 3 holes out of the four were stopped up. I have been drinking wine and grog from the first day, and altogether have astonished every body by not having had fever & co.' He was lucky not to suffer a secondary infection either from the ball or from the unsanitary practices of the surgeons. He liked to joke that drinking alcohol aided recovery from illness, but this may actually have been true as the polluted water was a major source of illness.

Many men died under similar conditions. Fitzjames wrote:

we have suffered much from sickness. In this ship we have 110 in the list and have lost many men from cholera. The 98th in the Belleisle lost about 70 from cholera and 11 died out of 17 who were struck down with the sun on the day of the affair at Ching-Kiang. But the 98th has been 7 months confined in a crowded ship, with little fresh food. Our friend the Colonel [Colin Campbell] was very ill at one time with dysentery, but since they have landed here and get fresh air and plenty of vegetables, both he and his Regiment are going on very well – he has quite recovered.

Fortunately for them, the Chinese government decided it would have to accept whatever terms Britain imposed and on that day hostilities ceased between China and Britain.

HMS *Cornwallis* was taken further upriver to Nanjiang (Nanking) and two days later, on 20 August 1842, it received the Chinese delegation on board. The British had insisted that the treaty should be signed on board the flagship rather than on shore, and used every opportunity to impress the Chinese with their military might. Fitzjames showed 'a Lieutenant General whose name I have been unable to get' over the ship's guns and recalled that the general was 'very curious to see everything' (see plate 26).

On 29 August 1842, the Treaty of Nanking was signed on board HMS *Cornwallis*. The Chinese delegation was received in the captain's cabin and the treaty signed. The scene was captured in a contemporary painting (see plate 27). It shows Gough and Parker, surrounded by their senior naval and army or Royal Marine officers. In his private journal, Lieutenant Le Vesconte of HMS *Clio* said that 'a limited number of officers from each ship was permitted to go on board the *Cornwallis* [to witness the signing of the Treaty] … I was one of the fortunate number …' The print is not an entirely lifelike scene. Fifty-eight people are present and the three sides of the cabin have been 'opened out' so that each person can be shown individually. Each individual was sketched as an individual portrait and the print was then constructed as a composite set of contemporary portraits. Several people whose lives would be wrecked or greatly affected by the disaster of the Franklin Expedition must be present, including Belcher, Collinson and Kellett, all of whom would sacrifice much in the forlorn search for the missing ships. At least two men who died on the expedition are present, including Le Vesconte. The figure standing in the crowd, fourth from the left, is a rather round-faced, smiling young man in a naval lieutenant's uniform with his left arm clearly strapped up under his coat. He will look strangely familiar to anyone who has studied the famous daguerreotypes of the Franklin Expedition's officers, taken just three years later. This was the 29-year-old James Fitzjames.

For Parker and for the British forces, the Chinese surrender came just in time. Disease was ravaging the British on land and sea. In his fascinating paper *Surgeons of the Opium War*, David McLean tells how:

> getting ships out of the Yangtze [Chang Jiang] from September 1842 onwards proved to be no easy matter. Most were so full of invalids that it was frequently difficult to manoeuvre properly. [Lieutenant William] Baker [Madras Artillery] confessed that he had never felt in so much peril as watching the few soldiers of his unit still on their feet trying to drift their troopship backwards on the current, unable to use the sails, whilst the ship's crew 'looked like living skeletons and were hardly able to crawl about the deck'. Jupiter, with Pine's twenty-sixth regiment aboard, could never hold her anchor because no-one well enough to be on deck was competent even to judge whether the ship was moving. Belleisle was among the first sent back to the sea where the fresh air might help restore her. She had carried more than 650 troops upriver in July; about 500 were still alive but many barely so and only 120 were healthy. Seventy-five of the ship's 250 sailors remained fit for duty and the entire lower deck had become an improvised hospital.

For Fitzjames the end of the war must have been welcome. Conditions on the *Cornwallis* can have been little better as Fitzjames slowly recovered from his wounds and the agonising operation he had endured. Recent commentators on the Franklin Expedition sometimes wonder why the officers and men on polar expeditions continued to volunteer when, to modern eyes, the chances of death or injury were so high. Having experienced service under conditions like this, officers and men who had served in China regarded the historic odds of survival on polar expeditions as quite attractive.

With the war now over and HMS *Cornwallis* safely away from the unhealthy rivers, Fitzjames recovered rapidly. He was accustomed to making long overland journeys, including his hike of 1,000 miles when he had brought the India mails from Lemlun to Beirut in 1836. Now he submitted a proposal for a far more ambitious land journey. Rather than come home on HMS *Cornwallis*, he requested permission to be allowed to return to London overland. He wanted to ascend the Chang Jiang and return via Tibet to Gaikar, Samarkand and Khiva, and from there travel through Russia. This would obviously have had great intelligence benefits for the British as it would take him through Russian-controlled Central Asia only three years after the disastrous First Afghan War. But the British plenipotentiary had enough issues to deal with in his negotiations and was not prepared to raise Fitzjames' request with the Chinese authorities. This would have been an extremely dangerous journey, but had he been permitted to make it, he almost certainly would not have been in a position to join the Franklin Expedition.

Cornwallis remained at anchor in the Chang Jiang estuary with her sailors confined to their ships and soldiers re-embarked. But, as Fitzjames, related officers were free to 'go up in large parties to the Porcelain Tower – the most glorious structure I have seen – beautiful in its proportions and its situation. It rears its head over the city of Nanking [Nanjiang] and certainly from the top one has a most splendid view of the whole city and surrounding country. We have not been allowed to go inside the walls.' He spent two days at the Porcelain Tower and made 'some rather poor sketches, the only ones I have in China, for I have not had much time or opportunity to sketch'. His modesty was perhaps false as one of the sketches was published in *The Chinese Repository*, 1844. Once the indemnity, which formed part of the treaty, on Nanjiang had been paid, he sailed with the fleet to the then new British possession of Hong Kong and arrived there on 18 November 1842.

Fitzjames' bravery in the China war has always been known by Franklin Expedition historians, but for Fitzjames, events which took place during the five days *Cornwallis* spent in Singapore late the previous year were even more significant.

We have already seen that Fitzjames credited his position on the *Cornwallis* to Sir John Barrow. This was how patronage relationships worked. Sir John Barrow had similar relationships with many hundreds of other officers, and Fitzjames had fulfilled his part of the bargain through his excellent conduct in the recent war. But by the time he returned to England, his relationship with Sir John Barrow had changed utterly and was on a completely different footing. The key to understanding why lies in the letter Fitzjames wrote to John Barrow junior from HMS *Cornwallis* at Nanjiang on 12 September 1842:

My dear Barrow,

Although we received the June mail some time since, we have only just received the May one which got delayed somewhere down the river.

By it I receive two letters from you, one of which 'came by Agincourt on business'. Now allow me to say that I do not see you have any particular cause to be so much obliged to me from lending your brother a hand when he was rather adrift. It surely would have been odd had I allowed any son of Sir John Barrow's to be in difficulty in such an out of the way place as Singapore while I could help him out of it. It was fortunate that I happened to arrive at the time, but what little money I advanced to him was I assure no inconvenience to me for on these long voyages one cannot spend money. Had it been at Portsmouth the case might have been different. As it is I am much obliged by your desire that I should immediately show for the amount which I should do to pacify you if I could remember the exact amount, but I have lost the memo I made of it. However, I told your brother to pay it in to Messrs. Gledstanes Kerr no. 11 Regent's Street. So if you will do that I shall be obliged and I shall be glad to hear of your brother's safe arrival in England without further troubles.

Fitzjames wrote this letter in reply to one Barrow had written to him from London in May. Mail took three to four months to travel from London to the Far East. So Barrow's letter of May must have been in response to one written early in 1842. This correspondence, therefore, refers to events which took place late in 1841 in Singapore. What happened? While in Singapore, Fitzjames says, he had been able to 'lend … your brother a hand when he was rather adrift' and he would naturally help 'any son of Sir John Barrow's' who was 'in difficulty … out of it'.

The unnamed brother must have been George Barrow, the future second baronet, who was 32 and unmarried at the time and was chief clerk of the Colonial Office. Fitzjames helping George Barrow 'out of it' had cost him quite a lot of money; enough for George Barrow to have to pay money back to him. John Barrow junior felt 'so much obliged' to Fitzjames for what he had been able to do. Precisely what this 'difficulty' was, Fitzjames does not mention and in a careful way he makes it clear that, now George Barrow is safely back in England, no record of the affair now exists as he (Fitzjames) has conveniently 'lost the memo' documenting the whole affair. Clearly, at the time, Fitzjames considered that what had happened was sufficiently serious that a formal written statement might be required.

It is difficult to see this as anything other than Fitzjames intervening to cover up what would otherwise have been a quite substantial scandal involving a hapless George Barrow; perhaps something which could have ended George Barrow's career at the Colonial Office or possibly even something which would threaten Sir John Barrow's position at the Admiralty? There are two more clues: this was something which might result in blackmail, otherwise why else would Fitzjames let it be known that the memo about it no longer existed? It seems also that this was not an unfortunate accident, but something for which George Barrow was the prime mover and culpable. But what? Corruption is unlikely, as Barrow and Fitzjames would be subject to British law at Singapore and it is difficult to see Fitzjames attempting to bribe a legal British official on behalf of George Barrow. It seems more likely to have been some sort of matter of honour or maybe even a homosexual incident. Of one thing we can be sure: Fitzjames, the man who hid his origins so successfully, knew how to keep a secret. We can be absolutely certain that he covered his tracks and that he thought this secret would die with him in the Arctic.

This is absolutely pivotal for understanding Fitzjames and his role on the Franklin Expedition. It explains why, from this point on, the patronage relationship seems to have reversed. From now on, Sir John Barrow acted as though it was he who was in debt to Fitzjames, rather than the other way around.

At the end of 1842, a flurry of official letters relating to Fitzjames was sent to Hong Kong from London. By then he was discharged from HMS *Cornwallis*, promoted to commander and appointed captain of HMS *Clio* over the heads of about half a dozen more senior and better qualified officers. Another remarkable fact about this, Fitzjames' fourth promotion in the Royal Navy, is that it was the first to be entirely regularly obtained.

Fitzjames related that Admiral Parker appeared as pleased to give him his new commission as he was to receive it. Parker suggested that Fitzjames try to exchange his new position with another captain whose commission had longer to run than the *Clio*, which was already nearly four years into her commission and would soon be ordered back to London. His seniority would be held back if he did not serve at least a full year on her. Fitzjames hankered after one of the new iron steamships. Ironically, when he left the China station, Admiral Parker let him know that had Barrow not intervened, Parker would have appointed him first lieutenant of HMS *Driver*, with *Driver*'s first lieutenant appointed to command the *Clio* and bring her back to England. Here was a second twist of fate: it was only because of Sir John Barrow's intervention that Fitzjames came to be in London at exactly the right (or wrong) time to be appointed to the Franklin Expedition.

There is no doubt that Barrow intended this appointment to *Clio* to be a reward. Bearing in mind the three-month delay in the transmission of letters between Hong Kong and London, this was promotion virtually by return of his letter in September to John Barrow junior. The unwanted little boy of twenty-eight years ago was now a valued commodity.

Nine

STEPS TOWARDS NEMESIS

Fitzjames had gone to China in the autumn of 1841 as a gunnery lieutenant. His career fitted the pattern of thousands of other officers. But eyebrows must have been raised when news of his promotion arrived in Hong Kong with HMS *Vixen* on 16 February 1843. This was accelerated promotion of a different order of magnitude from anything that had happened to him before. He wrote to Sir John on 20 March 1843, two days after his discharge from HMS *Cornwallis*, to thank him for his appointment to captain of HMS *Clio*. He recognised that 'my appointment to a Command could only have been obtained by your express application to the First Lord of the Admiralty ... over the heads of so many far more deserving than me'. He also wrote to John Barrow junior, saying that 'I really do not know how I can sufficiently thank you both ... Nothing but your father's express exertions could have got me such a distinction, and ... I can only hope that he may never have cause to repent of his kindness.'

He moved swiftly to make the most of this new turn of fortune. His problem was the surprising fact, to modern eyes, that nobody knew where HMS *Clio* actually was. The *Vixen* had seen the *Clio* earlier in the year at Calcutta, but that made it almost certain that she would not still be there. And even if she was, she was unlikely still to be there by the time Fitzjames could complete the journey from Hong Kong to Calcutta. The captain of HMS *Vixen* told Fitzjames he thought *Clio*'s next move had been to sail to Bombay, but he could not be certain. At Bombay she would fall under the orders of the governor-general, so there was no guarantee that she would still be there by the time he arrived if Fitzjames headed directly to Bombay. In other words, Fitzjames had his coveted command, but he had to find his ship first, and it could be almost anywhere in the 68 million square kilometres of the Indian Ocean.

There was also a further opportunity. At that time officers could sometimes 'exchange' their posting with an opposite number on another ship. For example, an officer who wished to stay on at a station when his ship was ordered home might exchange his position with another officer in a similar position on another ship coming out, if they both wished to and had the approval of their commanding officers. After the war, there were several captains who wished to get back to Britain as soon as possible, and the *Clio* was due home in less than a year. Fitzjames had no family ties with England and no desire to get back, so he might be able to exchange this posting to HMS *Clio* with another officer who wanted to get home. And perhaps he could 'trade up' to a more exciting ship? This would also save him the time-consuming and possibly embarrassing chore of finding HMS *Clio*. Despite telling John Barrow that money was of 'no inconvenience' to him, he was effectively broke and on half-pay from the date he was dismissed from HMS *Cornwallis* until he stepped aboard HMS *Clio*.

He wrote to the captains of HMS *Driver*, HMS *Serpent* and HMS *Wolverine*, having heard that they were all likely to want to get home soon. He had his eye especially on the *Driver* as she was a crack, modern steam frigate. As he said to Barrow junior: 'I hope my next letter will be from the Driver if I can only persuade Old Harmer to have the belly-ache, and want to get home. One of the chief of my ambitions has always been to command a steamship.'

Barrow tried to encourage him to write a book about the Chinese War. Fitzjames had already written a huge 10,000-word poem, 'The Cruise of the Cornwallis', which described the war in verse. It seems to have been written in stages and perhaps was originally recited over dinner for the amusement of his brother officers. After the war it was published anonymously in the *Nautical Magazine*, where it can be found still to the general bemusement of its occasional reader. Fitzjames was a fine poet, but this was not his best literary work. The subject matter can be extremely bloodthirsty but has flashes of quirky humour. Like this couplet, for example:

We get plenty of rice, fowls, egg and chow-chow;
But no milk to our tea, though so near to My-cow.

An asterisk at the bottom of the page explains that 'My-cow' means 'Macao'. Traditional Chinese cuisine does not include dairy products, so there we have it: 'No milk in Macao (= my cow).'

He published the poem anonymously and chose 'Tom Bowline' as his pseudonym. At that time 'Tom Bowline' was a generic name for a sailor, like 'Jack Tar' is and 'Tommy Atkins' would become for British soldiers. The name was popularised by a famous song, *Poor Tom Bowline*, by Charles Dibdin. Dibdin wrote it for his elder brother Tom who had been killed when he was struck by lightning at sea. This was not such an unusual occurrence then, as the traces of lightning conductor rod from the *Erebus* and the *Terror* found at Crozier's Landing will testify.

But as so often with Fitzjames, something which on the surface was light and even immature in its humour concealed a hidden meaning. The expression 'on a bowline' or 'on a taut bowline' had the meaning that a ship was sailing as close as possible to the wind. There was a further, more sinister meaning to the pseudonym. Today's Royal Navy has a dictionary of slang on its website. This tells us that:

> In the days when women were allowed on board during a ship's stay in port, the gun decks were often the scenes of debauchery; and if a male child was born he was called a Son of a Gun. An old description of such is 'he was begotten in the galley and born under a gun: every hair a rope yarn, every finger a fish-hook, every tooth a marline spike and his blood right good Stockholm tar'; he would be christened 'Tom Bowline' or 'Bill Backstay' or some such name. Tom Bowline was a famous character who died of wounds in 1790 and was buried at Haslar; he went ashore once in seventeen years.

So naval tradition actually retains to this day this subtle reference Fitzjames placed in his major published work acknowledging his illegitimacy. Fitzjames' swift mind worked with a sophistication that evaded most of his contemporaries and future readers.

But what extraordinary links with the past and the future Fitzjames' use of this name brings!

Dibdin had written the music for Garrick's play *The Padlock*, which opened as far back as 1768. Dibdin had acted in this play under the direction of Garrick. So Fitzjames' use of this pseudonym takes us back to the eighteenth-century London of Garrick and Samuel Johnson. The mournful song remained popular throughout the nineteenth century, although at some point it changed its name from *Tom Bowline* to *Tom Bowling*.

Then in 1905 Sir Henry Wood put together his *Fantasia on British Sea Songs* to celebrate the centenary of the Battle of Trafalgar. One of the songs he used was *Poor Tom Bowling* (sic). He performed this every year at the last of his promenade concerts in London. Since then the Proms have become world famous as one of the greatest music festivals of the world and the *Fantasia on British Sea Songs* has been performed every year until 2008 when, sadly, the BBC dropped it. And Sir Henry was not the only twentieth-century composer to use this song: it was a favourite of Benjamin Britten and Peter Pears, and an arrangement by Britten has also been published.

The tradition at the Proms was for the song to be played slowly with much weeping and mourning from the Proms audience. What a bizarre link this is to James Fitzjames!

Early in May 1843, Fitzjames set out as a passenger on the fast Honourable East India Company steam frigate *Phlegethon* from Hong Kong to Calcutta on what turned out to be a minor odyssey around the Far East – with no pay – before he managed to find HMS *Clio*. The *Phlegethon* was another Laird-built iron paddle frigate, a sister ship to the *Euphrates* and *Tigris*, and Fitzjames' old friend Cleaveland had been the captain who had brought her out to the Far East. Fitzjames arrived in Calcutta in June. This was his first visit to India and he found the heat and humidity extremely oppressive. The *Clio* was not in harbour and he heard that she had sailed, not to Bombay as he had been told, but to Trincomalee. If he tried to sail to Trincomalee he would almost certainly not get there in time, so rather than chase the *Clio* he decided to stay in Calcutta and await news of her. He moved into the house of a mutual acquaintance of John Barrow's and his, a Mr Sylvester. Fitzjames was dispirited by the humidity, as the rains had now started, and by his money problems, writing plaintively to John Barrow: 'are we to get any prize money from China, or are the medals meant as a sop?'

He waited for almost two months in this limbo with no news of the *Clio* and no money, until he decided to take a passage on the fast steamer *Queen*, which he heard would shortly be sailing to Bombay. He may also have found the tragedy which visited his friend Sylvester distressing. Sylvester's wife died unexpectedly, followed shortly afterwards by their newborn daughter. Sylvester himself, suddenly a widower with two young children, was 'quite inconsolable'. Fitzjames left his grieving friend and departed for Bombay on 8 August 1843.

After a voyage of nineteen days, the *Queen* arrived at Bombay and, to Fitzjames' great relief, he found HMS *Clio* tied up there. On the same day that he arrived, 27 August 1843, he took formal command of her. It was eighteen years to the day after he entered the Royal Navy as a second class volunteer and now, at the age of just 30, he had his first command. He was delighted and joked that, in the absence of any other ships on the west coast of India, this now made him 'senior officer, India'. He was given his own house with, as he noted, 'servants and furniture', which must have been a luxury. The last house he had lived in was William Coningham's in Regents Park over two years ago. His money problems also came to an end as he was paid his arrears of pay as a commander, due since 18 March.

He was introduced to the Governor of the Presidency of Bombay, Sir George Arthur. Sir George invited Fitzjames to stay with his family at his country residence in the hills at Dapoorie, near Poonah. He wrote: 'here I am living with a delightful family consisting of Lady Arthur, a married daughter, some unmarried ditto, a number of sons, Aide-de-Camps and co. Deer shooting, hounds, riding, driving & co. and above all doing just as one likes. The climate is delightfully cool and the country fine.' He remained almost two weeks, joking that this was 'as other senior officers have done' – a phrase which he delighted in underlining – before returning to Bombay. While he was clearly happy with his new position, he worried that if his period as captain of the *Clio* was less than a year, it would not count towards his seniority. At every opportunity he sought out other officers who wanted to return to England, so that he could exchange his short command for another longer command on another vessel. But as in Hong Kong, none were forthcoming. He wanted to extend *Clio*'s commission for at least a year, but did not want to risk the accusation that he was doing so for personal gain.

While staying with Sir George he heard that the new British Resident, Major Rawlinson, needed to be taken to Baghdad. Sir George was delighted to hear that Fitzjames knew the waters of the Persian Gulf and the Shatt el-Arab from his days on the Euphrates Expedition, and not surprisingly orders soon came through that the *Clio* should proceed to the Persian Gulf before sailing for home. This virtually ensured Fitzjames his seniority.

The post had been much delayed during his long chase around the Pacific and Indian Oceans to find HMS *Clio* and a long backlog of letters now caught up with him. Among them was one from Edward Charlewood, written from his Mexican paddle steamer. Anyone who has lost a close friend will empathise with Fitzjames' words: 'I am much greived [sic] to hear my dear old friend Cleaveland's death of yellow fever in the W. Indies.' The first of the great friends of Fitzjames' adulthood was dead.

Fitzjames made HMS *Clio* ready for sea. He already knew his first lieutenant, Henry Thomas Dundas Le Vesconte, from their days together at HMS *Excellent* in Portsmouth harbour in 1838, but now the two men became firm friends. Fitzjames said: 'I like the *Clio* and all in her – in fact, I am very happy. The 1st Lt, Le Vesconte, is just the man for me and I don't think we are in bad order.' They have both left accounts of this period of their lives and both have a slightly dreamlike quality. While British casualties in the actual fighting of the Chinese War had been relatively light, especially compared to the huge Chinese losses, the suffering and risk of death through illness had been very high. These were men relieved to be alive and recuperating after an extremely testing time. Although the ship was old, everything was to Fitzjames' taste: ship, ship's company, location and their work. The *Clio* was a small ship of 380 tons and obsolescent. She was entirely constructed of wood with no steam engine. She mounted just eighteen small-calibre, smooth-bored guns. Built in 1806, she was on her last commission. She was a sister ship of the famous HMS *Beagle*.

Fitzjames did not work the ship's company hard and looked after them. He relished his first command and his letters are full of fun. His high spirits are reflected even in the captain's log, which he was required to complete daily. Every day the ship was at anchor Fitzjames draw in a little picture of an anchor, making him one of the very few nineteenth-century Royal Naval captains to illustrate his logbook with cartoons. Under him, the *Clio* also acquired a mascot: a pet cheetah. The ship's company fed the big cat, which became acclimatised to life at sea and even used to climb up into the rigging with the men. It was considered to be an ideal pet because, unlike other big cats, the cheetah does not have retractable claws. Instead, it has permanently extended claws like a dog, so it is less able to injure people by swiping its paws. It must have been a remarkable sight and was a perfect symbol of Fitzjames' flamboyant leadership.

After a final fruitless attempt to find a captain who would exchange with him, Fitzjames set sail for the Persian Gulf to convey Major Rawlinson to Baghdad, leaving Bombay on 28 October 1843. Major Rawlinson was the Honourable East India Company's new Political Resident in Baghdad. *Clio* was a happy ship in healthy waters. Fitzjames said that 'of all delightful climates in the world I do think that the upper part of the P[ersian] Gulf and Mesopotamia is the most delightful, that is in the winter months. The air is cool and clean. Sun not too hot, thermometer in the mornings at Baghdad 28 degrees and up to about 50 in the day.' He added: 'I say nothing about the place in summer.'

After calling at Bushire and Basra, Fitzjames used his knowledge of the rivers from the Euphrates Expedition to take the *Clio* 56 miles beyond Basra, up the Tigris towards Baghdad. This was the furthest a Royal Navy man-of-war had ever sailed upriver at that time, as Fitzjames proudly noted; although Le Vesconte commented that it was 'effected with much difficulty from the shallowness of the water'. From this point, Fitzjames took Major Rawlinson with the *Clio*'s surgeon, the purser and a mate to Baghdad, arriving there on 25 November. To his delight, Fitzjames found the steamer *Nitocris* tied up at the British Residency. She was one of the smaller sister ships of the old *Euphrates* now plying the Tigris and Euphrates for the Honourable East India Company, and about to sail for Basra. He mentions meeting old friends at this point, and it seems likely that her captain was his old friend Lieutenant Lynch from the Euphrates Expedition, and that Lynch offered to take the party back to the *Clio* on the steamer. This was too good an opportunity to miss, so stopping only to retrieve the magnetic instruments from the Euphrates Expedition, which were still at the British Residency, Fitzjames and his officers sailed back downriver on board the *Nitocris* as passengers. The voyage only took four and a half days.

Before rejoining the *Clio*, Fitzjames took the party to Kerbala to visit the shrine of the prophet Husayn ibn Ali, grandson of the prophet Mohammed. He then led them up the Euphrates to Hillah to visit the remains of the great city of Babylon – the third time Fitzjames had been there.

Fitzjames felt at home in Mesopotamia and enjoyed 'seeing my old haunts and friends' again. He claimed to John Barrow that 'the road from this [Baghdad] to Kerbala is so safe as that from Dover to London'. He enjoyed himself hugely, writing that 'I was clean with only one attack of dysentery. The weather here is cold and delightful and very refreshing after the heat of Calcutta and Bombay.'

Le Vesconte was left in charge of HMS *Clio* and wrote that 'while they were away all this we were amusing ourselves as best we could in the marshes about the mudbrick ruinous city so often mentioned in the Arabian Nights ... Our great amusement was pig hunting in the marshes and we killed a great many fine fat fellows which gave good food to the men, for the time while the rest sailed down, kept them in a plentiful allowance for some months after.' When Fitzjames and his companions arrived back at the *Clio*, she sailed back downriver and crossed the Gulf to Bushire to collect more biscuit and bread. A significant quantity of the ship's stock of ammunition had been expended on Le Vesconte's razzia against the pigs, which Fitzjames coolly entered in the ship's books as expended in musketry exercises. He was pleased with the effect the better diet and climate had, saying that 'our men, who had been nearly dead in China, got so fat that they busted their jackets – and I have now [only] two men in the [sick] list – one of who is all with cold and the other an old woman with the rheumatism'. From Bushire, the *Clio* sailed west across the Gulf to Bahrain. Le Vesconte was entranced with Bahrain, writing that it was:

> an island famous for its pearl fishery and for the spring of fresh water which rises in the sea and can be brought up in skins by divers. There is also a fine breed of white donkeys on the island whose legs and tails are finely stained with henna giving them a bright orange tinge. We had a fine ride over the rocks on them first visiting a fine spring in the centre of the island which bubbles up from the bottom of a rocky basin about sixty feet deep filling it with a cool and very blue water. And is then carried off in a carefully made channel to supply water to the gardens. We were entertained … with a mess of fish, milk and dates – exquisite food. On returning we visited the extensive ruins of a Portuguese fort.

They continued their circumnavigation of the Gulf 'showing the flag' to the Sheikhs along the coast, visiting Bandar Abbas and Muscat, which the sailors called 'King of the Muskrats'. Even this place Le Vesconte found attractive:

> this town is completely a dwelling among the rocks. It is stuck in the bottom of a little cove, apparently beaten by the sea out of the broad front of high, black and utterly barren rocks which bound the coast. And yet barren as they are the prettiest little gazelle in the world lives on them. The King, or as he is improbably called in England the Imam of Muscat was at his island of Zanzibar on the African shore but we smoked a pipe with his son who was ruling in his absence and drank a glass of Port wine with the [Honourable East India] Company's Agent, Renham, a Jew and very civil man, who said there was only one word by which to describe Muscat and that was Jehanum – Hell.

One of the questions that Fitzjames was called upon to settle while in the Gulf was the loss of the merchantman *Mary Mallaby*. He wrote this up in an artfully written letter, which was published in the *Friend of India* at Calcutta on 14 March 1844, and it is an instructive story for anyone who might think of Fitzjames as a stereotypical imperial officer. The *Mary Mallaby* had been run ashore at Bandar Abbas, the implication being that this resulted from the carelessness of her officers. Fitzjames described how 'one fine afternoon (that is, in good weather and broad daylight) … a ship ran into the bay of Bunder Abbas with all sail set and grounded'. This ship was the *Mary Mallaby*, and after she grounded the Sheikh of Bandar Abbas wrote to the senior Indian naval officer to inform him that this had happened. At this, apparently, the master of the *Mary Mallaby* demanded 'what business it was of his!' Captain Porter, the senior naval officer, offered to help refloat the *Mary Mallaby*, but her master turned his help down as, in the meantime, he had sold the wreck to Abdul Rahman, the Sheikh of Kishur. Sheikh Rahman then sold the ship on to the Imam of Muscat, and the ship was refloated and sent to Muscat.

When the ship arrived at Muscat she was missing her anchors and 'two wooden boxes bound with iron'. The Imam of Muscat asked Sheikh Rahman to recover these and send them on to him. The boxes were opened, Fitzjames reported in his letter, 'in the presence of several respectable natives … the master of the barque Columbia and the second officer', who all signed affidavits in a 'Persian document' to confirm that the boxes contained nothing more valuable than stones.

His reason for reporting this in the press was that after selling his ship, the master of the *Mary Mallaby* had claimed the ship had been 'robbed of two boxes of treasure by the people of Bunder Abbas'. Presumably he asked the British authorities to have Fitzjames investigate and remedy this alleged theft. Fitzjames, having looked into it, clearly came to the view this was a 'try-on' by an untrustworthy man at the expense of the local rulers. He refused to enforce any claim against the people of Bandar Abbas and instead published an open letter which virtually accused the master of being incompetent and a liar.

Anyone today who would resort to knee-jerk assumptions that Fitzjames looked down on people of a different skin colour or faith, or did not respect non-British, non-Christian cultures, should study this event. Fitzjames could easily have used brute force to enforce the master's request for 'restitution'. Instead he spoke to the local leaders and trusted their account over that of an Englishman, and even then went to the trouble of openly ridiculing the master in the English language press.

At some point, the predictable problem of sailing on a small ship in the company of a large carnivorous cat manifested itself. One day, perhaps when he had his back to it and stooped, the cheetah attacked Fitzjames. It grabbed him from behind and would not let go until 'beaten with an iron bar'. After this the pet had to go, and it is a sign that Fitzjames had completely recovered from his bullet wounds that this assault did him no lasting damage.

This commission was relaxing, but Fitzjames was restless. He knew that Sir John Barrow would do everything he could to assist him in whatever he wanted to do. But Barrow was an old man. If Barrow retired before the *Clio* returned home then his patronage would be of no practical use.

In September 1843, HMS *Erebus* and HMS *Terror* had returned from their astonishingly successful three-year voyage to the Antarctic led by Sir James Ross. Fitzjames had volunteered for that voyage but the Admiralty had not let him go.

This time, with Sir John Barrow in his debt, there would be no question of that happening again. Everyone knew that Sir John Barrow's personal ambition was to achieve the final conquest of the North West Passage in his lifetime, and John Barrow junior sounded Fitzjames out about it. The original suggestion seems to have been that Ross should lead the expedition and Fitzjames serve as his deputy. Perhaps not realising the seriousness of the proposal, Fitzjames wrote back with an even more ambitious proposal:

> In one of your letters you hint about the North Pole. Nothing I should like better. But none of your N West Passage. I want to make a party of good walkers and reach the Pole itself, only going in the winter at night instead of the summer at day as Parry did and in consequence found the ice melting and drifting him south. I don't know whether they would trust me with the command of such a party, but I don't see why they shouldn't and I think I should make up in perseverance what I might want in sense. There ought to be two ships (for mutual protection) who ought to be ordered to go to the north of Spitzbergen and their [sic] land the North Pole party (under myself) and wait till they came back – though I think if I did reach the Pole, I would temporarily mistake the meridian and go down on the other side. It ought to consist of at least two boats (light) with each a crew of eight men, a wise man and a fool. The wise man to take the observations on the ice & co. and the fool to keep people in order, walk and do wise man occasionally, a doctor in one, and the head man in the other. This would make a party of 22. It is a mistake going in too small parties. While this party is going on, one of the two ships could be getting as far North as she could – the other waiting quiet. But all this is a matter of 'detail', as Chesney used to say.
>
> You see I am a great hand at building castles in the air. But I am not sanguine on anything. I have done so well by following the 'laisser allez' system that I wait for anything and think that whatever is – is best.

Fitzjames knew that successful ice captains like Parry, Ross and Franklin became household names with knighthoods. The two great prizes remaining were the North West Passage and the North Pole. With either of these, he would vault over all of them and could retire and marry advantageously, before even reaching the age of 40, as a knighted captain. It was a glittering prospect. After sending this letter, Fitzjames must have realised that by floating his North Pole idea he might prejudice his chances of a place on the North West Passage voyage, so less than a month later he wrote again making it clear that he would not turn down a position on a North West Passage expedition. He said:

> if there is any idea of sending Captain Ross to look for the N W Passage – I would go with him. I would go anywhere with Ross though I never saw

him – but I would not go second with anybody whose name begins with a B [presumably either George Back or Edward Belcher]. However, this is between you and I. The real part is, I should probably be too glad to get employed with any-one or any-where. Or I shall have to marry in a fit of desperation. I have had no letters from anyone. I expected answers from those written at Baghdad.

Fitzjames was not yet committed to the north. In May 1844 he wrote again to Barrow having heard that Admiral Sir Bladon Capel might be appointed to command the Royal Navy's Mediterranean station. He asked if Capel might 'have me in his eye as his Flag Captain'. He added that 'you may think this foolish but greater fools than I have been Flag Captain'. Capel was, of course, son of the Earl of Essex, the grand landowner of Cassiobury House in Hertfordshire and the man who had recruited Fitzjames for HMS *Winchester* in 1834. He ended this request for one of the most coveted positions in the entire Royal Navy with a candid admission that 'it looks absurd. But I am "ambitious"'. Fitzjames himself put the word 'ambitious' in quotation marks. In the event the rumour was unfounded and Capel did not win the appointment.

There was still work for the *Clio* in the Far East. In early May, a Captain Brown arrived in Bombay couriering the formal endorsement of the Treaty of Nanking, which had been signed by Queen Victoria in London, to China. But Brown arrived 'in such a state of nervous excitement from an illness which got hold of him in the Red Sea that he cannot go on'. Brown was sent home and HMS *Clio* dispatched to take the Treaty to Admiral Sir William Parker at Trincomalee so he could forward it to China. Fitzjames tried to find a way to exchange his commission with that of Captain Brown, but Brown had to be sent home to London. Fitzjames judged that Brown's 'monomania or hypochondria' was so bad that 'he can't eat and is altogether miserable, and I am sure he would die'. His last opportunity for an exchange had fallen through.

In late May 1844, HMS *Clio* sailed to Trincomalee for the rendezvous with Sir William Parker. Fitzjames and Le Vesconte met their old chief on HMS *Cornwallis* and Le Vesconte was struck by how effective Fitzjames was in winning the trust of his senior officers, commenting to his father on how 'fond' Sir William was of Fitzjames. One of Fitzjames' letters refers to returning home 'with a million', so it seems *Clio* took back to England a proportion of the massive indemnity the Chinese Empire had been forced to pay under the terms of the Treaty of Nanking.

They left Trincomalee and made a tremendously fast passage to the Cape 'with a furious breeze after us'. Rounding the Cape, the weather turned abruptly and the *Clio* sailed into Simon's Town in the teeth of an adverse gale. There the *Clio* picked up the officers and ship's company of HMS *Fawn*, who needed passage back to England as their ship had been condemned and was no longer seaworthy. On the long route around Africa to Portsmouth, the *Clio* had one final duty.

There had been an unseemly scramble to mine wealth of an unlikely type off the coast of what is now Namibia. 'White Gold' was the name given to colossal deposits of guano which had built up on the island of Ichaboe, where huge colonies of seabirds had congregated in the confined space of small offshore islands or rocky outcrops that sheltered them from natural predators. The dry climate meant that this guano retained its nutrients.

Fitzjames tersely stated in the record of his career that he 'visited Tcheroe (the guano island) on the west coast of Africa to settle the disturbances amongst the crews of the merchant vessels loading guano', which he did in August 1844. But Fitzjames and Le Vesconte were much more descriptive of its unique horrors in their private correspondence. Fitzjames described the island as 'the Father of all Dung-Hills' with a smell like 'rotten kittens'. Le Vesconte said:

> it is seven hundred feet long and the part above the waves is almost entirely formed by the guano which presents a smooth bounded surface and depth of thirty feet – landing can only be effected on the inshore side and the wind blows so much from the SW as to cause a continuous heavy sea to roll on this most barren reef-bound dangerous coast as there is no beach and even on the lee side the water is rough. The guano is brought to the boats over stages whose outer ends are hung to shears fixed among the rocks and secured with chains and heavy anchors. It is the most dirty miserable employment possible and attendant with frequent loss of life from the boats being dashed on the rocks. The guano itself has the appearance of very fine garden mould, but has a very pungent smell affecting the eyes and nose very much in simply walking over it and often drawing blood from the nostrils of those engaged in stowing it.

After the richness of this deposit was recognised in 1844, unscrupulous British and other ships descended on the island to loot guano. It is estimated that up to 800,000 tons was removed in only a few years. When the *Clio* arrived, Fitzjames found 130 ships scrambling over the 'white gold'. With no discipline, fights had broken out in a near-piratical situation. Fitzjames confiscated one ship which had attacked another and sent it back to England under the command of the first lieutenant of the *Fawn* and some of his ship's company. He arrested the ringleaders and took them back himself in irons, although they were released without charge when the *Clio* reached England.

Leaving Ichaboe behind, although the smell was apparent some way out to sea, the *Clio* had one last port of call before England: St Helena. 'Of course', said Le Vesconte, 'we all saw the place where Napoleon had rested and the stumps of the willows which were cut down by the French when they took away the body of their Emperor.' The unpleasantly situated house Napoleon had lived in had by then been converted into a granary and threshing floor, but 'the man who owns it makes you pay for seeing the rooms'. Fitzjames, Le Vesconte and all the officers attended a reception at the house of the governor, Colonel Trelawney, 'a very nice place among green slopes and forest trees about a thousand feet above the sea'.

Leaving St Helena on 22 August, by the end of September *Clio* was approaching England and the matter of Fitzjames' next position was still open. He wrote to John Barrow again:

> I am ready for the North Pole. Tell me what chance you think there is of Admiral Capel getting the Mediterranean. I said something about it in one of my letters to you. But on consideration I think I might as well have left it alone – it is too good. All I can say is if I don't get employed I shall get married – and perhaps thank if I do. If any decent body will have me. And clean. As I heard a man say the other day.

By the evening of 2 October 1844, HMS *Clio* had tied up at Spithead. The ship was paid off by 10 October 1844. She never sailed again and was broken up in 1845. There were many important people in Portsmouth at the time, as the King of France, Louis-Philippe, was returning from London after a state visit to Queen Victoria. The queen arrived in Portsmouth to see him off, although, ironically, the weather was so bad that she missed him and the king actually sailed home via Dover. Sir John Barrow and his son accompanied her and so were in Portsmouth when the *Clio* arrived. Le Vesconte and Fitzjames were now good friends and Fitzjames offered to introduce his paid-off lieutenant to the old man. They both seem to have thought that John Barrow junior would be appointed as his father's successor. Le Vesconte was pinning his hopes of an advantageous next appointment on his friendship with Fitzjames. He noticed Fitzjames' remarkably close relationship with the two Barrows, men to whom he had never previously been introduced.

Four men, whose different fates would be irrevocably linked with the Franklin Expedition, had now met.

Ten

FITZJAMES PREPARES

There is always a process of adjustment when a sailor returns home. But for Fitzjames his situation in the winter of 1844 was radically different.

On the credit side, he had now finally made his own position in the world. He had overcome the irregularities of his birth and the consequences of the dubious methods he had used to get the promotions he wanted. He had status now, as a Royal Navy commander, a former captain of one of Her Majesty's ships and a war hero.

But it is clear from his surviving letters that there was a darker side to the man who returned to England. He was much more mature and introspective. It can only have been on landing at Portsmouth that Fitzjames heard of the death of his true father, Sir James Gambier. Sir James had died in 1844 and this meant that Fitzjames' achievements could never now lead to any form of reconciliation with his natural father.

All of his foster family had passed away with the exception of William Coningham, and although Fitzjames and William were undoubtedly overjoyed to meet again, William was becoming a difficult man. Perhaps the early signs of the depressive illnesses which would dominate his later years were there. Fitzjames had last met William shortly after his marriage to Elizabeth Meyrick. While Fitzjames had been away, William's life had blossomed and Elizabeth and he now had two young children. Although Fitzjames was godfather to the elder, William now had something Fitzjames did not: a loving and supportive family. Fitzjames must have realised that something similar might at last be attainable for him.

As soon as William heard that the *Clio* had docked, he rushed to see Fitzjames, writing to his wife that 'I am just off to Portsmouth to see Fitz', adding that 'I shall ... probably sleep on board *Clio* in 14 inches of hammock'.

The reunion was emotional for all three. Fitzjames had lived for years on board ship and this masculine camaraderie contrasted very strongly with the gentler, loving family life which he now became a part of. On 12 October 1844, only two days after the *Clio* finally paid off, he wrote a remarkably personal letter to William's wife, Elizabeth Coningham, in which he described himself as having been 'thrown … on the world by circumstances over which I have no control, without one friend in it for whom I have any real affection except William'. He was delighted 'to find that his wife shares in the feelings of regard which he has always entertained for me. It might have been otherwise; had it been so, England would have been to me as a barren desert … I really do feel so completely bewildered and "adrift" – that I do not know what to be at first.'

Elizabeth and William Coningham were renting a house at 13 Royal Parade, Brighton, which was a fashionable newly developed town on the Sussex coast. They had two children, Elizabeth who was 4 and William who was 2. Getting to know the children made Fitzjames very conscious of his single status and there are several indications that he was chafing at this and hankered after marriage. In his letter to Elizabeth Coningham he had said: 'it is the first time in a long life that I have found myself completely my own Master, and I trust that it may be the last, which I fear is not probably'.

It is plain that the triangle between Fitzjames, Elizabeth Coningham and William Coningham was deep and complex. Fitzjames had met Elizabeth briefly before, when he came ashore between HMS *Ganges* and HMS *Cornwallis* in 1841, but then only for a matter of days. He moved into their home and, as none of them knew whether he would ever sail again, this could have been the start of a life together as a quasi-family.

William was fragile and already dependent emotionally on Elizabeth, as well as on Fitzjames. Underneath his tough veneer, Fitzjames was equally emotionally dependent on William as his de-facto sole relative. This threw the two virtual strangers, Elizabeth and Fitzjames, together as the third side of this complicated triangle of emotions, linked by their mutual love for William. These emotions spilled over after Elizabeth read a letter Fitzjames wrote to William expressing his sense of loss at parting with HMS *Clio*, her officers and men, and his wish to go to sea again. She seems to have thought he might be evading the challenge of sharing with her the task of caring for the fragile William. Fitzjames answered that he had only written this in 'a moment of despondency at leaving there [sic] company [i.e., the men of the *Clio*] when I have passed a very happy time as their Captain'. He continued that '[I] intend carrying out your intentions to the full' – presumably looking after William. 'But in the nature of things it is clear that I cannot always remain doing nothing.'

As always, Fitzjames was short of money. Within days of landing he had to borrow from William Coningham. Like his father Robert, William had always been unstinting in his financial support for Fitzjames. In 1843, when he had heard that Fitzjames might be returning to England, he had written to 'dearest Jim' saying 'do pray draw on me for anything that you want'. He yearned for Fitzjames to settle with Elizabeth, the children and him. Then he had written: 'why don't you come home all your friends will be glad to see you and with us you will find a home and the most affectionate welcome that hearts can give you?'

So, on 22 November 1844, James Fitzjames and William Coningham met at 37 Fleet Street at the offices of Messrs Hoare and Company, bankers. There Fitzjames was introduced by William Coningham and an account opened in his name. This was significant for several reasons. Hoare's was and still is one of the pre-eminent private bankers, so this helped confirm Fitzjames' personal status. Secondly, while William and Robert Coningham had had accounts at Hoare's for many years, Fitzjames' finances had been handled, up until now, by Gledstanes, the Coningham family trading business. And his father, Sir James Gambier, had been such a bad debtor that Hoare's had had to put his affairs into the hands of trustees. Hoare's acceptance of Fitzjames showed that, while he may come from the wrong side of the blanket, he was now very much on the right side of the banker's ledger.

William Coningham then transferred an annuity of £3,000, invested in Consols 3 per cent at the Bank of England, to Fitzjames. This would give Fitzjames an income of about £100 per annum. It is difficult to translate values fairly, but in terms of today's earnings that is a sum equivalent to over £2 million and the income equivalent to over £75,000. Was this simply altruism on William's part? Possibly; but it might, alternatively, be money which had been handed over to Robert Coningham by Sir James Gambier or by Fitzjames' mother's family at the time that Fitzjames was given over to his care. Unfortunately, bank records for Sir James Gambier and Robert Coningham for that period no longer survive, so it looks as though this can never be proved one way or another.

William Coningham was still engaged in amassing his huge collection of paintings and now had his own gallery to display them in Porchester Terrace, Bayswater. He had lost all his religious faith and, rare for those days, was openly atheist. Politically, he was moving more and more to the left and would shortly stand for Parliament. He described himself to Fitzjames as 'as bad a Radical as ever'.

Fitzjames embarked on a whirlwind tour of his old friends. He was reunited with Edward Charlewood, now starting his career on the railways. Charlewood had nursed the two men's great friend Richard Cleaveland as he died of yellow fever. Fitzjames also met, for the first time, his goddaughter Annie Sophie Charlewood, who was just 1 year old. He was not to know that her younger sister, to be born in 1850, would be named Alice Fitzjames Charlewood.

Charlewood had not abandoned his attempts to obtain another seagoing appointment with the Royal Navy and, with Fitzjames, the two old shipmates discussed the prospects of Charlewood skippering one of the two discovery ships, *Erebus* or *Terror*. Initially they hoped to be appointed as the two captains and Charlewood was, in Fitzjames' words, 'dolefully enthusiastic'. There was a problem with this which Fitzjames may not have been aware of. The United States government had taken an extremely dim view of the British sale of the armed paddle frigates *Guadeloupe* and *Montezuma*, and the secondment of Royal Navy personnel, including Charlewood and Cleaveland, to the Mexican navy in 1839. These ships had intervened in the Mexican Civil War and fought several sharp engagements with the embryonic Texan navy. It was while fighting for Mexico that Cleaveland had died of yellow fever. Since then, British relations with the United States had improved and Mexico's importance to Britain as an ally had lessened. But it appears that one condition of this warming was British acceptance of a United States condition that Charlewood, who was regarded as being close to a pirate, should never be sent to sea again by the Royal Navy. He never was, being given instead attractive jobs on the railways and in the coastguard. This condition may have prevented him from being employed on the Franklin Expedition and, therefore, had the unforeseen effect of saving his life.

Fitzjames also met Campbell relatives of the Coninghams and visited the graves of Louisa and Robert Coningham at Abbots Langley. But everywhere he went his mind was focused on his next challenge: the North West Passage. At Abbots Langley he met the current vicar, the Reverend Gee and his wife. Today Mrs Gee is remembered locally for founding a school, but Fitzjames was more impressed by her, describing her as a 'nice little cute body'.

It is clear that before the turn of the year 1844 he had been assured by Sir John Barrow that there would be a North West Passage expedition next year and that he, Fitzjames, would have a prominent position on it, if not actually lead it. Charlewood was promised the command of the second ship. Barrow also appears to have promised to arrange Fitzjames' promotion to full captain as soon as he could. From this point, all talk of walking to the North Pole or Mediterranean positions disappeared. The North West Passage dominated the rest of Fitzjames' life. He passed the word around his friends and acquaintances and bombarded the Admiralty with letters recommending officers for the new expedition.

But before the appointments could be formalised, the Board of the Admiralty would have to approve them. And here there was a problem. Barrow had his own reasons for wanting Fitzjames to be appointed and these were personal. He could not divulge them to the Board. And while Fitzjames was a capable officer, his knowledge of polar navigation was slight. In a letter to John Barrow junior, written on 2 January 1845, in which he was recommending officers to come with him, he made the following alarming statement:

I have been reading a French account of N P voyages from Zeno to Ross and Back. Which makes me quite au fait in the matter. It appears the Fury is broken up. So the Supernumerary Commander can't get her if he would. It does not appear clear to me what led Parry down Prince Regent's Inlet after having got as far as Melville Island before. The N W Passage is certainly to be gone through by Barrows Strait, but whether south or north of Parry's group remains to be proved. I am for North, sailing NW till in Long 140.

This fascinating but rather alarming letter shows us that Fitzjames was enthusiastically planning the expedition. There seems to have been a suggestion that he be taken along as 'Supernumerary Commander', the role in which he would eventually sail, with the mandate to locate the abandoned HMS *Fury*, refurbish her and then sail her back. Fitzjames had, after all, participated in the recovery of HMS *Terror* from the Portuguese coast in 1827. The *Fury* had been abandoned by Parry on 25 August 1825 at Creswell Bay on Somerset Island. But Somerset Island was very different from Portugal. Clearly Fitzjames massively underestimated the hostility of the Arctic. Even to have suggested this, he cannot have had any real idea of the dangers of the North West Passage and the power of the ice he would face. Sir John Ross or Crozier could have told him that the ice had ground the *Fury* to pieces so much that twelve years before, when Ross had visited Creswell Bay in 1833, he had found absolutely no trace of the ship at all, although a huge mound of her supplies remained.

Fitzjames did recognise that he needed to learn, and rapidly, about the ice and the Arctic, and he was reading up on the subject. He recognised that Parry's first voyage had come closest to achieving the passage but, no doubt influenced by Sir John Barrow, concluded that the route through the North West Passage would be found by sailing *north* from Barrow Strait. He seems to have accepted Sir John Barrow's view that an 'open Polar Sea' existed north of the ice, at least in the summer, and that if a ship could break through the pack ice surrounding it, she could then sail at will to a chosen longitude and break back south again through the pack.

At the time this seemed a reasonable view. Barrow believed that sea ice could only accumulate where there was land, in the same way that a snowflake or a raindrop accumulates around a speck of dust. In 1845 there appeared to be evidence to support this from the epic voyage of the *Erebus* and *Terror* under Ross and Crozier. Sailing south, they had come up against an apparently impenetrable barrier of pack ice on 5 January 1840. Unlike previous ships, theirs had been strengthened and had iron-reinforced bows. Franklin and Buchan had attempted to penetrate pack ice in 1818 but failed. This time, the *Erebus* and *Terror* had succeeded in breaking through a barrier of about 30 miles of closely packed ice and on the other side found open water. They sailed towards the magnetic South Pole in this virgin sea and appeared to encounter ice, the insuperable Ross Ice Shelf, only in front of land. Ross thought he could see mountains beyond the ice barrier, which he called the 'Parry Mountains'. We know that this was not evidence to support the existence of an 'open polar sea', but hindsight makes us all experts. At the time, the astonishing success of Ross and Crozier appeared to suggest that ice barriers, which had previously been impenetrable, might now be broken by the *Erebus* and the *Terror*, especially if they were given further reinforcement, determined leadership and steam engines.

Barrow was not able to win the appointment to command the expedition for Fitzjames, so the debate and the lobbying over who would lead it continued. Meanwhile, Fitzjames shuttled between Hertfordshire, London and Brighton.

He continued to put names forward as recommendations for whoever would eventually lead it. Not everyone he proposed was accepted, although Henry Le Vesconte was. A particular favourite of Fitzjames, D'Arcy Wynyard, was turned down. As January dragged on, Fitzjames became more and more frustrated that no decision was forthcoming. He knew that to have any chance of entering the ice at Lancaster Sound in 1845, the expedition must depart from England by May at the latest and felt that the continuing delays were jeopardising that prospect.

After Sir James Ross turned down Barrow's offer of command of the expedition, the two favourites for leadership were either Sir John Franklin or John Lort Stokes. Fitzjames hoped either for the captaincy of the second ship, if Charlewood was turned down, or to be second in command of the flagship. Fitzjames favoured Franklin over Stokes, although he does not seem to have known either man well. Stokes had captained HMS *Beagle* on her third voyage of discovery in the Pacific. One of Stokes' officers on this voyage had been Owen Stanley, the man who had befriended the young Pauline Helfer on the beach at Hierapolis back in 1834, and another was Graham Gore, who would sail with Fitzjames on the *Erebus*.

The eventual compromise on leadership was that Franklin would lead the expedition with Fitzjames as his commander and Charlewood as captain of HMS *Terror*. Charlewood received 'private intimation from the Admiralty that I was to be appointed'. But 'at the eleventh hour, Captain Crozier, an old Polar officer, who was then at Naples, observing in the newspapers that this expedition was fitting out, at once posted home, and proceeded to the Admiralty, claiming the right, as an old polar officer, to be appointed. The Admiralty felt the justice of his claim, and, about the day I expected the appointment to be finally made out for me, a note came to say that as Captain Crozier had tendered his services, the Admiralty felt bound in justice to appoint him.' The Admiralty may have found Crozier's appearance very convenient as it provided an excuse to avoid appointing Charlewood and inflaming anti-British feelings in the United States.

While Fitzjames fretted over the delay, he resurrected his earlier idea of making a fresh British attempt on the North Pole. Then a letter of 20 February 1845 makes it clear that he had privately been told of his fateful appointment. It seems that the Admiralty's concerns about Franklin's age, state of health and competence were alleviated by the knowledge that he would be backed up by the very capable Fitzjames as his commander or, in modern parlance, his executive officer. Franklin and Crozier's appointments were announced on 3 March 1845 with Fitzjames' on the following day. After all the lobbying, Fitzjames was going to become an Arctic officer.

Fitzjames wanted to use the expedition to make his name. By the end of March he had formulated a personal plan which would enable him to achieve the most from the expedition's voyage through the North West Passage. He took it as read that the well-equipped expedition would make it through to the Bering

Strait. Most people did. Even the more sanguine Lieutenant Fairholme thought that though the ships themselves would probably end up being abandoned, the expedition itself would complete the passage in open boats. Fitzjames knew that the news of the passage would be big in London and he wanted to be the first person to bring it home. In an expression of almost bravura showmanship, his intention was to be landed in Russia at the earliest possible opportunity and from there make his own way on land across Siberia and Russia, arriving home with the news before the ships did.

He wrote that 'in whatever year we do get through, the month will be August or September, so that these will be the times to go at once to Oshotk, and start off for St Petersburg ... Sir John tells me that he has thought of such a journey for one officer – and Col. Sabine says it would be highly desirable and interesting'.

This was an extremely astute move. Fitzjames would achieve a personal circumnavigation of the globe partly north of the Arctic Circle, like his earlier attempt to return to London from Hong Kong overland after the China war. Had it succeeded, it would have made him a household name in exploration, eclipsing Sir John Franklin, who would then have been just the captain of the first part of Fitzjames' remarkable journey. Now he had his mission.

The two famous ships chosen, HMS *Erebus* and HMS *Terror*, were fitted out. The *Erebus* and the *Terror* were 'bomb-ships', designed as dedicated shore bombardment vessels. They were very strongly built to absorb the recoil of the huge mortars bomb-ships mounted. Since the eighteenth century, the Royal Navy had used bomb-vessels as polar exploration vessels. Not until 1 February 1845 did the Admiralty commit to fit them with auxiliary steam engines. Time was short and the modifications were extensive. Early marine steam engines were huge and demanded frequent maintenance. Their engines had to be installed so they would not be damaged by ice and cold and would be useable for up to three years away from a dockyard. The decision to drive the ships with propellers rather than paddles was sensible but, for the day, quite radical. The engines used were two second-hand ex-railway locomotive engines, which were reconditioned by the famous firm of Maudslay. These were reliable and relatively compact power units capable of delivering at least 50hp.

Equipment was supplied for a whole series of magnetic and gravitational observations to be taken whenever ashore. An old friend Fitzjames met again at this time was Colonel Sabine, the army engineer officer who had trained up the Euphrates Expedition in magnetic observations, as he supervised magnetic equipment and training for the Franklin Expedition too. Franklin commissioned the construction of two special collapsible wooden huts to be used as observatories, which could be set up when needed, and Fitzjames was put in charge of magnetic observations.

As the ships took shape in Woolwich Dockyard Fitzjames again, and for the last time, moved out of Elizabeth and William Coningham's house in Brighton. He left all the possessions which he would not be taking with him in Brighton and took rooms at 14 Francis Street, close to the Royal Marine garrison at Woolwich and the ships. Such was the workload that complaints had been made about the hours of work, presumably by junior officers who were now living on board the ships, and on 19 March 1845, the Admiralty issued an instruction that the hours of work were to be limited – from 6 a.m. to 7 p.m., six days a week.

Just as he had been with HMS *Winchester* in 1834, Fitzjames was responsible for recruiting the officers and men. The ships would be very crowded, with *Erebus* taking seventy men and the slightly smaller *Terror* sixty-nine, eleven men more than they took to the Antarctic with Ross and Crozier. The additional men were an ice master, an engineer and three first-class stokers for each ship. Fitzjames was the eleventh extra man on *Erebus*. Most seem to have been volunteers and to have felt it was not especially dangerous. Le Vesconte did 'not think the danger or inconveniences are at all equal to China or the coast of Africa'. After all, 20 per cent of the original members of the Euphrates Expedition had died of disease. Le Vesconte had added, 'we are all hoping for promotion', and this was a major incentive for all the officers, as the careers of Franklin, Parry and James Ross had showed. The men had less of a career incentive but would receive double pay, better food than average and probably a slightly more relaxed disciplinary regime. If they failed to return, their arrears of double pay would be a valuable nest egg for their next of kin. We must not also discount the pure spirit of adventure, which was equally attractive to officers and men.

Fitzjames may have met Franklin in the Mediterranean in the early 1830s, but even if not he knew of him already. Franklin was famous, 'the Man who Ate his Boots' and, at 59, was half a generation older than Fitzjames and most of the men on the expedition. Like Admiral Lord Gambier, he combined a Royal Naval career with a driving Christian faith. He was a pillar of the Anglican Church who would happily deliver a forceful sermon whenever asked. To a worldly man like Fitzjames, who lived ashore in the household of an atheist, Franklin must have seemed very old fashioned. It is difficult to believe that, in the right company, the practised mimic Fitzjames did not deliver a devastatingly funny imitation of Sir John. But Fitzjames was skilled at winning the confidence of senior officers and the two of them seem to have had a good working relationship. While Fitzjames concentrated on recruitment Franklin, with his greater experience of the Arctic, seems to have supervised the stores, provisions and equipment for the ships. It was clear that, with the extra men and the engines, the ships could not sail across the Atlantic with three years' supplies so a transport ship, the *Baretto Junior*, was hired and an Admiralty agent, Lieutenant Griffiths, appointed to the ship. The exploration ships could then cross the Atlantic carrying just two years' provisions and the *Baretto Junior* would carry the remaining year's supplies for each ship. It was to transfer these supplies that the three ships rendezvoused off Greenland.

The other officer superior to Fitzjames on the expedition was the 48-year-old Francis Crozier. Fitzjames and Crozier had not met before, although Crozier's family were well acquainted with the family of Fitzjames' old boss Colonel Chesney. Chesney and Crozier had a similar Irish background.

Although one of the most experienced polar officers of the day, Crozier was shy and retiring and did not have Fitzjames' knack of winning the confidence of his superior officers. He was suffering from the strain of his last four years of voyages with Ross to the Antarctic. He was also lonely. He had twice asked for the hand of Franklin's niece Sophia Cracroft in marriage and twice been rejected. Like Fitzjames, he was not wealthy and must have felt that unless he joined this expedition he ran the risk of never getting another seagoing appointment.

Fitzjames has often been criticised in his choice of officers. He is said to have not taken anyone with polar experience and instead simply to have taken along friends. This criticism is completely wrong, as an analysis of the first set of officers appointed on 4 March 1845 shows. Charles Hamilton Osmer was appointed to HMS *Erebus* as paymaster and purser for the expedition. At 46 he was one of the oldest men on the expedition after Franklin and Crozier. He had extensive experience of the Arctic having served with Beechey on HMS *Blossom* in the Bering Strait and the Pacific from 1825 to 1828. Beechey had been sent to the Pacific to support Franklin's second overland exploration of the North West Passage and, at one point, her boats had reached within 150 miles of Franklin's further west position. Osmer joined despite having recently married and having a 1-year-old child. His assistant was Edwin Helpman, who had been Fitzjames' clerk-in-charge on HMS *Clio* and was appointed to HMS *Terror* as purser and paymaster. Le Vesconte was appointed to the *Erebus* and was delighted as he had prevaricated over other appointments so he could go on the expedition. Fitzjames selected a shipmate from the *Cornwallis*, Charles Des Voeux, as mate on the *Erebus*. Henry Collins was appointed second master to HMS *Erebus*. He had only recently been commissioned into the Royal Navy, in September 1843, but had eleven years' experience as a merchant marine officer. It is likely he had Arctic experience on whaling ships. Fitzjames selected another old China hand, George Hodgson, for HMS *Terror*. Hodgson had fought with distinction in the street fighting on the day Fitzjames had been shot and since had won a pitched battle with Malay pirates while serving on HMS *Wanderer*. Two more officers were appointed to the *Terror* that day: Frederick Hornby as mate and Edward Little as lieutenant. Fitzjames has no obvious link to either of them and it's not clear now why they were selected. They may simply have been volunteers looking for adventure who were in the wrong place at the right time.

The same pattern – a mix of former shipmates and men with Arctic experience – can be seen in the next round of appointments on 8 March 1845. Graham Gore, appointed lieutenant on HMS *Erebus*, had entered the Royal Navy five years before Fitzjames, in April 1820, and was older than him, but such was the effect of Sir John Barrow's accelerated promotion that Fitzjames was now senior to Gore. Gore had fought at Navarino and was an experienced Arctic officer, having sailed as mate on HMS *Terror* in Back's disastrous attempt on the North West Passage. He had also sailed on the famous *Beagle*'s third voyage under Stokes, when large parts of the Australian coast had been surveyed accurately for the first time.

Gore was the third generation of a remarkable line of seamen. His father John Gore was a senior naval officer who would retire as a rear admiral and who had sailed around the world as a boy. During this voyage Gore Point and the Gore Peninsula in the Alaskan Kenai fjords were named after him. His grandfather had sailed with Cook aboard HMS *Resolution* on Cook's third and final voyage. After the deaths of Cook and his second in command, Charles Clerke, grandfather Gore had taken command of the expedition and brought it back to England in 1780. Gore was ideally qualified for the voyage and, after Franklin's death, would become Fitzjames' second in command on *Erebus*.

As senior surgeon to the *Erebus*, Fitzjames arranged the appointment of Dr Stephen Stanley, who had been a surgeon on HMS *Cornwallis*. Possibly he was the man who had operated on Fitzjames to remove the musket ball from his back. Three other medics were carried. Acting surgeon John Peddie and assistant surgeon Alexander MacDonald were appointed to HMS *Terror*, with acting assistant surgeon Dr Harry Goodsir as Stanley's junior on HMS *Erebus*. Goodsir and Peddie were appointed on 6 March 1845. Peddie, Goodsir and MacDonald all seem to have known each other, having studied medicine at Edinburgh at the same time. Alexander MacDonald had already sailed to the Arctic on the whaler on which Eenoolooapik, a Greenland Inuk who had been induced to visit Aberdeen, was returning to his native land. MacDonald wrote a sympathetic memoir of Eenoolooapik and of his experiences in Aberdeen and Greenland. He presumably interested his fellow alumni from Edinburgh, John Peddie and Harry Goodsir, in the Arctic. Goodsir was a particularly important appointment. There was a long tradition of talented scientists being taken along on Royal Naval voyages of exploration. Cook had taken the brilliant scientist Sir Joseph Banks with him. More recently Charles Darwin had voyaged to the Galapagos and other exotic locations on the famous second voyage of exploration of HMS *Beagle*. Ross and Crozier had taken Joseph Hooker. Goodsir was a brilliant young medical and scientific researcher clearly in the mould of Hooker, Banks and Darwin, and he was friendly with Hooker and Darwin.

On 13 March, Fitzjames recruited Lieutenants Irving and Fairholme to the *Terror* and the *Erebus* respectively. Fitzjames had known Fairholme since both had served on HMS *Ganges* during the Syrian war. He was a very large man who had served eleven years in the Royal Navy. Unlike Charlewood and Fitzjames, he had been persuaded to join Trotter's ill-fated Niger Expedition and on it he had become so ill he had nearly died and was invalided home. He had also had the remarkable experience of being captured by Moors, after being shipwrecked off the coast of Africa while attempting to sail a captured slave ship which he had taken as a prize. He was subsequently rescued 'by some French negroes'. Couch, appointed on the following day, was another China hand who Fitzjames had known since they both trained on HMS *Excellent* in 1838.

The last significant set of officer appointments was the ice masters. Typically ex-whaling captains, their role was rather like that of a pilot, acting as an expert in ice conditions and advising the officers. James Reid was appointed to HMS *Erebus* on 26 March. Fitzjames liked him but made fun of his heavy Scottish accent, describing him as 'rough, intelligent, unpolished ... but not vulgar, good-humoured and honest'. As a gifted mimic, Fitzjames was always very aware of accents. The other officers did not like Reid, and Le Vesconte thought him 'a queer fellow ... Most of us think we should be better off without him but it appears the Admiralty are anxious to supply every thing that can be of use'.

The second acting ice master was Thomas Blanky, appointed to HMS *Terror*. He was a Yorkshireman with vast Arctic experience, having served on three earlier Royal Naval Arctic expeditions, the first two as an able seaman, as well as on whalers. He had served on Sir John Ross' Victory Expedition, the first attempt to force the North West Passage in a steamship. The story of the Victory Expedition was rather like the Franklin Expedition, in that the *Victory* had been trapped in ice for two years before being abandoned by the expedition. Blanky and the others had deserted the ship and dragged their boats 150 miles over snow and ice, living in a hut they built for shelter at Fury Beach and eating provisions left there after the wreck of the *Fury*. They finally reached open sea in their boats, but it had been a very narrow escape. Blanky had a wealth of valuable experience for the Franklin Expedition and it is noteworthy that despite what must have been a traumatic experience, he was willing to serve on this expedition. He was a rough diamond who, at one stage, had kept a public house in Whitby. The Arctic historian Glenn Stein, who uncovered this fact, has also shown that Blanky had something in common with Fitzjames: he concealed details of his birth. Blanky was Jewish and his real name was Blenkhorn or Blenkinhorn.

In addition to the officers, the *Erebus* took fifty non-commissioned crewmen and the *Terror* fifty-one. At least nine of these men, or almost 10 per cent of the total, can be shown to have served previously on the *Erebus* or *Terror* during the Antarctic cruise of 1839–43. The majority of the rest had previously worked on Royal Navy ships, although twenty-eight were listed as 'first entry', meaning that they had not previously served in the Royal Navy. As their average age was high, at 28 years old it seems most, if not all, of them were experienced merchant seamen, and it's probable many of them had Arctic experience from serving on whalers. Their careers are now extremely difficult to piece together, but on balance this suggests a ship's company reasonably well experienced in Arctic sailing. Some sailors followed particular officers or were sought out by them. Crozier especially selected Thomas Jopson as his servant and Fitzjames took Richard Aylmore, who had been his steward on HMS *Clio*.

Each ship also carried eight Royal Marines. They do not seem to have been volunteers, being instead drafted by the Royal Marine commandant at Woolwich, who had been asked to select candidates for the expedition from 'among those who are constitutionally best adapted to the service'. Unlike the rest of the crew they do not seem to have received double pay.

Fitzjames has been criticised persistently over these selections. Scott Cookman in *Ice Blink* says that 'officers and men rushed to enlist', yet 'only eight polar hands could be induced to re-enlist'. He claims that Irish, Scottish and non-English officers and men were weeded out so the expedition could be 'all English'. He does not mention any alleged anti-Welsh prejudice, which is a relief, but claims that 'not a single officer with previous Polar experience ... volunteered'.

It is quite clear that none of this is true. Fully one-third of the officers Fitzjames selected had prior polar sailing experience. Six of the eighteen seaman officers – Franklin, Crozier, Gore, Reid, Blanky and probably Collins – had prior experience of sailing in the Arctic or Antarctic. At least three – Osmer, MacDonald and Stanley – of the six non-seamen officers had prior Arctic experience also. In contrast, when Ross and Crozier had taken the *Erebus* and the *Terror* to the Antarctic in 1839, they had sailed with only two other officers with prior polar experience – Edward Bird and Archibald McMurdo. Altogether, only 15 per cent of their officers were polar veterans, whereas Fitzjames took more than double that proportion – over 30 per cent – for the Franklin Expedition.

It also made sense that many of the remainder were former messmates of Fitzjames. On a voyage where the ships would be isolated from the outside world for a long time, personal compatibility would be extremely important. Other voyages, before and since, are known to have been riven with dissent where officers' personalities clashed. Once he had a good selection of polar Arctic veterans, Fitzjames selected officers who he knew would be compatible. And since the China war had recently ended, and many of its veterans were back in England seeking new appointments, it's hardly surprising that the non-polar officers tended to be men who had come back from China.

Similarly, a significant proportion of the men seem to have had experience in polar sailing. Their extremely diverse origins show that any allegations of anti-Irish or pro-English bias are groundless. It did not occur to Fitzjames to analyse where within the British Isles they had come from. He told Elizabeth Coningham that he thought the ship's company was predominantly Scottish, although the largest single region represented was actually Kent. This is exactly what you would expect for ships that were fitted out and provisioned on the Kentish bank of the Thames estuary.

This is not to say that Fitzjames' selections were perfect. A modern officer in his position today would recruit in a completely different way. But it is simply wrong to claim that his recruitments were poor by the standards of the time, or that they were influenced by some mythical consideration of ethnicity.

The building work on the ships, if not the provisioning, seems to have been completed towards the end of April. Fitzjames was busy showing visitors over them, including the Barrow and Beaufort families. He even tried to engineer a visit by Queen Victoria, although that never took place. On 25 April, the Lords of the Admiralty formally inspected the ships and were hosted by Franklin and Fitzjames, but not Crozier, if *The Times*' report is correct. Crozier must surely have been present the following day when the *Terror* was towed out of Woolwich Dockyard and down to Deptford for final provisioning and fitting out. It is said that during this voyage, *Terror* cast off her towline and sailed under the power of her newly fitted engine. If so, then this would be the first time that Crozier had ever commanded a steamship. *Erebus* followed on Tuesday 29 April. The *Baretto Junior* docked at Woolwich the day after to pick up the remaining provisions and then sailed for Deptford to join the other two ships.

There seem to have been teething troubles with the engines and trials continued with representatives of Maudslays, the firm which supplied them.

Steamers were assigned to the expedition – HMS *Myrtle* to tow the transport ship *Baretto Junior* and HMS *Rattler* to tow both the *Erebus* and the *Terror*.

Formal sailing orders were issued on Saturday 3 May 1845. Fitzjames now had only two weeks left in England. The same day that the engines were tested for the last time, the Admiralty commissioned 1,000 copies of the position report forms which the expedition was ordered to complete and throw overboard in sealed metal cases or to deposit under cairns. At the same time, 200 tin cases were made up and supplied to the expedition. Paragraph 19 of Franklin's instructions referred to these 'copper cylinders or bottles [which] are frequently to be thrown overboard from the *Erebus* after the latitude of 65 degrees north has been passed; each cylinder is to contain one of the forms provided for the purpose. The form is to give the date and the position of the ship.' Three of these finished position records have been recovered, all completed by Fitzjames.

On Thursday 8 May, as the work of loading supplies continued, Franklin, Crozier and Fitzjames put on their dress uniforms and made their way to the Admiralty at Somerset House. Here, as the *Naval and Military Gazette* reported on 10 May, the entire Board of the Admiralty hosted a formal dinner for the three men. Also present was a glittering array of the British Arctic aristocracy, including Sir Edward Parry, Sir James Clark Ross, Sir John Pelly, Sir George Back, Sir John Barrow, Capt Beaufort, RN and Lt-Col Sabine, RA. At dinner, Fitzjames sat between the second sea lord, Sir William Gage, and Sir Edward Parry.

Many people have speculated on what conversation must have passed between these eminent men at probably the greatest assembly of early nineteenth-century polar explorers. Strangely, one of the most popular topics of conversation was Fitzjames' no doubt amusing reminiscences of his time on the island of guano,

Ichaboe. Sir William Gage was apparently so taken by this that he chuckled all evening and even passed a note about it to the First Lord of the Admiralty, Lord Haddington, who then made a series of puns around the double meaning of 'Caesar passing the Rubicon'. It was not all scatological humour, though. Parry assured Fitzjames that his planned assault on the geographical North Pole was perfectly feasible and 'everybody said I was to do it – when we come back'. After dinner, Sir John Barrow confirmed to Fitzjames that he had persuaded the Board of the Admiralty to support his promotion to captain.

This was followed on Friday by a more public inspection of the ships by the Admiralty and 'many ladies and gentlemen'. Public interest in the expedition was huge. Fitzjames said that during the day, 'we have crowds of people looking at the ships, who quite fill the vessels'. He was not involved in all these social engagements as he was spending a lot of his time at the Greenwich observatory practising magnetic and navigational techniques.

The following Monday both ships were towed out into the river again so that their machinery could be tested, but the results were still not satisfactory. A third trial was ordered the following day and the Admiralty accepted the need for a further first-class engineer and leading stoker. Presumably this final trial was acceptable. Lieutenant Irving noted that the ships could only make 4mph and that 'our engine once ran somewhat faster on the Birmingham line [although it made] the same dreadful puffings and screamings'.

After the ships sailed for Greenhithe, Fitzjames stayed at Woolwich until his magnetic training was finished, when he joined the ships with all the magnetic instruments.

Before leaving Woolwich, he visited the SS *Great Britain*, at that time the largest ship in the world, which was being fitted out on the Thames. That same day he had what was clearly an unexpected and emotional meeting with his true half-brother Robert Fitzgerald Gambier, who was one of Sir James Gambier's three legitimate sons. Fitzjames had called on the Barrow family to say goodbye and there, completely by chance, came face to face with Fitzgerald Gambier who, with his wife, had called on the Barrows at exactly the same time. The two men recognised each other for who they really were and their relationship was warm, although it is fruitless to speculate on what might or might not have been said. Fitzjames' comment was that 'I saw Fitzgerald Gambier and his wife to both of whom I really feel much attached for I cannot but be certain of their real regard for me'. He clearly hoped to build a more open relationship with his true family.

The tempo of preparation for the expedition did not let up in the final week. At this late stage Fitzjames engaged the 'first class engineers' requested a week ago in the form of James Thompson for HMS *Terror* and John Gregory for HMS *Erebus*, together with an additional stoker. It seems astonishing to modern eyes that men could be found who would sail with the expedition at a week's notice.

The interiors of the ships had to be refitted to accommodate so many people and, in fact, the work was still being completed as the ships sailed. Franklin insisted on special wine racks being fitted and bookcases had to be installed for the 1,000 books taken.

Shortly before they sailed, Fairholme described the atmosphere aboard in a letter to his father:

> All well with the expedition and very comfortable. Lady Franklin has given us, among other presents, a capital monkey, which with old Neptune, a Newfoundland dog which is coming and one cat will be all the pets allowed. At present, Saturday night seems to be kept up in due nautical form, around my cabin, a fiddle going on as hard as it can and 2 or 3 different songs from the forecastle; in short, all seems quite happy … I do not think there is a thing which is likely to be really wanted that I have not got.

The monkey, Lady Franklin's gift to the ship, was named Jacko, despite it being female. Neptune the Newfoundland dog and the ship's cat, whose name has not been recorded, were the only other pets.

The same evening, sitting in his cabin under the portrait of William Coningham, Fitzjames wrote a final letter to the man who had made it all possible for him and who had unknowingly condemned him to a miserable icy death:

> HMS Erebus, Greenhithe, 17th May, 1845
>
> My dear Sir John Barrow,
> I cannot leave England on the most interesting Expedition that has ever left her shores, without attempting to express to you how deeply grateful I am to you for all your acts of kindness – yes and exertions to secure my advancement in the Service.
>
> Whether I obtain the rank of Captain within a short time, or on our return, is a matter of small moment as I look upon it as a matter of certainty when we do return, and on looking back I perceive that I shall have risen to the highest attainable rank solely by your exertions on my behalf.
>
> I never can forget that it is to you, I owe my first footing, when you secured me the rating of Midshipman in the St Vincent, and in the time which I never otherwise could have hoped to have secured.
>
> To your recommendation I was appointed to Sir William Parker's flagship, which procured me the Commander's step; to your great exertions I was put in command of the Clio, and here I now am in a position which besides securing my final step, places me before the world in a most honourable point of view.

Pray you will express to Lady Barrow my grateful sense of her kindness, to your glorious son John I shall say nothing, because I can say nothing that would express my full affection for him, and with kind regards to Miss Barrow. Believe me, My dear Sir,
Yours most sincerely and gratefully,
James Fitzjames

Both men would be dead in a few years and neither realised the dreadful paradox that the older man, in attempting to help the younger, had signed his death warrant.

Fitzjames' life in England had just forty-eight hours to run.

Eleven

EXODUS

On Sunday 18 May 1845, Fitzjames joined every officer and man on the *Erebus'* deck for the first of what was to become a very familiar ritual for probably the next two years. Sir John was taking divine service. Franklin took his spiritual duties very seriously indeed and his family joined the congregation. It was an impressive service. Fitzjames wrote that 'Every one was struck with his extreme earnestness of manner, evidently proceeding from real conviction'. Fairholme said that Franklin had 'the most beautiful and impressive manner I ever heard, even in a clergyman', adding, with reference to Franklin's fervent Christian conviction, that 'the service here is very different from in most ships'. As well as a morning service every Sunday, Franklin took another service at 7 p.m. for men who were on duty in the morning and 'others who may wish to attend'.

This first service was interrupted by the arrival of a letter from the Admiralty permitting Osmer to release to the men their promised four-month advance of double pay. Fitzjames wittily noted that 'the men are quite satisfied at the prompt payment of their higher pay – although they never expressed any disatisfaction but much dis-approbation'.

On Monday 21 May 1845, and just over six months after he had brought the *Clio* into Portsmouth, the expedition sailed and Fitzjames left England for the last time. The ships cleared the Thames estuary and headed north into the teeth of the rapidly deteriorating weather and contrary winds. As well as the *Erebus* and *Terror*, there was the transport ship *Baretto Junior* and two steamers used as tugs, HMS *Monkey* and HMS *Rattler*. With steam power, the ships could fight their way through the force of the gale. Sometimes HMS *Rattler* towed the *Erebus* and the *Terror* at the same time, her 220hp Maudslay engine and Smith patent screw capable of forging through very rough seas. HMS *Monkey* was not powerful enough to tow the *Baretto Junior*, so the paddle frigate *Blazer* replaced her. The *Blazer* towed the *Baretto Junior* for the rest of the journey and sometimes, when the *Rattler* was not on station, towed the *Erebus* and *Terror* alternately. Owen Stanley was one of the *Blazer's* officers. As a sartorial footnote, it was in 1845 that the captain of the *Blazer* kitted his crew out in a standardised but rudimentary uniform of blue and white striped Guernseys with blue jackets. These jackets were named after the ship, which is reputed to be the origin of the name of the modern man's blazer. History does not record whether the crew wore these novel garments while towing the *Baretto Junior*.

At Aldeburgh the squadron anchored to ride out the worst of the storm. Here Fitzjames managed to post three last cheques drawn on his newly opened account at Hoare and Co. These were posted for him by Owen Stanley, who spent so long ashore that the *Blazer* almost sailed without him. The very last of these cheques was for £4 6s 0d made out to Captain Robert Gambier, his true second cousin and the man who had entered him into the Royal Navy on HMS *Pyramus* twenty years earlier.

North of the Farne Islands the weather became too bad for towing so the ships cast off and sailed independently to rendezvous at Stromness. *Erebus* hauled close in to the coast to avoid the worst of the weather and Fitzjames would have been able to see the lights of Montrose, which Fairholme saw in the distance on the port bow. Fitzjames found *Erebus* sailed better than he had expected, although the 'two old tubs ... pitch terribly. In the gale of Aldeburgh we were like little ships in musical clocks that bob up and down in a very solid green sea.' Fitzjames was impressed by the *Rattler*'s new-fangled screw and wrote prophetically that 'our cruise ought to settle for ever the efficacy of the screw. I doubt if any paddle box boat could have towed two old tubs like us – so heavy withal – 5 knots or 4 ½ against a rough sea and strong wind as she has done till the hawsers parted. Propeller Smith [a reference to Francis Pettit Smith, the British patentee of the propeller] who is on board must be delighted.'

At dinner on Thursday, Franklin toasted Smith and said he was looking forward to benefiting from the screws fitted to *Erebus* and *Terror* in the Arctic. *Rattler* sighted *Erebus* and *Terror* off Frazerborough and again took them in tow. By then the weather had ameliorated. Lieutenant Fairholme remembered:

[it was] a perfectly calm day, [and] we had a most delightful cruise along the NE coast of Scotland ... passing John O'Groats house about 6 in the evening. I never saw anything more lovely than the scene last night, as we ran through the narrow passages among these little islands. In themselves there is nothing of the beautiful, as they are perfectly bare, but there was such a sky, and such a summit or such a glass like sea that it was quite worthy of the Gulf of Smyrna.

The ships arrived at Stromness late in the evening of Saturday 31 May. Fitzjames was in very high spirits and encouraged by the way the expedition had overcome the weather. This would be their approach, he said, '"don't care" is the order of the day. I mean don't care for difficulties or stoppages – go ahead! is the wish. We look to the result not the means of attaining it.' Fitzjames was also thinking ahead to what would happen after the expedition cleared the North West Passage.

'I hope and trust that if we get through we shall land at Petropavlovsk – and I may be allowed to come home through Siberia. I shall do all in my power to urge Sir John Franklin to let me go and I do wish the Russian government had been asked to lend their services so that they may expect me and not oppose my going on.' He was still urging John Barrow that 'it is not now too late to send to St Petersburg. It could do no harm, and might do some good.' He was confident that the expedition would succeed in its objective, 'and if we don't, I do not think it will be our fault'.

He was getting on well with Franklin. 'Sir John is delightful – active, energetic and … full of conversation and interesting anecdotes of his former voyages. I would not lose him for the command of the expedition, for I have a real regard, I might say affection, for him and I believe this is felt by all of us.' It is clear that his relationship with Crozier was cooler. Fitzjames wrote cautiously: 'I have not seen much of Crozier yet, but what I have seen I like. And I think he is just made for a second to Sir John Franklin.'

Though the expedition arrived in Stromness harbour on Saturday evening, they stayed until Tuesday 3 June, much longer than planned. They had only stopped to replenish the water tanks of the *Baretto Junior*, replace the cattle that had been killed by the storm and offload passengers who had travelled on the exploration ships. Fitzjames was amused to record that the delay was caused by the God-fearing people of Stromness who, as they considered Saturday evening to be the Sabbath, would not trade cattle then and made the expedition wait until Monday.

Everyone knew Stromness would be their last sight of British soil for some time – in reality, of course, forever – and in their different ways they tried to make the most of it. They received mail and the news. The officers were keenly interested in the write-up of the expedition in the 24 May edition of the *Illustrated London News*, but Fairholme said the sketch of Fitzjames' cabin was 'very bad and [did] … not give any idea of the cabins' (see plate 29).

Officers off duty were free to go ashore, but the men were not because of their propensity to get drunk and desert. Crozier would not allow any of the men of HMS *Terror* off the ship. On *Erebus*, two men, 27-year-old Captain of the Foretop, Robert Sinclair, and 41-year-old Able Seaman Thomas Work, who both came from Orkney, approached Fitzjames. He wrote that 'two men wanted to see – one his wife whom he had not seen for four years, and the other his mother, whom he had not seen for seventeen – so I let them go to Kirkwall, fourteen miles off'. As Fitzjames had presumably not seen his mother for much longer, this must have touched his heartstrings.

He also allowed one man from each mess of the *Erebus* to go ashore to purchase fresh provisions. All came back to the ships as ordered. Then, although the ships were ready to sail, unfavourable winds delayed them in harbour overnight until Tuesday, so:

finding we were not going to sea till the following morning, four men (who probably had taken a leetle too much whiskey, among them was the little old man who had not seen his wife for four years) took a small boat that lay along-side and went on shore without leave. Their absence was soon discovered, and Fairholme, assisted by Baillie, and somebody or other, brought all on board by three o'clock in the morning. I firmly believe each intended coming on board (if he had been sober enough), especially the poor man with the wife – but, according to the rules of the service, these men should have been severely punished – one method being to stop their pay and give it to the constables, or others, who apprehended them. It struck me, however, that the punishment is intended to prevent misconduct in others, and not to revenge their individual misconduct – men know very well when they are in the wrong – and there is clearly no chance of any repetition of the offence until we get to Valparaiso, or the Sandwich Islands; so I got up at four o'clock, had everybody on deck, sent Gore and the Sergeant of Marines below, and searched the whole deck for spir-its, which were thrown overboard. This took two good hours; soon after which we up anchor, and made sail out. I said nothing to any of them. They evidently expected a rowing, and the old man with the wife looked very sheepish, and would not look me in the face; but nothing more was said, and the men have behaved not a bit the worse ever since.

This incident is interesting because of the light it sheds on the differences between Fitzjames and Crozier's attitude to indiscipline. To us Fitzjames' response seems a sensitive example of good leadership. Crozier simply thought *Erebus* was a 'slack' ship and in a letter to Ross he contrasted the disciplined way he ran the *Terror* with the more relaxed approach of the flagship.

The ships sailed on the morning of Tuesday 3 June 1845 for the Whale Fish Islands in Disko Bay, on the west coast of Greenland, where the supplies carried by the *Baretto Junior* would be transhipped to the *Erebus* and *Terror*. On 7 June, near the island of Rona 60 miles north-west of the Orkneys, the *Erebus*, *Terror* and *Baretto Junior* parted from the steamers (see plate 30).

[This was] a most exhilarating scene … which will doubtlessly remain in the memory of all that had the gratification of participating in the farewell cheer to the brave fellows that have volunteered in so laudable and perilous a service. At this time the Erebus and Terror, and Baretto Junior, transport, were hove-to, rolling heavily from the violent swell that the recent gales had produced; a signal flying from the mast-head of the Erebus indicated Sir J. Franklin's order for all Captains to proceed on board to receive their final instructions; this order having been completed, their return to their respective ships was the time chosen for manning the rigging of the two steamers in attendance. At the sound of the boatswain's pipe, the shrouds of the Rattler and Blazer were in one

instant lined by their crews, all anxious to out vie each other in the pleasing task
they were about to perform. The word was given, and three cheers, loud and
hearty as ever escaped the lungs of British tars, saluted the ears of Sir J. Franklin
and his gallant colleagues; in turn the crews of the discovery ships manned their
rigging, and with their respective commanders and officers on the quarter-deck
gave vent to cheers so long and powerful as to leave not the slightest doubt of
the physical energies of the men they came from, and their consequent fitness
to encounter the difficulties that may shortly surround them.

This moving scene was recorded in several sketches by Owen Stanley.

One man, Able Seaman John Brown of HMS *Terror*, was returned to London
on board HMS *Rattler*. It is possible the surgeons diagnosed tuberculosis during
the passage up the North Sea. They were certainly looking out for tuberculosis
and it was under active discussion. Fairholme wrote that 'the Doctor', presumably
Stephen Stanley, joked that 'Jacko [the *Erebus*' pet monkey] is in a rapid consumption'. He said that 'he certainly has a very bad cough, but the only other
symptom I see of it, is the rapid consumption of everything eatable he can lay his
paws on'.

The three sailing ships pushed out into the teeth of an Atlantic gale. The wind,
which had been fair, strengthened and veered to the north-west, with the sky
clear and the air 'fresh and bracing'. On Friday 3 June, Franklin assembled his
officers in his cabin and read out part of his orders to them. Fitzjames recalled:

> Sir John Franklin showed me such part of his instructions as related to the main
> purposes of our voyage, and the necessity of observing everything from a flea to
> a whale in the unknown regions we are to visit. He also told me I was especially
> charged with the magnetic observations. He then told all the officers that he
> was desired to claim all their remarks, Journals, sketches, etc., on our return to
> England, and read us some part of his instructions to the officers of the Trent, the
> first vessel he commanded, in 1818, with Captain Buchan, on an attempt to reach
> the North Pole, pointing out how desirable it is to note everything, and give
> one's individual opinion on it. He spoke delightfully of the zealous co-operation
> he expected from all, and his desire to do full justice to the exertions of each.

Fitzjames took care that the dispatches he sent back to Elizabeth Coningham
were strictly letters and not a journal, although they read very much as though
they were written with an eye to publication. If he succeeded in returning to
London via Russia before the ships these letters, combined with the journal of
his journey across Russia, would ensure him bestseller status. No wonder he
noted the rules so carefully.

Crozier was especially unimpressed by Clause 14 of Franklin's orders, which
read 'we have deemed it proper to request Lieut.-Colonel Sabine to allow

Commander Fitzjames to profit by his valuable instructions, and we direct you, therefore, to place this important branch of science [magnetic research] under the immediate charge of Commander Fitzjames'. Crozier, elected a Fellow of the Royal Society in 1843 for his earlier work in the field of magnetism, bridled and wrote to his close friend Sir James Clark Ross that 'I find by the instructions that Fitzjames is appointed to superintend the Mag. observations. I will therefore take just so much bother as may amuse, without considering myself as one of the Staff.' This incident again points to the difficult relationship between Fitzjames and Crozier.

On 8 June the wind direction changed to due aft and the ships took full advantage of it. *Erebus* led the little squadron with the *Baretto Junior* close by and *Terror* following some way aft. The mate of the *Baretto Junior* said that he had never seen ships carrying so much canvas under such conditions as *Erebus* and *Terror* were, yet Lieutenant Griffiths struggled to prevent his much faster ship *Baretto Junior* from outrunning them, despite carrying very little sail. The following Sunday, Franklin read his third sermon to the officers and ship's company of *Erebus*, which must have taken place on the lower deck, given the poor weather. Fitzjames commented: 'Sir John Franklin read the church service to-day and a sermon so very beautifully, that I defy any man not to feel the force of what he would convey.' Later, the officers worried that the strong winds would drive the ships straight into dangerous ice. Reid, the ice master aboard *Erebus*, assured Fitzjames that this was not a risk, saying:

'Ah! now, Mister Jems, we'll be having the weather fine, sir! Fine! No ice at arl about it, sir, unless it be the bergs – arl the ice'll be gone, sir, only the bergs, which I like to see. Let it come on to blow, look out for a big 'un. Get under his lee, and hold on to him fast, sir, fast. If he drifts near the land, why, he grounds afore you do.'

In the evening Fitzjames played Osmer at chess and Osmer won.

By now the officers and men had settled down in relative harmony in their tight wooden worlds. Fairholme described:

how comfortable we all were in this ship … We all now know each other probably as well as we ever shall and I really think there could hardly have been selected a set more likely to get on together. Sir John is a new man since we left. He has quite recovered from his severe cold, looks 10 years younger, and takes part in everything that goes on with as much interest as if he had not grown older since his first Expedition. We are all delighted to find how decided he is on all he resolves on, and he has such experience and judgement that we all look on his decisions, with the greatest respect. I never felt that the Captain was so much my companion with anyone I have sailed with before. He has certainly made a friend of every person on board, and I believe not a thing he has said or done has given rise to the slightest complaint.

Fitzjames is, as ever, a fine fellow. His time is principally devoted to magnetic observations. Gore does all the duties of 1st Lieut. Sir John still continues to receive three of us at dinner every day, and to dine with us on Sundays, and instead of the formal parties these are in most ships, one really looks forward with the greatest pleasure to meeting him.

Crozier's tart observation of Franklin's generosity with his table was very different. He wrote: 'I cannot bear going on board Erebus – Sir John is very kind and would have me there dining every day if I would go – he has Fitzjames and two officers every day.' Perhaps wisely, Crozier thought better of what he wrote next and inked out his next sentence. Franklin seems not to have noticed the tension between his two senior officers and ascribed Crozier's reluctance to socialise purely to the bad weather. At this point in the crossing, Fitzjames thought that Franklin was taking risks by insisting on sailing with too much canvas. The other officers agreed and during the night, while Franklin slept, Fitzjames turned out to order the *Erebus'* topsails reefed. The ships pitched severely. While the bullocks on *Baretto Junior*, already earmarked for slaughter, suffered terribly in their dark stalls on the pitching and rolling ship, Neptune, Jacko and the anonymous cat on *Erebus* fared better. Fairholme noticed that:

> Old Nep has lost much of his unwieldiness since we left and now runs up and down our stepladders with ease. He is the most loveable dog I ever knew and is a general favourite … The monkey continues to be the annoyance and pest of the whole ship, and yet not a person in here would hurt him for the whole world. He is a dreadful thief but such a very amusing one that his robberies bring very little sympathy for the unfortunate losers!

By the morning of 10 June, the weather had moderated with a mild wind and relatively smooth sea. Goodsir took the opportunity to net some molluscs and plankton. He drew the molluscs using his microscope and explained the significance of the plankton to the other officers. Fitzjames described them as 'blubber-like stuff, which … turns out to be whales' food and other animals'.

Franklin never had anything but praise for Fitzjames. One guesses that the ponderous and pious Franklin tried Fitzjames' patience, and he sometimes makes oblique references to Franklin's wordiness. Franklin talked a great deal about the injustices he felt he had suffered while Governor of Van Diemen's Land and he was flattered that Fitzjames asked to read the proofs of the polemic of self-justification which Franklin had written. Franklin saw himself as a father figure to Fitzjames and the other officers.

On Wednesday 11 June the weather worsened again. Fitzjames noted:

All ... day it blew very hard, with so much sea that we shipped one or two over the quarter-deck, by which I got a good drenching once. The sea is of the most perfect transparency – a beautiful, delicate, cold-looking green, or ultramarine. Long rollers, as if carved out of the essence of glass bottles, came rolling towards us; now and then topped with a beautiful pot-of-porter-looking head. At sunset the wind moderated, and was calm at night.

The following day the ships found themselves south of Iceland. For much of the day it was foggy, although this cleared later in the afternoon as the northerly wind strengthened. The ships made good progress with the favourable wind, but in the heavy Atlantic rollers the ships pitched badly. Not for nothing had Owen Stanley nicknamed them 'our friend and pitcher'.

In variable conditions over the next few days, officers and men became increasingly proficient in handling their ungainly ships. By Saturday 14 June, the ships were averaging 7¼ knots under sail in thick fog, with *Erebus* leading and *Terror* and *Baretto Junior* tucked close in either side of the flagship. With a strong and favourable wind, and carrying a lot of sail, the little squadron even worked up to 9 knots. That day, Fitzjames dined with Franklin, Reid the ice master and Osmer the purser. Fitzjames was the only unmarried man and was possibly piqued when Reid and Osmer pressed him to join them in the traditional Royal Naval toast 'Wives and Sweethearts', to which the reply is 'may they never meet'. Fitzjames riposted that 'I had not one and did not want the other'.

On Monday the sea was calm enough for officers of the two ships to visit each other. Fitzjames was rowed over to the *Terror* to talk to Crozier about his magnetic observations. Neither man left any record of the conversation. Fairholme and Le Vesconte experimented with the expedition's collapsible Halcott boat, as Fitzjames described it. Fairholme crossed to HMS *Terror*

on a calm day, about half way across [the Atlantic] in Peter Halkett's boat when the *Terror* was ¼ a mile from us and Le Visconte [sic] went with me and it carried us capitally. It holds just 3, and we got a board the *Terror*, paid our visit and got back again without the least wet or discomfort, altho we were of course sitting much below the level of the sea. The exertion of paddling is rather severe or rather it was so then from neither of us having had much practice lately.

That evening, Crozier and Little of the *Terror* and Griffiths from the *Baretto Junior* dined on board HMS *Erebus* with Fitzjames and Franklin.

By Tuesday 17 June, the sun was shining and the weather smooth. In the higher latitudes they were now sailing in the chill became more noticeable and the first signs of ice appeared. As night fell, a bright light could be seen reflected against the cloud to the north-east, which Fitzjames described as being 'like a large town on fire, twenty miles off'. He thought it might be caused by a strong sunset, while

Lieutenant Gore suggested instead that this strange light could be the Aurora Borealis. Reid, the ice master, knew better. He recognised this as 'ice-blink', caused by the reflection of sunlight off far-distant sea or land ice. Here was the first sight of the ice which would trap the ships and all aboard.

That evening was the thirtieth anniversary of the Battle of Waterloo and Franklin hosted a celebratory dinner. They toasted the Duke of Wellington, who was still very much alive at that time, and Fitzjames seems to have reflected on what he had left behind in England. He wrote to William Coningham that he had hoped his promotion to captain might have been made on that day and that he 'took a glass of brandy-and-water at ten o'clock, which allowing for difference of longitude, answers to half-past seven in London, and drank your health ...' While lost in these introspective thoughts, Reid the ice master challenged him, asking in his broad Scottish accent: 'Why, mister Jems, you never seem to me to sleep at arl; you're always writin!' Fitzjames responded by saying that when he *did* sleep, he slept twice as soundly as other people.

The next few days continued in similar vein: variable weather, the temperature steadily dropping and more ice blink in the sky. Franklin was by now worrying Fitzjames with his recklessness, which other officers noted too. Fitzjames wrote that 'I can scarcely get Sir John to shorten sail'.

Approaching the dangerous waters around Cape Farewell, the ominously named southern tip of Greenland, the temperature dropped further: another sign they were approaching the ice. On Saturday 21st June there was another heavy north-easterly gale which blew for three days. The weather did not depress Franklin, who at dinner regaled his officers with what Fitzjames described as 'most amusing anecdotes' from his first, disastrous expedition. On Sunday it was clear the days of open-air church services were over. Fitzjames wrote that 'we struggled through the church service on the lower deck, the ships rolling and tumbling much'. And on Monday 23 June, Fitzjames saw 'the highest sea I ever saw ... we had a few seas on our decks, one of which found its way down on to our table, just as we had done dinner. I dined at our mess to-day; Sir John finding his guests could not hold on and eat too. We are packed close, and can't move very far. But the good humour of every one is perfect; and we do dance before it so finely – I mean before the wind. It rained hard all yesterday and all night.'

This gale carried them right round the southern tip of Greenland and into the southern Davis Strait. The other officers certainly did not share Franklin's reck-lessness. In these very dangerous waters, not far from where the *Titanic* now lies broken in two on the seabed, officers of both ships immediately perceived that they had the potential to run into serious danger very quickly, just as the *Titanic* would sixty-five years later. Fairholme related how, as the gale continued to blow on Monday, 'we had rather an anxious time for there was a dense and continuous haze which scarcely even allowed of our seeing more than a mile ahead, and as we had expected to come on the ice long before, we never knew how soon a berg might be seen close to us. This obliged us to keep such a look out as I have never kept before, or than is generally necessary when running for land of which the position is well known.'

This passage should put to rest once and for all any doubts as to the competence of the companies of the *Erebus* and *Terror* as seamen. Although often accused of being inexperienced in Arctic navigation, Fitzjames and the other officers had immediately recognised the potential for danger and put in place a strategy to ensure they were protected against it. The contrast with Captain Smith and the officers of the *Titanic*, whose reaction to similar conditions in these waters was so ineffectual, is stark.

By Tuesday 24 June, the gale had passed. The ships were steering due north 90 miles west of Cape Farewell and closing with the Arctic Circle. Fitzjames had never crossed north of the Arctic Circle before and once he did, he was destined never to pass south of it again. By now, even at 10.30 p.m., the ships were still in broad daylight. The officers noted that the sea temperature was now dropping as well as the air temperature, and the men were aware of how cold it was getting. They marked it by secretly sewing a set of clothes, described as 'a blanket, frock, and trousers', for Jacko the monkey, who suddenly appeared on deck fully clothed.

On Wednesday 25 June visibility improved and the coast of Greenland could be seen 40 miles to the east. Simultaneously, they spotted their first iceberg 6–8 miles away. The sea was so perfectly calm that, said Fitzjames, 'the *Terror*'s mastheads are reflected close alongside, though she is half a mile off'. Morale was high. The ice masters and other polar veterans regaled their less experienced shipmates with stories of what they could expect. Fitzjames started his regular magnetic observations while Goodsir continued energetically 'catching the most extraordinary animals in a net, and is in ecstasies. Gore and des Voeux are over the side poking with nets and long poles, with cigars in their mouths, and Osmar [sic] is laughing; he is really an original, and a delightfully dry fellow.' Osmer and Fitzjames were becoming friends.

On Thursday 26 June, Crozier and Hodgson were rowed over from HMS *Terror* for dinner with Franklin and Fitzjames on board *Erebus*. Fitzjames thought Hodgson was 'looking very ill'.

Fitzjames noted a new scientific discovery: 'To-day has been hot and calm and delightful; got bottom in forty fathoms, and pulled up starfish and shells and strange beasts, and, what is better, pulled up plenty of codfish, enough for a good feed or two for all hands.' Fairholme added: 'These fish seem to be almost as numerous here as on the banks of Newfoundland, a fact scarcely known though we met with an Aberdeen brig out on a speculation for them and the salmon fishery inshore.' Wisely conserving their stores of food, the officers ordered nets to be put out and the two ships landed a substantial haul of cod. For several days the two ships' companies feasted on fresh fish. The captain of the brig which Fairholme referred to was exploring the potential of the cod fishery which the *Erebus* and

Terror had found, and also the potential of the fjords of Greenland for salmon. Fitzjames invited the captain on board and found that he came from Orkney. By a strange quirk of fate, he was a friend and former shipmate of Thomas Work, one of the men who had absented themselves without leave back at Stromness.

On 29 June, officers from *Erebus* were entertained to dinner on board *Terror*. Fitzjames noted that the illness which had afflicted Hodgson had passed and he appeared to be fit again. Sailing up the Davis Strait, a new chore defined itself. Clause 19 of Franklin's instructions tasked the expedition with completing and dropping overboard position report sheets. His instructions told him that 'after you have passed the latitude of 65 degrees north, and once every day when you shall be in an ascertained current, throw overboard a bottle or copper cylinder closely sealed, and containing a paper stating the date and position at which it is launched'. This latitude having been passed, Fitzjames prepared one of the sheets on HMS *Erebus*, probably at noon when the sun was sighted to confirm the position of the ships. He entered the name of the ship, its latitude, longitude and location and took it to Franklin, who signed it as captain. It was then placed in a specially made copper cylinder, which was sealed with solder by William Smith, the *Erebus'* blacksmith, and thrown over the side. The only report sheet that has ever been retrieved from the sea was the one Fitzjames completed and Franklin signed on 30 June 1845.

The three ships were now approaching the anchorage at Disko Bay, where the *Erebus* and *Terror* would take on the stores loaded on the *Baretto Junior* and the little squadron would separate. The Whale Fish Islands in Disko Bay were spotted overnight on 1–2 July, but, as Fairholme explained, getting to them involved

> threading our way through hundreds of icebergs, some of immense size. While passing near one of these, which I had just remarked was about the size of the North Foreland, it suddenly fell to pieces with an awful crash, sending the spray up to a great height, and leaving a field of sharp and broken ice. We saw many of them turn over, and indeed, in this weather, when the rain and sun are melting them fast, it is not safe to go near them.

Not reaching the islands in time before evening, the three ships stood off in safer waters overnight before trying to reach the anchorage again.

Setting sail the next morning, there was a mistake. *Erebus* led the little convoy from their overnight anchorage towards where they had seen the Whale Fish Islands the previous day, but Reid the ice master believed that their correct course lay to the north. Franklin and Fitzjames deferred to his experience despite some doubts, so the three ships headed in the wrong direction. Only by midday, when they had sailed right into Disko Bay, did Reid realise his initial error. Following in *Terror*, Crozier had realised that *Erebus* was sailing in the wrong direction, but he did not signal this to *Erebus*. Instead, he and Griffiths in the *Baretto Junior* simply followed the flagship. Fitzjames was severely embarrassed. And when they finally arrived at what they thought was the correct anchorage, none of them could make it out with certainty. So Le Vesconte was rowed out in *Erebus'* gig to reconnoitre. His gig was met by five Inuit, paddling kayaks which seemed very small to the sailors, and two of the Inuit kayaks piloted first *Erebus*, and then the other two ships, to their anchorages. Their anchorage was in a narrow channel just four times the ship's breadth, and perfectly landlocked. The nearby settlement was tiny. Fairholme described it as 'two or three small houses on a low point immediately under the high land. It certainly does not look inviting for winter quarters.'

That evening, with the ships safely at anchor, Fitzjames went on board *Terror* and seems to have challenged Crozier about the confusion over the location of the anchorage. Crozier disingenuously claimed that he had thought Franklin and Fitzjames had decided to anchor somewhere else, although that is not what he said in a private letter to Ross. The episode embarrassed Fitzjames, Franklin and Reid and cannot have improved the respect the officers on *Erebus* had for Reid, their uncouth north-country ice master. Nor can it have improved the relationship between Fitzjames and Crozier. It looks rather as though Crozier had been willing to let the expedition waste almost a whole day in order to score a point over Franklin and Fitzjames. But as far as we can tell, the matter ended there and nothing further was said.

With all three ships moored, the work of transhipping the *Baretto Junior's* stores onto the *Erebus* and *Terror* started. This took six full days' work, the men working a fourteen-hour day. The problem was less the physical effort involved and more in finding stowage on *Erebus* and *Terror* for the sheer quantities involved (see plate 31).

While the men continued this work, the scientific research programme progressed. The prefabricated wooden houses which had been especially designed for the very sensitive magnetic and gravitational instruments were unshipped and foundations for them prepared ashore on a small island. Fitzjames selected Fairholme and Le Vesconte to help him with this work. On Saturday morning, less than twenty-four hours after arriving, Fairholme and Fitzjames were taking regular readings of magnetic strength, dip and variation. Fitzjames dryly noted: 'very large mosquitos biting us'. It was just a year since Fitzjames and Le Vesconte had been riding the white henna-tinted donkeys in the blinding heat of Bahrain.

The following day, Sunday, was a day of rest so the work of transhipping stopped. Franklin took the service in the morning. Le Vesconte and Fitzjames were ashore at 6 a.m. engaged in surveying. The men were allowed ashore as well and enjoyed the fine sunny weather, as well as the opportunity to forage for fresh food, especially eider duck and their eggs. Attendance at Franklin's evening service must have been large that day.

On Monday, the backbreaking work of transhipping stores started at 4 a.m. and went on until 6 p.m. By Wednesday 9 July, Crozier was worried about the risk of

overloading the ships. Lieutenant Griffiths of the *Baretto Junior* said that when all
the boats were hauled back onto *Erebus* and the anchors weighed, the ship actually drew 17ft of water. Fitzjames commented: 'we are now full – very – having 3
years' provisions and coals, besides the engine. The deck is covered with coals and
casks, leaving a small passage fore and aft, and we are very deep in the water.'

Goodsir and Fairholme visited the Inuit settlement, where Goodsir spent
several hours putting together a dictionary which the expedition could use to
communicate with the Inuit people it encountered on the voyage through the
North West Passage. During the day, Fairholme, Fitzjames and Le Vesconte took
regular readings at the observatory from 6 a.m. until 4–5 p.m.

Fitzjames and the others were intrigued by the Inuit kayaks. The Inuit let them
try out the kayaks, but this was not without incident. Fairholme found that the
'canoes are so small that had I seen one on shore I should have thought it was a
model, but having succeeded so well with Halkett's boat, I was determined to try
this also'. Fairholme was a large man and could not get into one, so he inserted
one beefy leg into each kayak and paddled around in two. Although well-built,
Fitzjames was smaller than Fairholme and more lithe. He managed to squeeze
into the kayak by taking off his trousers, and 'paddled about for some time' in
the bay. Any canoeist will know that with ambition comes the risk of overturn-
ing the canoe and sure enough, 'at last over I went head downwards where I
remained until rescued'.

On Thursday 10 July, with all the provisions transhipped, Lieutenant Griffiths
dined on board HMS *Erebus* as Franklin's guest, while the officers tested the quality of the tinned foods. Griffiths recalled 'partaking at the officers' table of some
of the meats which had been opened for trial, as also some of the vegetables. The
carrots really were as good as if just removed from the ground; the potatoes also
were good and sweet, but certainly with little flavour of the potato.'

The ships, especially the smaller and older *Terror*, had not been able to pack in
everything the *Baretto Junior* had brought and Lieutenant Griffiths reported that
'we brought Home 2 Bower Anchors, 2 Chain Cables, 1 Boat, 2 Hawsers, some
casks of Rum, Beef and Pork, Coals and various Return Stores not required'.
Last letters were written and sewn into mailbags to be taken back to Britain.
Franklin, Fitzjames and Crozier all speculated on their next step, uncertain how
best to cross the ice-choked Davis Strait and push west into the Lancaster Sound.
The ice conditions would be, Fitzjames said, 'a lottery'. The magnetic and other
instruments were packed up and the ships 'swung' so that their compasses could
be used.

Before leaving, four further crew members were discharged and sent back to
Britain on board the *Baretto Junior*. We do not know why. Crozier said that 'two
were ill and two completely useless', although Griffiths described all four men
as 'invalided'. This meant that *Erebus* was down to sixty-seven men and *Terror*
sixty-two, against their establishments of seventy and sixty-nine respectively. The

Terror sailed short of three able seamen, its armourer, its sail-maker and one of its mates. Griffiths thought the *Terror* appeared undermanned and asked Crozier if he would like him to 'volunteer' two of the *Baretto Junior's* company to replace those the *Terror* was losing. Crozier was more concerned about running short of provisions than manpower and replied: 'No, my good fellow; I would rather have their provisions than their company; we shall be very well manned without them.'

Fitzjames wrote his last letter to survive to John Barrow junior on 11 July 1845. It was hurried and optimistic and included this passage:

> And now you have us as far as Disko, and by the time you get this we shall I trust be well into our work – where we may be God knows. Give my kindest regards to Sir John and Lady Barrow. We intend to drink Sir John's health on the day we go through Behring's Straits. If we get through this season we shall have to land somewhere or other to discharge our cargo – for it will not be safe to go into the Pacific laden as we are.

On Saturday 12 July, Franklin hosted a final dinner for Lieutenant Griffiths on board the *Erebus*. They ate 'some beef ... of excellent quality, which Mr Osmer, the paymaster and purser, told me had been expressly cured for them'. Sitting opposite Osmer, Griffiths asked him for his opinion on the quality of the provisions. Osmer described them as 'very good indeed', adding that 'I should like you to tell Mr Meek [the then comptroller of victualling] when you get home'. Griffiths says that this request 'elicited an expression of satisfaction from the officers at mess, that they were, in the opinion of their purser, so well supplied'.

Not all the officers were content with the stowage of their stores. Officers took substantial stores of their own, as well as animals for fresh food, on the initial stages of the voyage. Crozier recounted an unhappy event to Ross. He was smarting from the absence of some of the stores which he had bought, and wrote that 'my sugar and tea have not made their appearance. The sugar is a great loss to me but the tea I can not forgive. I cannot at all accounts say much for Fortnum and Masons punctuality – they directed my things to Captain Fitzjames' *Terror* but by some strange accident they discovered my name sufficiently accurately to send me the Bill and I was fool enough to pay it from their declaring that the things were absolutely delivered on board.'

One hopes that Crozier saw the funny side of this confusion between the two officers and that Fitzjames returned Crozier's stores before the ships sailed. Lieutenant Griffiths reported that as well as the official provisions, the officers also carried at least six dozen hens, some pigs and a few sheep. Despite embarking a dozen heifers in Greenhithe, and making their numbers up again at Stromness after the depredations of the storm in the North Sea, it seems that the Atlantic crossing killed seven head of cattle. The crew of the *Baretto Junior* 'killed three bullocks two days before leaving, and I think each ship had three or four quarters of beef hung up to their mainstay for the express purpose, as Sir John Franklin himself told me, to be kept for their forthcoming Christmas entertainment'. Unfortunately, the weather was so warm that the beef started to deteriorate, so when Lieutenant Griffiths departed he saw the crews of the *Erebus* and *Terror* starting to eat into the meat they had hoped to keep for Christmas.

Rising from dinner in Franklin's cabin on Saturday 12 July, Lieutenant Griffiths returned to the *Baretto Junior* and sailed for Britain that afternoon with a heavy heart. He regretted not being part of the expedition himself. He had developed a huge affection for the officers and men on the *Erebus* and *Terror*, writing that he 'felt quite low spirited at leaving Sir John and his officers', and saying that 'finer fellows never breathed'.

The *Baretto Junior* arrived back at Deptford on 11 August 1845, by which time the *Erebus* and *Terror* were well on their way into the Lancaster Sound. HMS *Erebus* and *Terror* raised anchor on the morning of Sunday 13 July, presumably after morning service, and followed the *Baretto Junior* out from Disko Bay. As the *Baretto Junior* sailed back south along the Greenland coastline, the *Erebus* and *Terror* started to thread their way north through the pack ice of the Davis Strait, hugging the coast until they could reach the Lancaster Sound and the North West Passage.

A week later, the ships were probably sighted by Captain Stratton of the whaler *Eagle* on Saturday 19 July at 72° 45' North, 58° West, sailing in a westerly direction. They were definitely sighted on Friday 25 July, moored alongside an iceberg in the eastern part of Baffin Bay at 75° 12' N, 61° 6' W. Here they were joined by the whalers *Prince of Wales*, commanded by Captain Dannet, and *Enterprise*, commanded by Captain Martin. All four ships were awaiting the break-up of the ice so they could proceed on their different missions. The *Enterprise* closed with the *Erebus* and Captain Martin hailed Sir John Franklin and Ice Master James Reid. The three men held a shouted conversation from the decks of their respective ships. Probably on Saturday 26 July (or possibly 28 July), several of *Erebus*' officers came on board the *Enterprise* and met Captain Martin. They were in high spirits. Captain Martin was invited to dinner with Franklin on *Erebus* the following day, but he had to decline as the ice was starting to break up and the time when the ships would part was fast approaching. On 26 July, Captain Dannet of the *Prince of Wales* had been visited by ten officers from the expedition, one of whom he thought was James Fitzjames. Like Captain Martin, Captain Dannet was invited to dinner on the *Erebus*, but declined as he had decided to sail. Visibility was excellent and Captain Martin believed he could still just make out the tips of the masts of the *Erebus* and *Terror* on the horizon until either 29 or 31 July 1845. After that the ships disappeared.

And that was the last the outside world ever saw of Commander James Fitzjames.

Twelve

AFTER LIFE

Fifteen years later, on 2 March 1860, the 45-year-old Liberal MP for Brighton addressed the House of Commons:

> May I remind the noble Viscount [Sir Francis Baring, bart.] that Sir John Franklin had gone forth on no volunteer expedition; he was called on by his country to undertake the expedition in which he lost his life; and it was because the Government had not taken the proper measures to search for him and his gallant companions – because they had not adequately fulfilled their duties – that Lady Franklin had sacrificed almost her entire private resources. The search hitherto made had been chiefly conducted by sea, and I was told by Dr Rae, no mean authority on questions of this kind, that the only real and effectual search for the remains and journals of the officers engaged in the expedition would be by land and during summer; and there would be no danger whatever, he understood, in such an expedition. The only danger would be if the expedition were compelled to pass the winter in those desert regions. Not only those who were interested in Polar discovery, but the great bulk of this nation and the civilized world were interested in obtaining all the information that could be collected as to the fate and history of Sir John Franklin's expedition; and I really think the Government would be wanting in their duty to the relatives and memory of those whom they had sent out on such dangerous adventures if they did not take steps to recover what traces they could of their history and endurance.

William Coningham MP might have been a controversial eccentric, but he was no fool. Coningham made this statement during a debate on the Franklin Expedition. It was said that he had tried to dissuade Fitzjames from going and this statement shows that, too late, he understood exactly what risks Fitzjames had taken. Rae had told him that the Arctic was accessible to small, well-trained parties travelling light and living Inuit-style on the land, but sending two large ships with massive crews had been very foolhardy. He now knew that Fitzjames had been trapped and had died on an unnecessary venture.

William's bitterness shines through every word. After Fitzjames left, William had amassed the country's largest collection of Italian great masters at his private gallery in Porchester Terrace, Bayswater. He became heavily involved in the National Gallery. But he does not seem to have derived any lasting happiness from this. He engaged in bitter rows over the management, or, as he saw it, mismanagement, of the National Gallery and the Royal Academy. Whether the argument was over the location of the gallery, the collections it should hold or the cleaning of old masters, his aggressive approach never helped his case. He was extremely critical of Turner. At one point he argued that the National Gallery's sole motive in cleaning his beloved 'Old Masters' was to make them look worse in comparison with what he called 'Turner's chalky absurdities'. The wealth that gave him freedom also freed him from intellectual and emotional constraint.

Then, on 9 June 1849, he abruptly announced to an astonished London that he was selling his entire collection. He never gave a reason for this, never visited his gallery and never even saw his collection in the sale room. A door into what had been a major part of his life had simply slammed shut. Was it a coincidence that by then, mid-1849, the Franklin Expedition was twelve months overdue? William must have realised that this time James Fitzjames would not be coming back.

Coningham became more politically active and aligned himself with the views from which socialism would emerge. He developed a very strong antipathy towards the ruling class. The most extreme example of this came in 1851. In a staggering display, and while rowing with the elements in the arts world he despised, he privately circulated a political pamphlet so shocking that it was suppressed. In it he accused Prince Albert of unconstitutional interference in British politics and of engineering the dismissal of Lord Palmerston as part of a coup on behalf of mysterious German royal interests. He withdrew the pamphlet and events soon demonstrated that it was completely misjudged. But it was not the work of a happy man or a level mind. His instability must have been enhanced by his complete loss of religious faith – he was an avowed atheist – and the contradiction that much of his immense wealth was derived from slavery.

Coningham argued every position he took forcefully, although no doubt with impeccable manners and without raising his voice. His wealth meant that when he wrote he had no need for publishers; he simply produced his material privately. Some of his positions look principled now, like his hatred of slavery, while others seemed crazy then and still do today, like his opposition to public inoculation against disease. As an MP for Brighton, he had a platform from which he could argue his views. When he clashed with the Royal Naval authorities, he found himself being contradicted by Captain Lord Clarence Paget MP, who, nearly thirty years before, had been one of the 'pullers', along with Fitzjames, who had rowed King Otto ashore at Nauplia.

Death stalked William Coningham. His parents died young and two years after his election to the House of Commons his beloved daughter Elizabeth, Fitzjames' goddaughter, died at the age of 17. This must have been a devastating blow. He resigned his seat in 1863, forcing a by-election, and gave up his political career at the age of 48. His health collapsed. In 1877 his wife Elizabeth wrote 'how shattered his health and spirits have become, and how (to see if it would do him any good) we have wandered, from one place to another; and with no cheering result'. When he died in 1881, it was said that he had been ill for twenty-five years. He was survived by his son William, his wife Elizabeth and her elder sister, the 81-year-old unmarried Hester Meyrick. With their deaths, many of the connections to James Fitzjames died also. Only a few years after that the Markhams were able to claim that Elizabeth Meyrick and James Fitzjames had been sister and brother. No one contradicted them.

Coningham published two separate collections of letters privately. Both were from men he greatly loved and admired, and both had died young. One was the ascetic writer and thinker John Sterling, and the other was the dashing, laughing seaman and now explorer James Fitzjames.

In 1969 the National Maritime Museum received a bequest from an old lady called Mrs Ronnie Wathen. It was the magnificent cup awarded to James Fitzjames for saving the life of James Dickinson, the man who had fallen into the Mersey 135 years before. She had been a widow since 1957 when her husband of forty-five years, Major Ronnie Wathen, had died. Her maiden name had been Hester Coningham and she was William Coningham's granddaughter. With the bequest came a single volume of James Fitzjames' journal covering his life from February 1833 to October 1834, and inside the front cover someone had written:

Cloaths are left in James' drawers
11 calico shirts
3 Irish do
6 white pt headscarfs
7 pair short stockings

The people who had moved in Fitzjames' circle met wildly different fates. He had tried to take two young friends with him on the Franklin Expedition: D'Arcy Wynyard and John Commerell. Sir Clements Markham related Wynyard's peculiar fate. Markham knew Wynyard and said he 'worshipped Fitzjames and gave … a good deal of insight into his almost perfect character'. Wynyard was described to Markham (allegedly) as 'a daring little chap, no end of go in him, giving every promise of making a first rate officer, a favourite with his shipmates'. But he caught fever 'from exposure to the sun and imprudent bathing' and died on HMS *Pandora* off the coast of Costa Rica in March 1849. He was buried at sea aged just 18.

Commerell lived to become Admiral Sir John Commerell, VC. He addressed the lunch held by the Royal Geographical Society in 1895 to mark the fiftieth anniversary of the sailing of the Franklin Expedition. At the lunch Commerell said, with some feeling one imagines, 'I volunteered to go with Sir John Franklin in 1845. Lieutenant le Visconte [sic] whom I was serving with at that time, and Captain Fitzjames, whom I served with in a ship previously, did the best they could with Sir John to give me a chance of going; but, ladies and gentlemen, I am happy to tell you that I was too young at that time.'

A less serene fate awaited Fitzjames' childhood friend John Boyd, whose brother had died in a hail of bullets on the beach at Málaga in 1831. He has the unusual distinction of having owned a dog which became a ghost. Almost thirty years to the day after his brother was shot, John Boyd, then captain of HMS *Ajax*, was drowned in one of the greatest storms ever to hit the east coast of Ireland. Some men from the *Ajax* accompanied Boyd and his Newfoundland dog in one of the ship's boats in an attempt to rescue some shipwrecked sailors who had been washed onto some rocks outside Dún Laoghaire harbour. Boyd and three of his men were washed off the rocks back into the sea by a giant wave and were drowned. The only survivor was Boyd's dog, which was found still alive and waiting for him in the boat.

Boyd's body was recovered and he was given one of the biggest funerals ever seen in Dublin. The dog accompanied Boyd's coffin to his funeral and afterwards to his grave, which it refused to leave, eventually dying there of starvation. A magnificent statue of Boyd was later erected in Dublin and the spectre of his dog has allegedly been seen sitting near its base. This ghostly Newfoundland has also been sighted lying on Boyd's grave at Glasnevin Cemetery, although apparently not since 1950.

No such rumours surround Sir John Barrow. He died, happily never knowing the extent of the disaster he had inflicted on Fitzjames, in the autumn of 1848. Fitzjames' last public act, almost certainly, in reality, posthumous, had been to contribute £5 0s 0d in 1851 to the construction of the memorial to Sir John Barrow erected above his home town of Ulverston. The real donor must have been John Barrow junior. Such was his respect for James Fitzjames that he clearly felt his friend might yet emerge from the ice, even after six years.

Whatever Fitzjames covered up for George Barrow in Singapore in 1842 remained covered. George became Sir George, second baronet, on the death of his father. He married, fathered eight children and rose to become chief clerk to the Colonial Office. He died in 1876. John Barrow, Fitzjames' friend, lived until 1898. He had written a number of travel books to places such as Iceland and Germany, and risen to be a colonel in the Volunteers. Fitzjames' correspondence with him passed to Sir Clements Markham and, after his death in 1916, was archived at the Royal Geographical Society.

Fitzjames' childhood friend Sophia Percy married Charles Bagot in 1846. She did not die until 1908. As an old lady she boasted that she was one of the few people alive in the twentieth century who had danced with a partner of Queen Marie Antoinette of France, who had been guillotined in 1793. She wrote that she had found it very hard to accept that Fitzjames had been snuffed out by the ice, saying that 'for long we could never believe he had perished at the North Pole – death and he appeared to have nothing in common'.

Despite the fact that Fitzjames' achievements were mainly in the Mediterranean or the South China Sea, it is as an Arctic explorer that he has been remembered, even though his credentials as one are completely unknown. When John Barrow commissioned his friend Stephen Pearce to paint 'The Arctic Council Discussing the Plan of Search for Sir John Franklin', he made sure that Fitzjames had a place in it. Much discussion has been generated by this painting as no actual 'Arctic Council' ever existed. The painting was simply a method of grouping together all the people John Barrow wanted to portray, including Bird, Ross and Richardson. Sir John Barrow and Sir John Franklin look down at the 'Council' from large portraits hanging on the wall, and between them is hung a rather smaller portrait of James Fitzjames. The unfairness of excluding Crozier from this depiction has often been commented on. Yet Crozier had never been a friend of John Barrow; James Fitzjames had been. As Barrow was paying for the painting, he had had his father and his friend included.

Fitzjames' memory was put to some strange uses at the close of the nineteenth century. Sir Clements Markham was the somewhat maniacal inspiration for the resumption of polar exploration by the Royal Navy at the turn of the twentieth century. With the exception of the unsuccessful Nares Expedition of 1876, on which Sir Albert Markham served, the Royal Navy had turned its back on the ice with the end of its searches for the Franklin Expedition in the 1850s. Markham wanted the Royal Navy to re-engage in polar exploration and he needed a model of his 'ideal' officer. Fitzjames became this model and was idolised in Markham's writing. Markham could do this precisely because so little was known about the real Fitzjames and the resulting image bore little resemblance to reality. Nares would have been a better model – at least he had had the sense to withdraw his party from their attempt to reach the North Pole before dietary deficiencies and cold killed all of them, but that sort of prudence was not the kind of model Markham admired. Captain Scott was the officer Markham selected to aspire to this image, with results as disastrous for him and the four men of his polar party as they had been for the 129 men of the Franklin Expedition.

Many people have been amazed by the apparent composure with which Scott and his companions met their end: 'we have been to the Pole and we shall die like gentlemen. I regret only for the women we leave behind.' Did Scott, Wilson and Bowers want to avoid any posthumous comparison with the apparent physical and moral disintegration of the Franklin Expedition on King William Island? The Franklin Expedition seems to have abandoned groups of sick and crippled men as the survivors desperately struggled to stay alive. Scott and his companions may have felt they could face similar criticism over the abandonment of Petty Officer Evans and Captain Oates. Scott emphasised that Oates voluntarily left his expedition to die, but if you imagine that Oates' comment 'I am just going out and may be some time' was the sarcastic response to an unrecorded order to commit suicide, then it has a rather different meaning. Such thoughts are unworthy of the memory of very brave men, but the problem is that the spectres of the Franklin disaster cast long shadows then and still do today. The memory of Fitzjames became trapped in some very strange distortions.

The Coningham family and Fitzjames' friends, men like Edward Charlewood and John Barrow, wrote no distortions. They simply did not refer to their friend's cavalier approach to his career and would not have done anything to draw attention to his illegitimacy. But Fitzjames' memory was undoubtedly wilfully distorted by Markham. Some of his fabrications have persisted until now. Markham died in 1916 when he accidentally set fire to his own bedclothes. By then Fitzjames had been gone for over seventy years and had passed out of living memory. The confusions in Fitzjames' naval records, caused by his illegitimacy and the dubious methods he used to pursue promotion, made it difficult for later Franklin Expedition historians, such as Richard Cyriax, to uncover the original source material, so until now Markham has been largely trusted.

Markham wrote about Fitzjames in detail. He makes out that it was simply Fitzjames' brilliance which attracted Sir John Barrow to him. Yet for twenty years, Markham possessed Fitzjames' letter to John Barrow junior. This made it perfectly clear that Sir John Barrow's favouritism towards Fitzjames was because Fitzjames had paid off some blackmailer, or otherwise dug George Barrow out of a hole of his own making, in Singapore. It is difficult to believe that Markham could not have understood this letter. Especially when he writes that 'Sir William Parker gave him the *Clio* brig' – a statement which is directly contradicted in another letter that Markham possessed for twenty years. There are other places where it seems the Markhams are deliberately fabricating falsehoods about Fitzjames. Sir Albert claimed, in the first chapter of his unpublished book, that Elizabeth Coningham was Fitzjames' sister. The Markhams must have known this was untrue.

A major cause of the break between the reality and the myth of James Fitzjames was the Crimean War. This created a huge lacuna in Victorian society. After it, the Franklin Expedition and those who died on it seemed to be the martyrs of a more innocent 'pre-war' age, in the same way that the sacrifices and adventures of Scott and Shackleton paled for British society once the First World War unfolded. It is very revealing how Shackleton was received in 1917 when he returned, as if from the dead, in the midst of that terrible war. Was he, who had voluntarily gone to the ends of the Earth and consequently suffered, more of a hero than the members of every family in the land who were being killed, maimed and disfigured every day? What meaning can the death of a few self-selected adventurers have when the whole of society is being devastated by the holocaust of war? Many of Fitzjames' friends fought in the Crimean War as he would undoubtedly have done. None had a 'better war' than Fitzjames' friend Colin Campbell, who he last met when Campbell was a colonel in China. On 24 October 1854,

Campbell rallied his Highland 93rd Regiment at the Battle of Balaklava to face a massed charge by Russian cavalry. As the Russian cavalry bore down on them, Campbell told his regiment: 'there is no retreat from here, men; you must die where you stand.' To which the soldier in the most vulnerable position of all, on the extreme right of the line, replied: 'Ay, Sir Colin, an' needs be, we'll do that.' That soldier was a hero whose spirit Fitzjames would have recognised. *The Times* correspondent, W.H. Russell, who saw the action, described Campbell's regiment as a 'thin red streak tipped with a line of steel' and thus originated the phrase 'the thin red line'. Campbell fought through the Crimean War and the Indian Mutiny and ended his days as Field Marshal Lord Clyde, dying in 1863.

Fitzjames' friends started to mourn him as it became clear in the late 1840s that he would never return from the ice. But what happened to him? He left a few traces of his path through the Arctic.

The last clear evidence of James Fitzjames is the famous Victory Point note, which he wrote with Francis Crozier on the bleak shore of King William Island in April 1848, as the two men were about to start their death march after abandoning their ships. On the Victory Point note, Fitzjames' signature and writing is cramped compared with his beautiful and distinctive handwriting before he sailed, and betrays the strain he was under. The note tells us that he became captain of the *Erebus* after the death of Sir John Franklin.

There is a final possible trace of James Fitzjames in a very confused set of documents known as the 'Peglar Pocket book'. This was recovered from the skeleton of a man dressed in the uniform of a ship's steward, which was found by Leopold McClintock lying face down close to the south coast of King William Island. The Pocket Book this steward was carrying had originally belonged to a seaman called Henry Peglar, hence its name, but seems to have passed to the steward after Peglar died. It consists of a confused mass of papers written at different times during the expedition by several people. It is extremely difficult to read, but recent high-quality digital images taken by the National Maritime Museum make some slightly clearer interpretations possible.

One sheet is a reused envelope with a sentence on it written in a circle. This is not completely decipherable, but seems to read: 'He … money a thought going ar bouart the harmonic'. It is not clear now what 'many have thought going about the harmonic' might mean, but the meaning of the words inside the circle is possibly clearer:

… Erebus
Tell the Cap[tain]
You … Peglar
… Lord our God
… the Terror camp
… be clear.

This just might be a message to the captain of the *Erebus'* survivors from the 'Terror camp', to say that the 'Terror camp' is now clear. The reference to Peglar and 'Lord our God' would suggest that Peglar had, by that time, died. It seems reasonable that the survivors of each ship would stay together on land, given that they had lived for so long together on their separate ships. So if Fitzjames was still alive at this point, this appears to be a message to him ('Erebus ... Cap[tain]') from the 'Terror camp'. Recent scholarship, principally by Glenn Stein, has suggested that the skeleton on which the Pocket Book was found may have been that of William Gibson, subordinate officer's steward on HMS *Terror*. An officer's steward was exactly the person who would be expected to take messages from one officer to another. If so, this grim little note is the last surviving letter to Fitzjames.

Fitzjames and his comrades had all had the greatest confidence in the success and safety of the expedition, although it is said William Coningham tried to dissuade him from going. We can now see, as William Coningham came to see, that they took much greater risks than they understood and that a whole series of climatological, geographical and disease factors were stacked against them. Fitzjames may have been joking when he wrote to John Barrow junior that 'I always fancied an iceberg was a great big transparent-looking lump of ice, instead of a white beautiful twelfth cake looking thing as it is – odd shapes, though, some of them'.

But perhaps not. His comment was typical of the thinking of the whole expedition. Big ships like HMS *Erebus* and HMS *Terror* should never have been sent. When they became locked in the ice off King William Island on 12 September 1846 there was only one chance to free their ships, in the summer of 1847. After that, the expedition was condemned either to walk to safety or starve where they sat. Their supplies and equipment were enough to get them into trouble, but not to get them out. The Admiralty gave no consideration at all to how the expedition would move if the ships were trapped and took no steps to rescue them until it was too late. When the expedition had been fitting out in 1845, a Mr J.R. Crowe had written to the Admiralty suggesting that it should be equipped with 'snow shoes and clothes or Lapland coats & co.' The Admiralty had not even bothered to reply until after the expedition sailed. The side arms they carried were Royal Marines' muskets and officers' personal shotguns. They carried no hunting rifles. Muskets and shotguns are of limited use for hunting seal, musk ox or polar bears, all of which demand weapons with accuracy, range and stopping power. A polar bear was shot and killed at Beechey Island by one of the later expeditions searching for Franklin and his men. When dissected, a musket ball was found lodged in its skin, which must have been fired from a Franklin Expedition musket during the winter of 1845–46. It is significant that this ball, which must have been fired from a fairly close range given the inaccuracy of the musket, failed to penetrate the animal's pelt and did not even seriously injure it.

Disease was another contributor, although it has probably been overestimated by some researchers. There is evidence of TB, lead poisoning and scurvy. Each of these was very serious and, in aggregate, they reduced the men's already slim chances of survival. One of the effects of scurvy is to degrade scar tissue, resulting in the opening up of old wounds. If scurvy got a hold on Fitzjames, the consequences would have been very grim, given the severe wounds he suffered in the China war. It was scurvy which sealed the fate of Captain Oates on Scott's disastrous expedition.

All these factors stacked the deck further against Fitzjames and his shipmates, but the fundamental cause of his death was the ice. While his ship retained its mobility, he and his men could sail anywhere. The sea had been the medium through which Fitzjames had advanced his career and overcome all the obstacles fate had placed in front of him. But when this same sea froze solid in September 1846 and did not release the *Erebus* or *Terror* in 1847, it became his tomb.

The date of Sir John Barrow's death, 23 November 1848, may be around the date James Fitzjames died. Probably by then the majority of the men who set out with him were dead. The expedition seems to have broken up into groups of desperate, freezing, exhausted and dying men on the margins of life in the Arctic. While Sir John Barrow earned a funeral with the full panoply of Victorian mourning, Fitzjames' last resting place is unknown. His bones may lie in a shallow grave or may lie, scattered in fragments, somewhere in the Canadian Arctic. For all we know, fragments of James Fitzjames may be among the samples analysed by Owen Beattie and his team.

So what do we now know of James Fitzjames?

He should not be remembered as a footnote to the Franklin tragedy. His great achievement was to create for himself the life he craved, that of a naval officer, despite his very uncertain origins. He was the illegitimate son of a dissolute bankrupt, probably born of a Portuguese or Brazilian mother. It would vastly amuse him that many who have criticised the Franklin Expedition for its alleged ethnic prejudices have singled him out as the quintessential Englishman. How ironic that in reality he was born in the shadow of the Sugar Loaf Mountain, possibly of a Native American mother!

He was not born with 'friends in the right places' or with a silver spoon in his mouth. Actually, as he put it, he was 'thrown ... on the world by circumstances over which [he had] no control, without one friend in it'. The Gambier family did obtain for him his first position in the Royal Navy, but within twelve months they were off the scene with Robert Gambier's resignation and they offered him no practical help at all thereafter. Fitzjames' continued position in the Royal Navy in 1826, and his subsequent promotion from volunteer of the second class to captain in just twenty years, owed nothing to wealth or family connections and everything to himself. Only his own great determination enabled him to continue his career in 1830, when the Royal Navy would only accept him as a master's assistant – not an officer at all. His family and friends were power-less to gain him an officer's position. It was his personal interview with Captain Senhouse that won him his position as a midshipman on HMS *Asia* in 1831, combined with his and Robert Coningham's scheming that ran rings round the flat-footed naval bureaucracy.

His future success was entirely due to his education, his intelligence, his per-sonal charisma and his bravery. In the light of this, almost every single word of Scott Cookman's description of him, as 'well-educated, aristocratic, wealthy, of good family, Church of England, fast rising in the service – and thumpingly, lisp-ingly English to the core', simply could not be more wrong.

Let's examine each in turn.

James Fitzjames was well-educated – better than his peers – but this is because his foster parents were intellectuals with a passion for education, especially that of women, and it owed nothing to privilege. He was emphatically not aristocratic, nor was he wealthy; in fact, he seems to have been completely broke for most of his life. And not only was he not 'of good family' – he didn't have one at all! Like every naval officer of the time, he was a member of the Church of England. It is a misunderstanding of his career to describe him as 'fast rising'. Sir John Barrow certainly favoured Fitzjames in the last years of his life, but only from 1842 onwards. Until then, Barrow was more likely to have regarded the man as an embarrassment. Barrow had done nothing at all to help Fitzjames' career before he had saved George Barrow from … something. And, lastly, he was not, in the way that Cookman means it, English. Though his father was an Englishman, his mother was almost certainly either Portuguese or Brazilian and he was born in Brazil.

Fitzjames was not an anachronism. He was actually a very modern figure who made himself what he wanted to be and earned his position through bravery, flair and brains. He was a talented artist with a particular sensitivity to and apprecia-tion of Islamic culture, which is clear both through his respectful descriptions of, for example, Kerbala, as well as his drawings. He wrote well with wit and insight. And while much of his poetry to survive is close to doggerel, more designed to amuse his peers than anything else, it is always witty and carefully crafted and he was capable of writing sensitive poetry too.

Fitzjames' riotous sense of fun and his robust practical jokes made a big impres-sion on his contemporaries. But they all missed the real point of what he was saying. And they still do today. Fitzjames' jokes were at the expense of people, then and now, who judge by appearance. He pokes fun at the ludicrous racial stereotyping of today as much as he did at its counterpart in his day. When he dressed as a sleazy missionary, a pompous religious bigot, a rich Jew or a poor Turk, and then revealed himself as an English Royal Naval officer, his contem-poraries laughed. But what he was really saying was that the appearance of a man is not necessarily what one should judge. 'Look at me', he was saying, as he grinningly cast off his disguise and adopted the demeanour and uniform of an officer of the Royal Navy; 'you all think I'm an English aristocrat, yet actually I'm a half-breed Latin American bastard'.

And even today nobody gets the joke.

Markham's distortions and the reluctance of Fitzjames' friends, like Edward Charlewood and William Coningham, to risk drawing attention to his origins have masked his true achievement. This was to overcome the accident of his illegitimacy and build himself a naval career in the face of prejudice. In the light of this, it is doubly unfair that he has come to personify ingrained aristocratic and family-based privilege for so many writers. If there is an afterlife, I have no doubt that Fitzjames will be enjoying that particular irony. But these misrepresentations of the man mean that no one has understood his other achievements in war and on the Euphrates Expedition. They have also masked his influence on the Franklin Expedition and distorted historians' understanding of how and why Franklin and the other officers were selected.

Modern scholarship has given us the opportunity to strip away almost 200 years of prejudice and misconception. Let us hope that we can, and now celebrate a portrait of a talented and charismatic man who overcame prejudice to create for himself the life he was determined to lead. It was mainly the Franklin Expedition that brought him into the public eye – he would not feature in a Clive Cussler novel for any other reason – and joining the expedition was the only big mistake he ever made which he couldn't overcome. His life shows that however talented and lucky we seem to be, just one mistake can be fatal.

The last word should go to Edward Charlewood, one of the few of Fitzjames' close friends to die in bed, who wondered why, when 'Fitzjames and all hands belonging to both ships have all perished in those dreary regions ... I, who bitterly deplored my hard fate at losing the appointment, am still alive ...'

A NOTE ON SOURCES

Since this is the first book written specifically about Fitzjames, there is no single source for him in existence. I have wanted to present his life as a biography and have not broken the narrative up with too much description of sources, so the key published sources are given in the Bibliography.

The principal unpublished sources are letters to, from and about Fitzjames held on microfilm at the National Maritime Museum (reference MRF/89) and the Scott Polar Research Institute in Cambridge (reference GB15), and the letters he sent to John Barrow junior held at the Royal Geographical Society (reference LMS F 6 1829–45). A final very important primary source is the single volume of Fitzjames' journal held in the National Maritime Museum archive under the reference JOD/86. The enormous Admiralty archive at The National Archives at Kew contains letters and other material relating to Fitzjames' career as well, especially in the series ADM2, ADM12, ADM35 and ADM37. Specific significant papers in the ADM archive will be referenced in the appropriate place below.

I have avoided footnotes and endnotes and list below the specific sources for quotations and other information.

Dedication
Admiral Charlewood's words come from Charlewood, 1869.

Foreword
Fitzjames' letter and questionnaire response to O'Byrne is an important document in the British Library archive, reference Add 38039 – 38054 and gives Fitzjames' own account of his background and career.

Introduction: James Fitzjames and Me
All the books which contain the varying published accounts of his life and career are given in the Bibliography. The account of the 'boat place' in Fleming, 1999 is based on McClintock, 1860. McClintock was paid by Lady Franklin and made no reference to cannibalism in his book, but from the context and subsequent

archaeological research, it is quite clear that it had taken place. Stereotypical references to Fitzjames will be found in a surprising number of books about the Franklin Expedition and other Franklin personalities, especially in Cookman, Smith, Cussler and Simmons.

The ships' plans for the *Erebus* and *Terror* are held at the National Maritime Museum.

Incidentally, the description 'handsomest man in the Navy' frequently said to be a reference to Fitzjames was actually said of Sir James Clark Ross.

Barrow's life can be read best in Lloyd, 1970 and Barrow, 1847.

Copies of the Victory Point note are widely available but many transcriptions ignore the punctuation or, even worse, put in punctuation of their own. Always refer to images of it. For a discussion of some of its ambiguities please refer to my blog post 'Is the Conventional Interpretation of the "Victory Point" note wrong?' at http://hidden-tracks-book.blogspot.com/2009/04/is-conventional-interpretation-of.html.

The Markhams' comments on Fitzjames are contained mainly in Markham, 1909 and Markham, 1891. Markham, 1921, published posthumously, is rather confused and this seems more to be a reflection of the author's great age than anything else. The principal alternative source for his career is O'Byrne, 1848. This was used by Chesney, for example.

Fitzjames' passing certificate is not (or was not when I last looked) indexed at The National Archives at Kew, although it is in the ADM archive. This is one reason why researchers have had so much difficulty tracing his career prior to 1838. The detailed reasons for this are discussed in Chapter 3. The muster books are all available at The National Archives. The relevant references for HMS *St Vincent* are ADM37/8374, ADM37/8375, ADM37/8370, ADM37/8369, ADM37/8371, ADM37/8372 and ADM37/8373. The references for HMS *Asia* are ADM37/7870 and ADM37/7871.

One: Tracking Down James Fitzjames

The surviving daguerreotype of Fitzjames is at the Scott Polar Research Institute. The National Maritime Museum holds a photograph of the other, which has been lost. Both are accessible via the internet. Many authorities state that the second daguerreotype is held at the Derbyshire County archive in Matlock, but this is not so. Derbyshire holds what appears to be an early copy of this daguerreotype, possibly a collotype rather than a photograph. More investigation is needed into the story behind these daguerreotypes. A lot of people claim to see a faint smile on his face in one of them, but to me the two expressions seem very similar.

Fitzjames' baptismal certificate can be seen in the National Maritime Museum and Scott Polar Research Institute microfilms and there is a record of his baptism also on microfilm at the London Metropolitan Archive in Islington. Elizabeth

Coningham's birth is recorded at Burford in Oxfordshire and her family and ancestry is clear at the two main genealogists' websites www.familysearch.net and www.ancestry.co.uk. Professor Robin Coningham and Janet Lash have both helped in clarifying some matters relating to the Coningham family.

An example of a letter where both Robert Coningham and James Fitzjames make it clear that they are in no way related can be found in the file ADM1/4609, Letter F10.

There is little written about Sir James Gambier. His life can be reconstructed from standard genealogical resources, from *The Complete Peerage of England, Scotland, Ireland, Great Britain and the United Kingdom, Extant, Extinct or Dormant*, new edn, 13 volumes in 14 (1910–59; reprint in 6 volumes, Gloucester, UK: Alan Sutton Publishing, 2000), volume I. The description of 'Bolto Togo' and other references to Sir James Gambier in Brazil come from the diary of Elizabeth MacQuarie, held at MacQuarie University in Sydney.

Pamela Hunter, the Hoare and Company archivist, was very helpful in untangling Sir James Gambier's financial affairs.

Sophia Percy's recollection of the bloodstained coat is in Bagot, 1901. The Church of England's records give scant details of Robert Coningham's career as he never took a living, but do confirm his curacy. I can find no source for the life and death of his infant son John, but was given this information by Coningham family genealogists.

The reference to Fitzjames being fluent in Portuguese is in Captain Sartorius' reference about him in the ADM archive. It is perhaps significant that Robert Coningham and Robert Gambier both refer to Spanish rather than French, presumably seeking not to associate Fitzjames too closely with Portugal.

I was greatly helped in finding information about Rose Hill and its environment in the 1820s and 1830s by the Abbots Langley Local History Society, and especially by Professor Richard Simon. Sophia Bagot's description of life in rural Hertfordshire at the time comes from Bagot, 1901, which is such a great read it really deserves a reprint. The online Carlyle letters archive at http://carlyleletters. dukejournals.org/ is the source for much to do with Robert Coningham's intellectual circle. Information about Louisa Coningham and her father Colonel Capper comes from the *Dictionary of National Biography*. Robert Coningham's life is summarised in the online Cambridge University database of its alumni. Fitzjames' later references to Hertfordshire are peppered throughout his correspondence (op. cit.).

The Campbells can be very confusing, especially given their liking down the generations for the forenames Colin and Elizabeth. Pauline Connolly, the Australian historian, helped me a great deal with them. They were also sensitive of the origins of Colin Campbell, later Field Marshal Lord Clyde.

More information is available about John Sterling, for example in Carlyle, 1851 and Boyd-Carpenter, 1911. The online Carlyle letters website at http://carlyleletters.dukejournals.org/ is also extremely valuable.

Reference to the Coninghams' travel comes from the Fitzjames letter archive at the National Maritime Museum.

Two: Mr Fitzjames Goes to Sea

Gambier's letter entering Fitzjames to HMS *Pyramus* is at ADM 1/1865/A682. For the career of a conventional naval officer of the time, the ADM records at The National Archives in Kew would be the sole source. One would expect to find his career prior to passing his lieutenant's exam on his passing certificate, which is at ADM107/74 and his career thereafter in the ADM196 files. Anyone who has read Chapter 2 will understand why these records are not complete. In practical terms ADM107/74 is fairly reliable but omits mention of HMS *Asia*. The two muster books of HMS *Asia*, ADM37/7870 and ADM37/7871, provide confirmation that he was entered on this ship on either 9 or 12 February 1831 and dismissed on 23 February 1831.

The reconstruction of Fitzjames' career on HMS *Pyramus* comes from his letters and his brief account in the O'Byrne questionnaire. Information on the Sartorius and Gambier families comes from standard genealogical web resources.

Information on Sir Robert Ker Porter and M. Morier comes from web searches. They would make fascinating subjects for original research, but are peripheral for this study. The description of the sailors singing in the masts comes from Bagot, 1901, and the evidence from sailors' skeletons from Boston and Loe. The attempted abduction of John Williams, the alleged runaway slave at Barbados, and Captain Gambier and James Stephen's intervention on his side, is detailed in file CO28/99 at The National Archives.

Fitzjames' skill as a linguist is mentioned by Robert Coningham in the National Maritime Museum correspondence archive, which also contains Sartorius' confirmation that he spoke Portuguese fluently. I strongly suspect that in Lisbon he had contact with his maternal family, but can find no evidence. There are several places in his letters to Robert Coningham where he shows some dislike of Miguel.

Evidence for William Barrow as a member of the Experimental Squadron comes from Barrow, 1850.

Eton College has limited information on boys of William Coningham's age at that time, but were able to confirm the dates.

The events leading up to the tragedy of General Torrijos and Robert Boyd can be found mostly in Carlyle, 1851 and Boyd-Carpenter, 1911, as well as in the Fitzjames correspondence archive at the National Maritime Museum.

The reconstruction of Fitzjames' appointment as a master's assistant to HMS *St Vincent*, and then his dubious promotion to midshipman, comes mostly from correspondence between Robert Coningham and him in the National Maritime Museum, validated by the muster books for *St Vincent* (ADM37/8369-75) and HMS *Asia* 37/8373 (ADM37/7870 and ADM37/7871). There is also a limited amount of Admiralty correspondence in ADM2 and ADM12. John Barrow junior's correspondence involving Fitzjames has not survived, which strongly suggests the two men were not friends at this stage.

Three: 'A Sailor's Life'

The title verse comes from Fitzjames' untitled poem, reproduced in the Appendix, which can be found in the back of his journal at the National Maritime Museum (reference JOD/86).

His letters to and from the Coninghams in the National Maritime Museum inform this chapter, backed up by muster book corroboration. All quotes come from these sources or his journal, JOD/86, unless otherwise noted. Unfortunately, no Royal Naval records relating to the cutter *Hind* have survived, so the service of John Boyd and James Fitzjames on this vessel has to come from indirect sources – principally the letter archives.

Information on the Boyd family and the tragedy of Robert Boyd comes from several sources. Fitzjames kept the letters John Boyd sent him, including Robert Boyd's last poem, and these are preserved in microfilms at the National Maritime Museum and the Scott Polar Research Institute. There is some very interesting supporting material in Carlyle, 1851 and in Boyd-Carpenter, 1911, which also gives descriptions of Alicia Campbell and clarifies a lot of the relationships between the Boyds and the Campbells.

As with his appointment to midshipman, the ADM records give a very confused account of his passing of his lieutenant exams and the story has been reconstructed from the letters Fitzjames and Robert Coningham exchanged. Senhouse's letter 'there would be some trouble …' is in the Fitzjames correspondence archive at the National Maritime Museum and was, for obvious reasons, not officially recorded.

Fitzjames' description of amateur dramatics comes from his journal, and the full script of the play *Chrononhotonthologos* can be found at www.chrononhotonthologos.com/script.htm. This is certainly a play overdue revival.

There is a reference to the close relationship between Colin Campbell, the future Lord Clyde, and the Coninghams and Barrows in 1833 and 1834 in Shadwell, 1881; for example, 'The remainder of this year [1833] was spent in visits to his relations the Coninghams and the family of Mr Clutterbuck, whose wife was a sister of Mrs R Coningham, at Watford. The year 1834 found Colin Campbell still unemployed. After paying a visit to Portsmouth … he met his intimate friends William and John Barrow', which ties in exactly with Fitzjames' letters and journal.

Fitzjames' movements for the rest of the year are less easy to pin down as he only intermittently completed his journal, but they can be cross-referenced with official records in the ADM series, notably ADM1/2561/S130.

Four: Colonel Chesney: 'A Most Determined Man'

There is one modern and very good account of the Euphrates Expedition: Guest, 1992. Otherwise, the excellent memoirs of various participants have been used, principally Charlewood, 1869, Chesney, 1850 and 1868, Ainsworth, 1838 and 1888, Nostitz, 1878 and Lane-Poole, 1885.

The extensive unflattering description of Col. Chesney comes from Lane-Poole, 1885.

Extracts from Fitzjames' journal are incorporated into some of these and some letters to and from him of this period survive in the National Maritime Museum and the Scott Polar Research Institute archives. I am also grateful to the archivists at the Wirral Archives, who showed me the original records, such as they exist, relating to the *Euphrates* and *Tigris* steamboats. There are limited records in the British Library and in the Gloucestershire archive at Gloucester relating to Colonel Chesney, but much of what they include is actually given in the published records already cited.

The most detailed information on the 'affair in the Mersey' is in Fitzjames' own correspondence in the National Maritime Museum and in Charlewood, 1869. The cup, complete with its soldered repair, is now in the National Maritime Museum with the reference PLT0048 and a photograph of it is reproduced in this book.

The description of the demolition of the Arab house comes, as with many other colourful stories, from Charlewood, 1869.

The changing plans and objectives of the expedition are convoluted and not fully explained in this chapter. For more background please refer to Guest, 1992.

Five: Steaming on the Great Rivers

Here the sources are exactly as for Chapter 4.

Six: The Rivers of Babylon

The sources for much of this chapter are the same also. Fitzjames' letter describing his hair-raising journey across Mesopotamia is reproduced in Chesney's book and also exists in the British Library archive. David K. Brown's book *Before the Ironclad* gives a very interesting account of the near-disaster which almost sank the *Nemesis* in the Indian Ocean, and which seems to have been very similar to the damage suffered by the *Euphrates* during Colonel Chesney's ill-advised attempt to take the river steamer to sea.

The hostile village of Lemlun seems to have vanished from modern maps, perhaps with the draining of the marshes or a change in the course of the Euphrates.

The story of his practical joke dressed as a Turk comes from Fanshawe, 1904 and is typical of the stories of his outrageous jokes which circulated in the Royal Navy for the next fifty years after his death.

Chesney's wish to repopulate his kennels comes from Lane-Poole, 1885.

Seven: 'A Huge Gingham Umbrella'

The statistics on the fatalities suffered by the expedition come from Estcourt's handwritten notes on the original commission of the expedition which is deposited in the Gloucester County Archives and is also given in Chesney, 1868.

Information on William Coningham's wealth derived mainly from the will of Walter Coningham, which is held at the Hertfordshire County Archives, and also from perusal of his account books at Hoare and Company.

Most of the firsthand accounts in this chapter come from Charlewood, 1869. The two stories of Fitzjames' extended practical joke at Charlewood's expense on board HMS *Excellent* come from Charlewood's memoirs, with some supporting information in Lane-Poole, 1885.

The papers recording the convoluted progress of Fitzjames' eventual promotion to lieutenant are at The National Archives under references ADM1/3920.

The muster books for HMS *Excellent* give the dates of his service and his rank there and also confirm other future members of the Franklin Expedition, notably Le Vesconte and Couch, as having served there at the same time.

Fitzjames' friendship with John Barrow junior seems to date from this time, as from now on his correspondence with Barrow, held at the Royal Geographical Society archive, is a major first-hand source.

Fitzjames' outrageous impersonation of the aides of Sir Moses Montefiore was apparently a story still doing the rounds when Sir Albert Markham was a naval officer and was recorded in Markham, 1891.

Fitzjames' passage on the *Great Liverpool* was noted in the *Asian Journal* of 1 June 1841, and his solitary entry on the British census can be found online.

Eight: Fitzjames' Chinese Puzzle

The general accounts of the background to the war come from modern analysis on the internet. The accounts of the fighting in which Fitzjames took part are from contemporary accounts, principally Hall and Bernard, 1847, Loch, 1843 and Ouchterlony, 1844.

Fitzjames was by then in regular correspondence with John Barrow junior and these letters in the RGS archive provide the firsthand accounts, backed up by his letters to William Coningham in the National Maritime Museum. Fitzjames' poetic account of the Chinese war, published in instalments in the *Nautical Journal*, also gives some additional colour. Regrettably, at over 10,000 words, it is too long to include in this book. Simmons in *The Terror* suggests that Fitzjames wrote this to recite to his messmates as a prank, and this may well be true.

Letters from Fairholme and Le Vesconte also add colour. Fairholme's letters are in the Derbyshire County archive at Matlock and Le Vesconte's are at the Provincial Archives of Newfoundland and Labrador at St John's Newfoundland. I am grateful to Lieutenant Le Vesconte's great-grandnephew William H. Wills of Ontario for providing me with an electronic copy of these. Susan Alexander, of the Fish Hoek and Masiphumelele Libraries in Cape Province, kindly visited William Barrow's grave there and corroborated Fitzjames' account of its location.

Also valuable is David McLean's paper *Surgeons of the Opium War*, which describes the appalling health experience of the British forces and how lucky Fitzjames was to survive.

The critically important information relating to George Barrow is all in one letter Fitzjames sent to John Barrow junior held in the Royal Geographical Society archive.

Nine: Steps Towards Nemesis

This chapter is again based on Fitzjames' letters to John Barrow junior in the RGS and on Fitzjames' own letters held at the National Maritime Museum and the Scott Polar Research Institute, supplemented by letters of Lieutenant Fairholme held at the Derbyshire County archive at Matlock and the Le Vesconte archive at Halifax, kindly sourced via Mr William Wills.

Markham, 1891, adds the detail about the cheetah.

Fitzjames' letter describing the circumstances of the loss of the *Mary Mallaby* was published in the *Friend of India* newspaper at Calcutta on 14 March 1844.

Ten: Fitzjames Prepares

Again, Fitzjames' letters to Barrow are a primary source, although Charlewood's private memoir and Le Vesconte and Fairholme's letters give useful additional detail. Once he opened his bank account at Hoare and Company, their archive gives full details of his financial affairs. Unfortunately, he was not a rich man and he only wrote a few cheques. His will is in The National Archives, and the Bank of England archive confirms that the only asset he held, his investment in Consols 3 per cent, had been transferred to him by William Coningham in November 1844.

His relationship with Elizabeth and William Coningham can be tracked through the Fitzjames correspondence in the National Maritime Museum.

The details of the *Erebus* and the *Terror* come from their plans held at the National Maritime Museum and from Ware, 1994.

The chronology of Sir John Barrow and the Admiralty's decisions in finalising who should lead the Franklin Expedition is complex and comes from Fitzjames' private correspondence with John Barrow junior, cross referenced with Cyriax, 1939 and standard sources on the Franklin Expedition.

The biographical sketches of Franklin and Crozier come from their recent biographies, Beardsley and Smith respectively, and the information about the other officers and members of the crews mainly comes from Ralph Lloyd-Jones' two papers: *The Men who Sailed with Franklin* and *The Royal Marines on Franklin's Last Expedition.* These have been supplemented by my own research into the ships' muster books at The National Archives. Information about the Ross Expedition to the Antarctic is drawn from Ross, 1984 and Ross, 1992. Other sources include the letters of Lieutenant Irving, which were published in Bell, 1881, and Crozier's letters, which are now in the Scott Polar Research Institute. Some additional information comes from various editions of *The Times*, the *Nautical Journal* and the *Illustrated London News*. I have found that many new insights come from looking at all of this material and cross referencing it, especially with the correspondence of Fitzjames, Fairholme and Le Vesconte. One good example of this is Fitzjames' meeting with Robert Fitzgerald Gambier and his wife at the Barrows'. One wonders how coincidental this meeting really was.

Eleven: Exodus

The voyage of the expedition has been reconstructed mainly from the letters of Fitzjames, Le Vesconte and Fairholme, which together give a very detailed account. Crozier's letters to Sir James Clark Ross in the Scott Polar Research Institute are also used.

Almost the final source is the reminiscences of Lieutenant Griffiths, the Royal Navy's agent on board the *Baretto Junior*, whose letters are mainly at the RGS tucked into the back of John Barrow junior's letter book, although some were also published in *The Times*, notably on 12 January 1852. The last sightings of the ships by Captains Dannet and Martin were reported in *The Times*.

Twelve: After Life

William Coningham's speech was recorded in Hansard, and the description of him is gleaned mostly from Francis Haskell's papers relating to him in the archive of the National Gallery, and references to him in the writings of others such as Carlyle and George Elliott.

I am grateful to the National Maritime Museum for enabling me to clarify the nature of its bequest from Mrs Wathen.

The list of clothes in 'James' drawers' is in the flyleaf of JOD/86 at the National Maritime Museum.

My good friend, Glenn Stein, drew my attention to Commerell's speech at the lunch to mark the fiftieth anniversary of the sailing of the Franklin Expedition. The Markhams' views and comments come from their papers in the RGS archive and the published sources.

Boyd's fate comes partly from internet sources of Dublin ghost stories and partly from Boyd-Carpenter, 1911.

The 'Peglar Pocket book' is kept at the National Maritime Museum. The speculative interpretation of it is my own.

The brief discussion of the causes of the Franklin disaster come from my own research and thinking. Mr Crowe's reference to Lapland clothes is in ADM1/446 at The National Archives.

Appendix I

THE 'OTHER' JAMES
FITZJAMES

Officers in the Royal Navy during the period Fitzjames lived did not hold a permanent commission until they reached the rank of lieutenant. Like the crews, junior officers were commissioned only temporarily for the time that the ship they served in was in commission. When a young man had served as a volunteer and a mate, he was eligible to apply to become a lieutenant and to have a permanent commission. As a permanently commissioned officer, he would then retain his rank whether or not he was appointed to a specific ship, although he would be on 'half-pay' when not appointed to a ship.

The Admiralty kept service records for every officer once they reached the rank of lieutenant, but did not do so for more junior officers or for non-commissioned men. Their records were kept in the ships' muster books and pay books, which were maintained by each ship for the period when it was in commission. When a candidate wanted to become a lieutenant, he had to demonstrate that he had sufficient service to qualify him and provide other details including the date and place of his birth. Records of men who had attained the rank of lieutenant or higher list each officer's prior service, up to the point where he was promoted. All of these records are kept together in the Admiralty's files. Through a quirk of the indexing, the record of James Fitzjames' service prior to lieutenant was missed out from the index. This is why many authors, trying to reconstruct Fitzjames' service, have not been able to do so. In time, I found Fitzjames' service records by looking through the relevant muster books.

But to my surprise, the index directed me to a certificate for another James Fitzjames who passed for lieutenant in 1821. Who was this 'first' James Fitzjames? An astonishing story is revealed in the file, which includes this attached affidavit:

The Reverend Dawson Warren vicar of Edmonton in the county of Middlesex maketh oath and saith that he hath known James Fitzjames Midshipman on board his majesty's ship Protector (Lieutenant Hewitt commander) from his infancy and verily believes he is now upwards of nineteen years of age. And this deponent further saith that he verily believes that the said James Fitzjames was born in the early part of the month of April in the year one thousand eight hundred and two for this Deponent saith that he was intimately acquainted with the reputed father of the said James Fitzjames who in the said year one thousand eight hundred and two and shortly after the said month of April conversed with the Deponent respecting the said James Fitzjames stating amongst other things that the said James Fitzjames had been registered in the Baptismal Register of the Parish (as well as this Deponent from the length of time can now recollect) of St George's Hanover Square but this Deponent hath lately examined carefully the said register and no such entry can be found. And this Deponent further saith that the reputed Father of the said James Fitzjames is dead. And this Deponent verily believes that no better or more accurate information can be obtained on the subject of the Birth of the said James Fitzjames than as above.

From the Mansion House London the 1st day of May 1821, before me John Thomas Thorpe, Mayor

A little sleuthing revealed that the Rev. Dawson Warren was vicar of Edmonton at that time, Lieutenant Hewitt was captain of HMS *Protector* and John Thorpe was no less than the Lord Mayor of London. So who was *this* James Fitzjames?

The answer becomes clear once we analyse Dawson Warren's career. He was a very worldly cleric. He moved in elite circles and had met Napoleon while accompanying the British delegation to Paris to negotiate the Treaty of Amiens in 1804, where apparently he 'astonished Napoleon by appearing at the Tuileries in the full canonicals of an Anglican divine'.

In 1802 he had been a personal chaplain to the Duke of York, who was the famous 'Grand Old Duke of York' of nursery rhyme fame. The Duke of York was a powerful political figure, a younger brother of the Prince Regent and commander-in-chief of the British army. He was gluttonous, drunken and promiscuous. The duties of personal chaplain to the Duke of York clearly included the periodic disposal and fostering of illegitimate children. It seems that this James Fitzjames was either the illegitimate son of the duke or of someone in his circle, and that the Rev. Warren arranged foster parents for him. This clearly has parallels with the story of the younger James Fitzjames.

There are some strange coincidences. Both boys were called James Fitzjames, though in neither case was it their real name. Both joined the Royal Navy at the age of 12. The elder boy, who I shall call James Fitzjames I, joined as volunteer first class, whereas the younger, James Fitzjames II, had to join as a volunteer second class. James Fitzjames I served from 1814 to 1821, during which time he seems to have met Napoleon in exile on St Helena in 1817.

In spring 1821 he was appointed to HMS *Protector*, a sister ship of HMS *Clio*, strangely enough. It seems that it was at this point that James Fitzjames I realised that his father had never registered his birth, so asked the Rev. Warren to provide an affidavit vouching for his birth and age. For good measure, he arranged for it to be witnessed by the Lord Mayor of London. He then rejoined his ship. HMS *Protector* was assigned to survey work in the Greek archipelago, again a strange link with the career of James Fitzjames II. Sadly, James Fitzjames I was drowned with a group of sailors from the *Protector* when their boat was lost in a storm. There does seem to have been some trouble when his death became known, as the original captain's log of the *Protector*, for the period immediately after his drowning, is missing and was subsequently rewritten by Lieutenant Hewitt. Also, someone later weeded his lieutenancy file and removed any references to HMS *Protector*.

There are strange parallels between the two James Fitzjameses beyond the apparent coincidence of their unusual shared name. Both were unwanted babies with concealed parentage. At least James Fitzjames II had his birth registered, although his parents' names were faked. Both boys were fostered. Both had problems achieving their promotion to lieutenant. Both served in the Mediterranean and died away from home on active service. Both simply disappeared with neither body ever being recovered.

Could there be more to this than coincidence? Perhaps they shared a father in James Gambier? It is unlikely that the affair which resulted in the birth of James Fitzjames II was the only time James Gambier broke his marital vows. At the time that James Fitzjames I was conceived Gambier was an army officer and the Duke of York was commander-in-chief of the army. Perhaps James Gambier was the person who fathered an unwanted baby by a woman in the circle of the Duke of York, and his resignation of his army commission and move to Portugal was part of the hushing up of the scandal? We will never know for sure, but it is an intriguing possibility.

A SAILOR'S LIFE

We hear from those who cannot know
The pleasures of a sailor's life
That when we on the waters go
We pass our days in useless strife
But I contend that one may be
Happier than anywhere else at sea.

The breeze is fair, the sails are full
The ship moves steadily along
Main lands glance swiftly by our lee
The sailors shew their joy in song
While all around is purely bright
Oh blessed is a moon light night.

The wind blows through, and the land
That lately we admired is past
The sails are quickly brought to hand
While keenly blows the Northern blast
Still are we happy, for the wind
Swells on the joys we left behind.

The night is dark down pours the rain
In torrents on the jaded crew
The vessel rolling on the main
The storm but ends to blow anew
Yet once below and in the berth
The sailors cares are drowned in mirth.

A calm succeeds, the blazing sun
Warms with his blessed rays the men
They idly stroll, their work is done
They wish a storm of wind again
But as the glassy decks we roam
We dream of those we left at home.

And now the lovely light of morn
Breaks on our free and fertile isle
Three years of happiness are gone
Our toils are ended for a while
When? Landsman! Tell me where find you
The joy that fills a sailor's mind.

Poem written by James Fitzjames in the back of his journal at Portsmouth on 20 August 1834, at '12 o'clock at night — I have entered 7 men today'.

Appendix III

MAPS

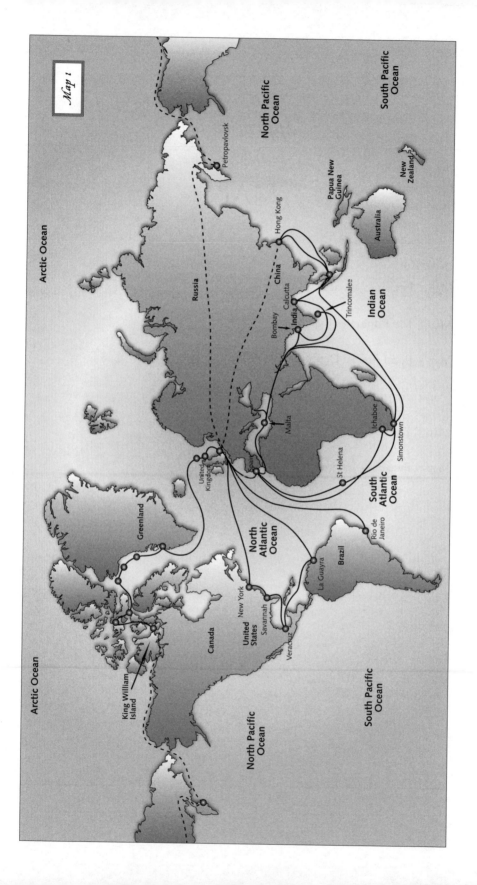

Map 1

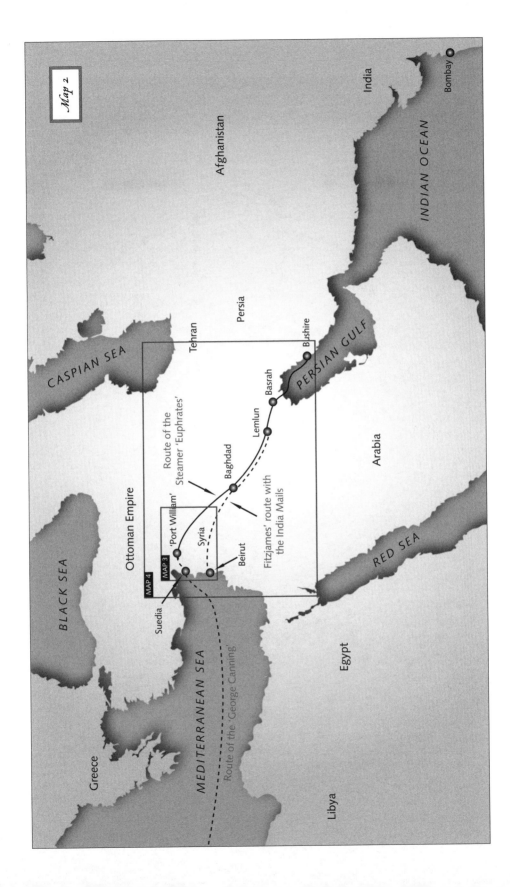

Map 2

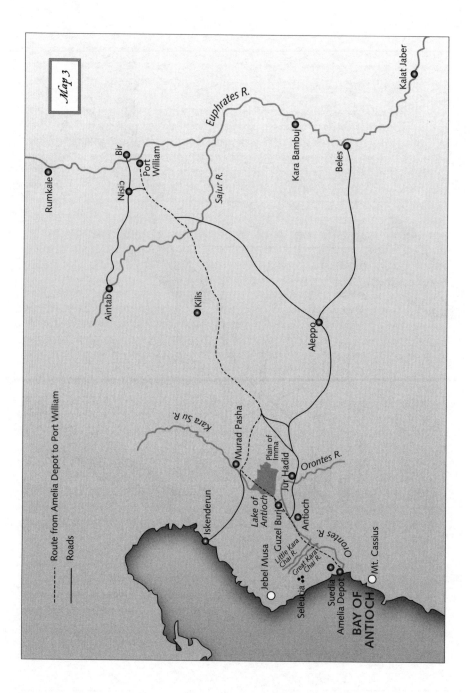

Map 3

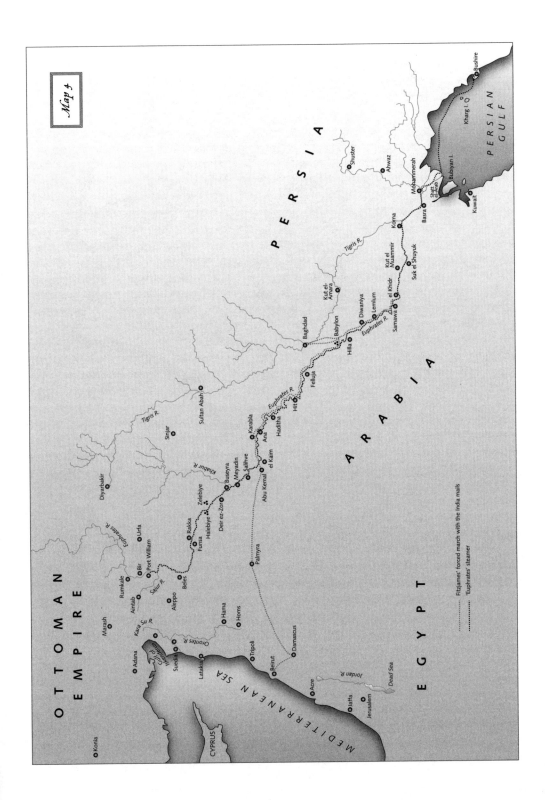

Map 4

OTTOMAN EMPIRE

PERSIA

ARABIA

EGYPT

PERSIAN GULF

MEDITERRANEAN SEA

CYPRUS

Konia
Adana
Marash
Aintab
Rumkale
Suedia
Latakia
Bir
Port William
Urfa
Diyarbakir
Sinjar
Sultan Abah
Beles
Aleppo
Rakka
Funsa
Halebiye
Zelebiye
Deir ez-Zor
Buseyra
Meyadin
Salihye
Abu Kemal
el Kaim
Karabla
Ana
Haditha
Hit
Felluja
Hilla
Babylon
Baghdad
Kut-el-Amara
Hama
Homs
Tripoli
Beirut
Damascus
Acre
Jaffa
Jerusalem
Palmyra
Diwaniya
Lemlum
Zaab el Khidr
Samawa
Suk el Shuyuk
Kut el Muammir
Korna
Basra
Kuwait
Shatt el Arab
Bubyan I.
Mohammerah
Ahwaz
Shuster
Kharg I.
Bushire

Tigris R.
Euphrates R.
Khabur R.
Kara Su R.
Sajur R.
Orontes R.
Jordan R.
Dead Sea

Fitzjames' forced march with the India mails
'Euphrates' steamer

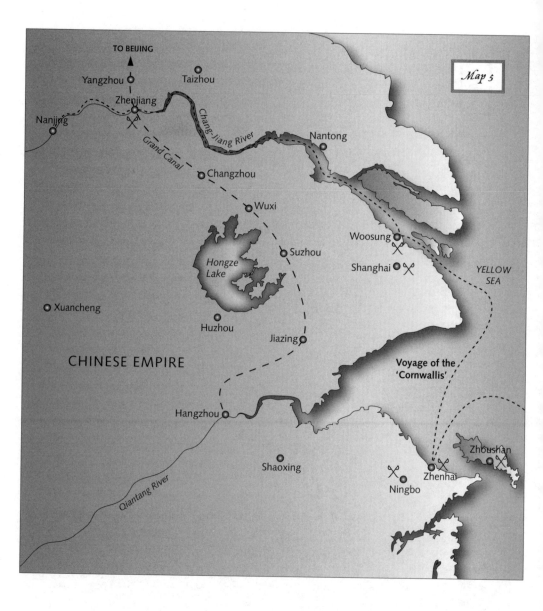

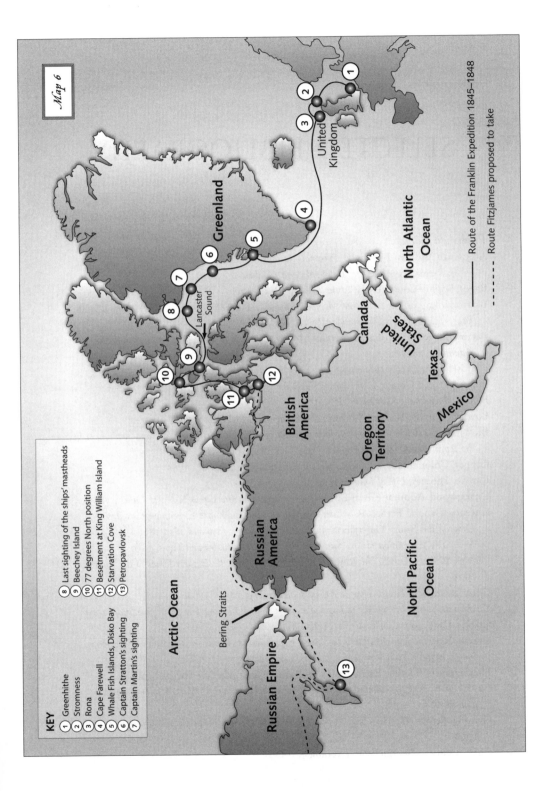

Map 6

KEY
1. Greenhithe
2. Stromness
3. Rona
4. Cape Farewell
5. Whale Fish Islands, Disko Bay
6. Captain Stratton's sighting
7. Captain Martin's sighting
8. Last sighting of the ships' mastheads
9. Beechey Island
10. 77 degrees North position
11. Besetment at King William Island
12. Starvation Cove
13. Petropavlovsk

Arctic Ocean

Russian Empire

Russian America

Bering Straits

North Pacific Ocean

Mexico

Texas

Oregon Territory

United States

British America

Canada

North Atlantic Ocean

United Kingdom

Greenland

Lancaster Sound

——— Route of the Franklin Expedition 1845–1848
- - - - - Route Fitzjames proposed to take

SELECTED BIBLIOGRAPHY

Published Books

Ainsworth, William Francis, *A Personal Narrative of the Euphrates Expedition*, 1888

———, *Researches in Assyria, Babylonia and Chaldea* ..., 1838

Bagot, Sophie Louisa Percy, *Links with the Past*, 1901

Barrow, John, junior, *A Private Memoir of the Life and Service of the Late William Barrow, Esq., (HMS Rose), Commander Royal Navy*, 1850

Barrow, Sir John, *An Autobiographical Memoir Of Sir John Barrow, Bart., Late Of The Admiralty*, 1847

Beardsley, M., *Deadly Winter: the life of Sir John Franklin*, 2002

Beattie, O. and Geiger, J., *Frozen in Time: the fate of the Franklin Expedition*, 1988

Bell, B., *Lieutenant John Irving, RN*, 1881

Boyd-Carpenter, Rt Rev. William, *Some Pages of My Life*, 1911

Brown, D.K., *Before the Ironclad. Development of Ship Design, Propulsion and Armament in the Royal Navy, 1815–60*, 1990

Capper, Colonel James, *Observations on the Passage to India* ..., 1785

Carlyle, Thomas, *Life of John Sterling*, 1851

Charlewood, Admiral Edward Phillips, *Passages from the Life of a Naval Officer*, 1869

Chesney, General Francis Rawdon, *Narrative of the Euphrates Expedition carried on by Order of the British Government during the years 1835, 1836 and 1837*, 1868

———, *The Expedition for the Survey of the Rivers Euphrates and Tigris*, 1850

Clowes, William Laird, *The Royal Navy, A History from the Earliest Times to the Present*, 1901

Coningham, William, *Twelve Letters by John Sterling*, 1851

Cookman, Scott, *Ice Blink: the tragic fate of Sir John Franklin's lost polar expedition*, 2005

Cussler, Clive and Cussler, Dirk, *Arctic Drift*, 2008

Cyriax, R.J., *Sir John Franklin's last Arctic expedition: a chapter in the history of the Royal Navy*, 1939

Eber, Dorothy Harley, *Encounters on the Passage: Inuit Meet the Explorers*, 2008

Fanshawe, Alice E.J., *Admiral Sir Edward Gennys Fanshawe, G.C.B. A record. Notes, journals, letters*, 1904

Fleming, Fergus, *Barrow's Boys. A Stirring Story of Daring, Fortitude and Outright Lunacy*, 1999

Guest, John S., *The Euphrates Expedition*, 1992

Gurney, W.B., *Minutes of a Court Martial holden on board his Majesty's ship Gladiator ...*, 1809

Hall, Captain W.H., RN, and Bernard, W.D., *The Nemesis in China, comprising a History of the Late War in that Country; with an Account of the Colony of Hong Kong*, 1847

Lane-Poole, Stanley (ed.), 'His wife and daughter', *The Life of the Late General F.R. Chesney*, 1885

Latta, Jeffrey Blair, *The Franklin Conspiracy. Cover-up, Betrayal, and the Astonishing Secret Behind the Lost Arctic Expedition*, 2001

Lloyd, Christopher, *Mr Barrow of the Admiralty; a Life of Sir John Barrow, 1764–1848*, 1970

Loch, Captain Granville G., RN, *The Closing Events of the Campaign in China*, 1843

Markham, Sir Albert Hastings, *Life of Sir John Franklin and the North-West Passage*, unpublished, 1891

Markham, Sir Clements R., *The Lands of Silence*, 1921

———, *The Life of Admiral Sir Leopold M. McClintock*, 1909

McClintock, Admiral Sir Leopold, *The Voyage of the Fox*, 1860

McGoogan, Ken, *Fatal Passage*, 2001

———, *Lady Franklin's Revenge*, 2005

Nostitz, Countess Mathilde Pauline, *Pauline Helfer's 'Travels of a Doctor and Madame Helfer in Syria, Mesopotamia, Burmah and other lands' ... Rendered into English by Mrs G. Sturge*, 1878

O'Byrne, William, *Naval Biography*, 2 vols, 1848

Ouchterlony, Lt John, F.G.S., *Chinese War: An Account of all the Operations of the British Forces from the Commencement to the Treaty of Nanking*, 1844

Pappalardo, Bruno, *Tracing your Naval Ancestors*, 2003

Ross, Rear-Admiral M.J., *Polar Pioneers: John Ross and James Clark Ross*, 1994

———, *Ross in the Antarctic*, 1982

Savours, Ann, *The Search for the North West Passage*, 1999

Shadwell, Lawrence, *The Life of Colin Campbell, Lord Clyde*, 1881

Smith, Michael, *Captain Francis Crozier. Last Man Standing?* 2006

Traill, Rev. H.D., *The Life of Sir John Franklin, RN*, 1896

Ware, Chris, *The Bomb Vessel. Shore Bombardment Ships of the Age of Sail*, 1994

Warren, Dawson and Broadley, Alexander Meyrick, *The Journal of a British Chaplain in Paris During the Peace Negotiations of 1801–2*, 2001

Woodman, D.C., *Strangers Among Us*, 1995

———, *Unravelling the Franklin Mystery*, 1991

It is an interesting reflection on the age of this material that despite the huge recent outpouring of research into the Franklin Expedition, the average date of publication of a book cited in this bibliography is 1923.

Journals and Papers

Boston, Ceridwen and Loe, Dr Louise, 'The Royal Hospital Greenwich, Archaeological Report' in *Oxford Archaeological Unit, Ltd.*, 2007

Denny, Sir Henry Lyttleton Lyster, 'Pedigrees of Coningham and Sterling' in *Genealogists' Magazine*, 1929

Haskell, Francis, 'William Coningham and His Collection of Old Masters' in *Burlington Magazine*, 1991

Lloyd-Jones, Ralph, 'The Men who Sailed with Franklin' in *Polar Record*, 2005

————, 'The Royal Marines on Franklin's last expedition' in *Polar Record*, 2004

McLean, David, 'Surgeons of the Opium War: the Navy on the China Coast, 1840–42' in *The English Historical Review 2006 CXXI(491):487-504; doi:10.1093/ehr/cel005*, 2006

Mariners' Mirror
Gentleman's Magazine
Illustrated London News
Nautical Magazine
The Times

Websites

Abbots Langley Local History Society,

The Franklin Trail, <www.netscapades.com/franklintrail/index.htm>

Hidden Tracks, <http://hidden-tracks-book.blogspot.com/>

Late 18th, 19th and early 20th Century Naval and Naval Social History – Index, <www.pbenyon.plus.com/Naval.html>

National Maritime Museum, Franklin relics, <www.nmm.ac.uk/collections/explore/index.cfm/category/franklinrelics>

Scott Polar Research Institute, University of Cambridge,

Visions of the North, <http://visionsnorth.blogspot.com/>

INDEX